THE CONSTITUTIONAL PROTECTION OF EXPRESSION

Richard Moon

In this book, Richard Moon puts forward an account of freedom of expression that emphasizes its social character. Such freedom does not simply protect an individual's liberty from state interference; it also protects the individual's right to communicate with others. Communication is an activity that is deeply social in character, and that involves socially created languages and the use of community resources such as parks, streets, and broadcast stations. Moon argues that recognition of the social dynamic of communication is critical to understanding the potential value and harm of language and to addressing questions about the scope and limits on individual rights to freedom of expression.

Moon examines the tension between the demands for freedom of expression and the structure of constitutional adjudication in the Canadian context. The book discusses many of the standard freedom of expression issues, such as the regulation of advertising, election spending ceilings, the restriction of hate promotion and pornography, state-compelled expression, freedom of the press, access to state and private property, and state support for expression. It examines several important Supreme Court of Canada decisions, including *Irwin Toy, Dolphin Delivery, RJR Macdonald, Keegstra,* and *Butler.*

RICHARD MOON is Prof

The Constitutional Protection of Freedom of Expression

RICHARD MOON

UNIVERSITY OF TORONTO PRESS
Toronto Buffalo London

© University of Toronto Incorporated 2000
Toronto Buffalo London
Printed in Canada

ISBN: 0-8020-0851-8 (cloth)
ISBN: 0-8020-7836-2 (paper)

Canadian Cataloguing in Publication Data

Moon, Richard, 1954–
The constitutional protection of freedom of expression

Includes bibliographical references and index.
ISBN 0-8020-0851-8 (bound)   ISBN 0-8020-7836-2 (pbk.)

1. Freedom of speech – Canada.   2. Freedom of speech –
Canada – Cases.   I. Title.

KE4418.M66 2000   342.71'0853   C00-931945-X
KF4483.C524M66 2000

This book has been published with the help of a grant from the Humanities
and Social Sciences Federation of Canada, using funds provided by the
Social Sciences and Humanities Research Council of Canada.

The University of Toronto Press acknowledges the financial assistance to its
publishing program of the Canada Council for the Arts and the
Ontario Arts Council.

University of Toronto Press acknowledges the financial support for its
publishing activities of the Government of Canada through the
Book Publishing Industry Development Program (BPIDP).

To Sibyl, Ellen, and Hope.
Words cannot do justice.

Contents

Acknowledgments

Many of the ideas expressed in this book can be traced back to articles published over the last fifteen years. Most obviously, Chapter 2 bears a strong resemblance to 'The Supreme Court of Canada on the Structure of Freedom of Expression Adjudication,' *University of Toronto Law Journal* 45 (1995), 419, and Chapter 4 is a revised version of '*R. v. Butler.* The Limits of the Supreme Court's Feminist Re-Interpretation of s.163' *Ottawa Law Journal* 25 (1993), 361. I am grateful to both journals for permitting me to reprint parts of these articles.

Grants from the Law Foundation of Ontario and the Justice Department of the Government of Canada enabled me to employ capable research students over the last three summers. Invaluable research assistance was provided by Mike Perry, Bernadette Corpuz, Mark Polley, Chris Stanek, and Phil Shaer. I am also grateful to the Humanities Research Group of the University of Windsor for the award of a Research Fellowship several years ago, which enabled me to start this project. Finally, I want to thank the friends and colleagues who were kind enough to read and offer comments on several of the book's chapters. I owe thanks to Bill Bogart, Bill Conklin, and David Schneiderman. I am particularly indebted to Julie Macfarlane.

THE CONSTITUTIONAL PROTECTION OF
FREEDOM OF EXPRESSION

Introduction

To some readers the first words of this book's rather bland sounding title, 'the constitutional protection,' might seem superfluous. In much of the writing about freedom of expression, particularly that from the United States, no distinction is drawn between freedom of expression as a moral or political ideal and as a constitutional right. To write about freedom of expression is to write about its constitutional protection.

Yet, as the book's title is meant to suggest, it matters whether we are talking about freedom of expression as political claim or constitutional right. In very general terms, this book is about the tension between the demands of freedom of expression and the structure of constitutional adjudication. The chapters that follow consider the ways in which the concept of freedom of expression is compressed within the parameters of constitutional adjudication and the ways in which the boundaries of constitutional adjudication are stretched (and the competence of courts is strained) by the courts' efforts to give significant meaning to the freedom.

The book considers many of the standard freedom of expression issues, such as the regulation of advertising, hate promotion and pornography, election spending ceilings, access to state and private property, state support for expression, and compelled expression. It does not, however, offer ready-made answers to these issues. Indeed, I believe it shows why there are no simple and clear answers to most of them.

Freedom of expression does not simply protect individual liberty from state interference. Rather, it protects the individual's freedom to communicate with others. The right of the individual is to participate in an activity that is deeply social in character, that involves socially created languages and the use of community resources such as parks, streets, and broadcast stations. Yet the structure of constitutional adjudication, reinforced by an individual rights culture, tends to suppress the social or relational character of freedom of expression and its distributive demands (concern about the individual's effective opportunity to communicate with others).

Recognition of the social character of freedom of expression is critical to understanding both the value and potential harm of expression and to addressing questions about the freedom's scope and limits. Freedom of expression is valuable because human agency and identity emerge in discourse. We become individuals capable of thought and judgment and we develop as rational and feeling persons when we join in conversation with others. The social emergence of human thought, feeling, and identity can be expressed in the language of truth or individual autonomy or democratic self-government. Each of the tra-ditional accounts of the value of freedom of expression (democratic-, truth-, and self-realization-based accounts) represents a particular perspective on, or dimension of, the constitution of human agency in community life. At the same time, the variety of these accounts reflects the diverse role that expression plays in the life of individual and community – that different relationships and different forms of communication contribute to the realization of human agency and the formation of individual identity. While the social character of human agency is seldom mentioned in the traditional accounts of the value of freedom of expression, it is the unstated premise of each. Each account is incomplete without some recognition that individual agency is realized in social interaction; this dimension has simply been pushed below the surface by the weight of the dominant individualist understanding of rights and agency.

Recognition that individual agency and identity emerge in communicative interaction is crucial to understanding not only the value of expression but also its potential for harm. Our dependence on expression means that words can sometimes be hurtful. Our identity is shaped by what we say and by what others say to us and about us. Expression can cause fear, it can harass, and it can undermine self-esteem. Expression can also be deceptive or manipulative. Human reflection and judgment are dependent on socially created languages, which give shape to thought and feeling. While language enables us to formulate and communicate our ideas and to understand the ideas of others, it is not a transparent vehicle, an instrument that lies within our perfect control.

But if expression is never fully transparent, neither is it entirely opaque, a 'cause' that simply impacts upon its audience. Some instances of expression encourage reflection and insight even about some of our most basic assumptions, while others by-pass or discourage reflection. This distinction, however, is a relative one. There is no clear line between manipulative and rational expression. How we label a particular act of expression, as rational or manipulative, will depend on its form but also on its social/economic circumstances, including the distribution of communicative power.

The Canadian freedom of expression decisions are characterized by a tension between the general faith in individual freedom and rationality that underlies established theory and doctrine and a recognition that different forms of expression or different social and economic circumstances may discourage or constrain judgment. Freedom of expression doctrine is built on an understanding of the individual as free and rational and on an understanding of expression as the transparent communication of opinion and information, which takes place either face-to-face or in books, newspapers, and other generally accessible media. This understanding of agency and expression has left the courts unable to account for the harm (or to justify the restriction) of expression and ill-prepared to respond to either the rise of visually based commercial advertising as the paradigm of public expression or to the concentration of communicative power. If individuals are free and rational, capable of determining what they will believe and what values they will hold, and if expression is simply transparent, how could freedom of expression ever be harmful? Expression would have no tangible effects; it would simply provide ideas and information that an individual listener might decide to accept or reject.

Traditional freedom of expression doctrine has always permitted the restriction of manipulative expression (or expression that incites). Expression may be viewed as manipulative when it takes a form or occurs in conditions that limit the audience's ability to rationally assess the claims being made and the implications of acting on those claims. A commitment to freedom of expression means that individuals should be free to express their views and to hear and assess the views of others. The conventional assumption is that a restriction is not justified simply because we think that the restricted expression 'causes' harm or that the audience's reason cannot be trusted. To be consistent with the constitutional commitment to free expression a limitation must rest, at least in part, on the presence of exceptional conditions or circumstances that undermine the audience's ability to freely or rationally assess the views expressed.

The difficulty, however, is that these conditions or circumstances may be difficult to isolate. Because there is no condition of pure human reason and perfect independence it is impossible to identify clear deviations from the proper and ordinary conditions of free choice and rational judgment. The line between rational and manipulative expression becomes even more difficult to draw once we recognize that some of the factors that may impair autonomy and reason are systemic – for example, the domination of public discourse by the advertising form or the private ownership of key parts of the public sphere. Because the courts are unable (and the legislature is unwilling) to address these systemic problems directly (by opening public discourse up to a wider range of voices and views) they are treated by the courts as part of the context within which freedom of expression operates, as factors that affect individual reason and autonomy.

The Canadian courts have tried to by-pass these difficult issues by adopting a behavioural approach to the justification of limits on expression. The courts have often upheld limits on freedom of expression without explaining why the freedom's defining faith in the free and rational judgment of the individual does not apply in the particular circumstance. Instead, they have simply asked whether the expression 'causes' harm. When expression takes place in a context in which individual judgment seems distorted or constrained, it is simpler for a court to label and treat the expression as a form of action that 'impacts' upon the individual than to try to isolate the exceptional character or circumstances of the expression. In addition, because 'cause' is difficult to prove the courts have either fallen back on 'common sense' or deferred to legislative judgment to 'complete' the causal link between expression and harm.

However, if the courts support the restriction of potentially harmful expression without explaining why the judgment of the audience is not to be trusted in the particular circumstance, and without acknowledging the costs of removing certain matters from the scope of public discourse, the right to free expression will have ceased to play any obvious role in their decision making. Freedom of expression has little substance if our trust in the 'autonomous' judgment of the individual is the exception – a condition that must be established. It has no substance if it is 'protected' only when we agree with the message or consider the message to be harmless. The nearly impossible task for the courts is to define a reasonably clear space for freedom of expression that does not depend (simply) on our agreement with the message communicated or our judgment that no harm will be caused if the message is accepted. The task is difficult not just because reason is imperfect and autonomy is relative but because freedom of expression operates against a background of communicative inequality that seems to lie outside the domain of constitutional review.

This points to the other tension apparent in the Canadian freedom of expression decisions: the tension between the conventional understanding of freedom of expression as a right of the individual to be free from state interference and the recognition that freedom of expression has implications for the distribution of communicative resources.

Traditional accounts of freedom of expression emphasize the importance of protecting the individual's personal sphere from interference by the state. When the state interferes with the individual's freedom to express him/herself, a court must decide whether the state has good and strong reasons for its action. However, if expression is a valuable activity, the courts should not be concerned solely with direct state censorship. They should also be sensitive to the real opportunities that individuals have to express themselves and to participate in public discourse – opportunities that depend upon the distribution of communicative resources.

Yet any attempt to read the constitutional right to free expression as requiring the expansion of communicative opportunities for some members of the community runs up against both the conventional understanding of the freedom as a 'negative' right against state interference and the structural constraints on the courts' capacity to engage in a significant or coherent redistribution of communicative power. This tension between the distributive demands of freedom of expression and the structure of constitutional adjudication is apparent in the courts' attempts to define a right of communicative access to government property. While this right rests on concerns about communicative opportunity, it is narrowly defined and awkwardly framed in the constitutional language of state interference with individual liberty.

Chapter One

Truth, Democracy, and Autonomy

1. Introduction: Common Ground

There are many arguments for protecting freedom of expression, but all seem to focus on one or a combination of three values: truth, democracy, and individual autonomy. Freedom of expression must be protected because it contributes to the public's recognition of truth or to the growth of public knowledge; or because it is necessary to the operation of a democratic form of government; or because it is important to individual self-realization, or because it is an important aspect of individual autonomy. Some arguments emphasize one value over the others. In these single-value accounts the other values are seen as either derived from the primary value or as independent but of marginal significance only.[1] However, most accounts assume that a commitment to freedom of expression, which extends protection to political, artistic, scientific, and intimate expression, must rest on the contribution that freedom of expression makes to all three values.[2] Freedom of expression, like other important rights, is supported by a number of overlapping justifications.

In this chapter, I will argue that the different accounts of the value of freedom of expression rest on common ground. While emphasizing different values or concerns, these accounts rest on a common recognition that human agency emerges in communicative interaction. We become individuals capable of thought and judgment, we flourish as rational and feeling persons, when we join in conversation with others and participate in the life of the community. The social emergence of human agency and individual identity can be expressed in the language of truth/knowledge, individual self-realization/autonomy, or democratic self-government. Each account of freedom of expression represents a particular perspective on, or dimension of, the constitution of human agency in community life.

This recognition of the social character of freedom of expression does not represent a general or novel account of the freedom's value under which all other accounts can be located. The wide variety of accounts offered to justify the constitutional protection of freedom of expression suggests the rich and varied role that expression plays in the life of individual and community. Different relationships and different kinds of discourse are critical to the realization of human agency and the formation of individual identity. Any account of the value of freedom of expression must recognize the complexity of human agency and the diverse forms of human engagement in community.

While the social character of human agency is seldom mentioned in the different accounts of the freedom's value, it is the unstated premise of each. Each account is incomplete without some recognition that individual agency is realized in social interaction. This dimension of the freedom has simply been pushed below the surface by the weight of the dominant individualist understanding of rights and agency. As a consequence, most accounts of freedom of expression consist of little more than abstract statements that give little shape to our intuitions about the value of expression and provide very little guidance in the resolution of particular disputes concerning the scope and limits of the freedom.[3] My hope is that making explicit the social character of freedom of expression will enable better understanding of the value and potential harm of expression and better judgment about the scope and limits of the freedom.

2. Truth and Knowledge

The most familiar version of the truth-based argument for freedom of expression is that of J.S. Mill, who thought that the general public would be more likely to recognize truth if they were permitted to hear all available views, even those thought by many or most to be false.[4] In *On Liberty*, Mill (1982 [1859]) argued that censorship inhibits the progress of human knowledge because no censor is infallible. Even when it acts in good faith (which is certainly not always the case), the state will make mistakes and sometimes suppress truth rather than falsehood (Mill 1982, 77). The risk that censorship will inhibit the search for truth is significant, according to Mill, because public debate is not simply a competition between true and false ideas. Even the apparently false idea often contains at least a grain of truth, which will be suppressed if the idea is censored (Mill 1982, 108). In Mill's view, the progress of public knowledge occurs through the synthesis of competing ideas.

Mill dismissed the argument that fallible state censors might still be in a better position than the general public to distinguish truth from falsehood. In his view, individual judgment isolated from the process of open debate is unreliable. We can only have confidence in our judgments about what is true when there is free and open expression of competing views, when determinations of truth and falsity are left to the general public.[5] Mill's fallibility argument rests on a faith in public reason.[6] It assumes that the public, when permitted to engage in free and open debate, is capable over the long run of distinguishing truth from falsehood.

For Mill, even if the state censor happens to judge correctly and suppresses only false views, something is still lost. The expression of false views has value because the 'collision' of truth with error gives us a 'clearer perception and livelier impression of truth' (Mill 1982, 76). We will gain a better understanding of the truth if we must address competing views and decide why we believe a particular view to be true or false. Our truthful opinions will be stronger and less vulnerable to superficial attack if they are based on reasoned judgment (Ten 1980, 126).

Mill is generally understood as having made an instrumental argument for freedom of expression.[7] Freedom of expression is valuable because it advances the goal of truth. Members of the community are more likely to recognize what is true and what is false, at least over the long run, if freedom of expression is protected. Yet, as many have suggested, this empirical claim is contestable. We have plenty of reasons to be sceptical about the reliability of public reason when exercised in particular social/economic contexts (Meiklejohn 1975, 19; Baker 1989, 6). In addition, even if, as a general rule, truth is more likely to emerge when there is debate rather than dogma, there is certainly a case to be made that some false or objectionable views could be excluded from public discussion (although perhaps not from expert debate) without any noticeable decrease in publicly recognized truth. This case has greater strength once we recall how often members of the public base their 'opinions' on the authority of experts rather than on an independent evaluation of the evidence or arguments. Instead of being subject to a general or presumptive ban, restrictions on expression could be considered on a case-by-case basis to determine whether their benefits to public knowledge outweigh their costs (Smith 1987, 695). If dialogue leads to truth, as Mill argued, then eventually, on some questions at least, the truth may be realized, at which point opposing views may simply be mischievous or misleading.[8] Provided we are not in the grip of a profound scepticism, we might decide to hold on to the truth we have achieved by suppressing false ideas. The difficulty, admittedly, would be knowing when that moment of practical certainty had been reached.

Along these lines, Chief Justice Dickson for the majority of the Supreme Court of Canada in *Keegstra* (1990, 762) said:

> Taken to its extreme, this argument [for truth] would require us to permit the communication of all expression, it being impossible to know with absolute certainty which factual statements are true, or which ideas obtain the greatest good. The problem with this extreme position, however, is that the greater the degree of certainty that a statement is erroneous or mendacious, the less its value in the quest for truth. Indeed, expression can be used to the detriment of our search for truth; the state should not be the sole arbiter of truth, but neither should we overplay the view that rationality will overcome all falsehoods in the unregulated marketplace of ideas.

Dickson C.J. suggested that the hateful views of James Keegstra could be denied constitutional protection because they were so 'obviously' false.[9] Yet obviously false views are unlikely to be seen as a concern and to attract censorship. If the views are obviously false, few will be persuaded by them. Indeed, if many people are convinced, the views cannot be so 'obviously' false and the risks of censorship may be significant. The problem with the views of James Keegstra and others is that they are not obviously false to some members of the community. The issue is whether and when the governing authorities should be permitted to suppress views that *they* recognize as obviously false. Perhaps the ground for censoring the false views of Keegstra and others is not the obviousness of their falsity but rather their appeal to the irrational (a matter of the form and social context of expression) or some combination of the irrationality of the appeal and the seriousness of the harm that might follow acceptance of these views by some members of the community.[10]

If Mill's concern was simply that true opinions gain general acceptance (so that society is in a better position to act in ways that increase the welfare of its members), then it would not matter how these ideas were spread. As long as true opinions achieve general currency in the community it should not matter whether this occurs through persuasion or through indoctrination. The only argument against manipulation or indoctrination is that, in contrast to rational persuasion, they are inefficient tools in the spread of truth.

Mill, however, had other concerns. His argument is not simply that freedom of expression is valuable as an instrument to the realization of public knowledge or the public recognition of truth. It involves much more than an empirical claim that truth will emerge from free and open discussion. Beneath the instrumental and empirical form of Mill's argument, and its concern for the achievement of the social good of public knowledge, is a belief that participation in public discourse is necessary to the development of the individual as a rational agent and a commitment to a way of life that involves reasoned judgment and the effort to discover truth through discussion with others (Ten 1980, 124).

For Mill it mattered not only that we, as a community, hold true opinions but also that we, as individual community members, hold these opinions in a particular way. He was concerned that the individual think and act 'as a rational being,' one who understands the grounds for his or her opinions (Mill 1982, 97).[11] He wanted the individual to participate in the truth, in the sense of being able to distinguish truth from falsehood and knowing the grounds for her/his opinion. More generally, Mill valued the 'cultivation of intellect and judgement' and believed that this would occur through the individual's participation in public discussion and the collective effort to discover the truth (Mill 1982, 97).[12]

Seen in this way, Mill's argument cannot really be described as instrumental rather than intrinsic or as concerned with the collective rather than with the individual.[13] Truth is valued as something recognized or realized by human agents, by individual members of the community exercising their reasoned judgment. The life of truth (or knowledge) is in human reflection and judgment. But reflection and judgment are not simply private processes. Truth is achieved through collective deliberation, through the sharing of ideas and information among community members. Public discussion is valuable to the community, which comes to have greater knowledge, and to individuals, who come to know truth as community members, to develop as rational agents capable of recognizing true opinions, and to live in a community where the pursuit of truth/knowledge is valued.

In the United States, the metaphor of 'the marketplace of ideas' is sometimes used to express the kind of truth-based argument made by Mill: that truth will emerge from a free and open exchange of ideas.[14] Sometimes, however, this metaphor is meant to express an argument that is more sceptical about truth claims. Justice Holmes argued that 'the ultimate good desired is better reached by the free trade in ideas ... that the best test of truth is the power of the thought to get itself accepted in the competition of the market' (*Abrams* 1919, 630). In Holmes's account 'truth' may be simply that which emerges from the marketplace of ideas, the outcome of unrestricted discussion among members of the community.

This sceptical form of argument has been criticized on several grounds. If we are deeply sceptical about the possibility of truth or knowledge, why should we attach the label of truth, indeed why should we attach any value, to whatever conclusions may emerge from free and open discussion? If the product ('truth') has value, this value must be based on the process of its production. Freedom of expression is valuable not because it produces truth but because it is the right or fair way to decide social questions or to achieve public consensus. This is very different from the conventional truth-based argument, in which the value of free expression depends on its production of truth, independently or objectively determined. In its sceptical form the marketplace of ideas argument resembles the democratic account of freedom of expression, with its focus on the process of deliberation and consensus building.

For at least two reasons the idea of democratic deliberation has advantages over the marketplace of ideas metaphor. First, the 'marketplace' image (and its laissez-faire connotations) discourages consideration of the appropriate conditions for achieving social consensus. Most importantly, it does not address the question of the background distribution of wealth and communicative power. The distribution of communicative power should be a central issue in an account concerned with the process of community consensus building. We do not enter the public market as equals: greater voice is given to those with greater economic power. The marketplace metaphor, however, encourages us to think of the existing distribution of communicative power as a fixed background to the free exchange of information and ideas among citizens. It assumes that the public sphere should operate in the same way as the market for goods: controlled by those with resources.

The other difficulty with the metaphor is that the exchange of ideas and information is not analogous to the exchange of goods and services (Shiffrin 1990, 91). Public discourse is not simply about the provision of information and ideas that enable individuals to advance their desires and preferences. Participation in public discourse is vital to the formation of preferences and choices. Human desires, preferences, and purposes are not presocial, formed independently of debate and discussion, but are instead given form in public discourse.

3. Democracy

The argument that freedom of expression is necessary to the operation of democratic government is appealing for a number of reasons. First, it accounts for the central role that political expression seems to play in our understanding of the scope of freedom of expression. Second, it offers a way to justify the constitutional entrenchment of freedom of expression as a limitation on the actions of a democratically elected government. If we accept that freedom of expression is a basic condition of democracy, then the tension between judicial review and democracy seems to dissolve. According to this view, freedom of expression is a necessary constraint on the majority's will and is appropriately enforced by a judiciary insulated from political pressure.

The democratic argument is an American creation, intended to give content and legitimacy to the constitutionally entrenched right to free speech. Its most important proponent, Alexander Meiklejohn, argued that '[t]he principle of freedom of speech springs from the necessities of the program of self-government' (Meiklejohn 1965, 27).[15] This principle is not 'a Law of Nature or of Reason in the abstract'; it is instead 'a deduction from the basic American agreement that public issues shall be decided by universal suffrage' (Meiklejohn 1965, 27).[16] The adoption of a democratic form of government carries with it an obligation to protect freedom of expression. The exercise of self-government requires the free and open flow of ideas and information concerning public issues. If men and women are prevented from hearing 'information or opinion or doubt or disbelief or criticism' relevant to a public issue under consideration, their efforts to advance the common good will be ill-considered and ill-balanced: '[T]he thinking process of the community' will be distorted (Meiklejohn 1965, 27) and the government's democratic authority will be lost.

In Meiklejohn's account, the purpose of the First Amendment is to ensure the 'voting of wise decisions' and this means that voters must be made 'as wise as possible' (Meiklejohn 1965, 26). The responsibility for deciding public issues lies with the citizens, who must, therefore, be given the opportunity to consider these issues. The focus of Meiklejohn's account is thus on 'the minds of the hearers' rather than 'the words of the speaker.' What matters 'is not that everyone shall speak, but that everything worth saying shall be said' (Meiklejohn 1965, 26). As well, in this account, the First Amendment protects only speech that bears, 'directly or indirectly,' upon issues with which voters have to deal. Speech that does not contribute to the consideration of public issues is not protected. 'Private speech' (and 'private interest in speech') has no claim to First Amendment protection (Meiklejohn 1965, 79). However, the protection of 'public' or political speech 'admits of no exceptions' (Meiklejohn 1965, 20).[17] Within its proper scope the freedom is absolute.

For Meiklejohn, the principle of 'self-government' provides a generally accepted and constitutionally recognized premise from which the protection of 'political' discussion follows. Yet what self-government involves or requires is the subject of considerable debate. Certainly the category of speech necessary to the operation of representative government is anything but clear and uncontroversial.

While political expression lies at the core of our understanding of freedom of expression, other forms of expression – notably artistic, scientific, and even intimate expression – also figure in our intuitions about the freedom's scope. It may be that political expression occupies this central role not because it is somehow more valuable than other kinds of expression, but simply because it has been the most vulnerable to state censorship. Many accounts of the value and constitutional protection of freedom of expression focus on the partiality of the government's decision to censor political expression alleged to be untruthful or harmful.[18] These accounts recognize that governments may not judge well the value or harm of political expression and may sometimes be tempted to suppress criticism of their policies. Regardless of whether political expression is more valuable than other forms of expression, there are particular reasons for ensuring independent (judicial) scrutiny of legislative decisions to censor it.

Most advocates of the democratic account of freedom of expression accept that intimate and artistic expression deserve some protection and have sought to fit these other forms of expression into the democratic account. One approach has been simply to supplement the account with a recognition that freedom of expression contributes to other values, such as truth and self-realization. Cass Sunstein, for example, argues that while political speech lies at the core of freedom of expression, which is principally concerned with democratic deliberation, other forms of expression, such as works of art, lie at its margins, protected because they contribute to values such as individual autonomy (Sunstein 1993, 123). For Sunstein, the centrality of democratic values and the consequent focus on political expression is a matter of constitutional interpretation rather than moral or rights theory. It stems from the structure, history, and text of the First Amendment, which establishes the right to free speech as a constitutional limit on state action.

Meiklejohn adopts a different strategy for extending protection to speech that is not directly concerned with political issues. In his original statement of the democratic account, Meiklejohn had argued that the First Amendment only protected speech that related directly or indirectly to issues that voters had to decide, to matters of public interest. Many criticized his account for failing to protect works of literature, science, and philosophy. In his later writings, however, Meiklejohn argues that such criticism was unfair and that his democratic account of the First Amendment extended protection to these different forms of expression because they contributed to the wisdom and sensitivity of voters. According to Meiklejohn, '[s]elf-government can exist only insofar as the voters acquire the intelligence, integrity, sensitivity and generous devotion to the general welfare that, in theory, casting a ballot is assumed to express' (Meiklejohn 1975, 11). Voters derive this 'knowledge ... [and] sensitivity to human values' from many forms of expression, including philosophy and the sciences as well as literature and the arts (Meiklejohn 1975, 12).[19]

The most obvious problem with Meiklejohn's broad understanding of the category of political speech (speech that contributes to democratic deliberation) is that his already difficult claim that the freedom is absolute in its protection of political expression now seems stretched beyond breaking point. If freedom of speech is this broad, it must often come into conflict with other important interests and must sometimes give way to them. Meiklejohn avoids this conclusion and maintains the claim of absolute protection by denying the label of political speech to any communication that is deceptive, manipulative, or personally offensive, even though its content may be political.[20] While we may be prepared to accept Meiklejohn's claim that these forms of speech do not contribute to political deliberation, and in particular to the listener's ability to make wise political judgments, there is no easily defined or clearly bounded category of manipulative, deceptive, disruptive, or offensive speech. The determination that speech is manipulative or disruptive and so falls outside the scope of the First Amendment involves a difficult contextual assessment of factors that contribute to, or detract from, the audience's ability to exercise independent judgment. Furthermore, while deliberative democracy may require some restriction of disruptive or offensive expression, the exclusion of these forms of expression may also be seen as limiting the individual's opportunity to contribute to political discourse and to hear strongly held views.[21] Meiklejohn's category of 'political speech' may be protected absolutely and not balanced against competing interests. However, something very like balancing may enter at the stage of defining the scope of the protected category.

Meiklejohn's broad view of the scope of political speech highlights the difficulty that democratic theorists have in keeping the focus of their account on the operation of democratic government. First, if the concern of democratic theorists is with self-government, and with the equal right of citizens to participate in the decisions that affect their lives and the life of their community, this concern could easily extend to other sites of social interaction and power, such as the workplace, the school, or the marketplace, which are of central importance in the life of the individual.[22] While the workplace, for example, may not be organized on the same principles as the governing process (i.e., on the basis of free and equal participation by members), it should, perhaps, be more open, with employees having the right to discuss working conditions, product quality, or management organization.[23] The workplace is an 'important site for the forging of personal bonds' between individuals from diverse backgrounds and 'it affords a space in which individuals cultivate some of the values, habits and traits that carry over to their role as citizens' (Estlund 1997, 727). The focus in the democratic account of freedom of expression on political speech and the workings of representative government stems not so much from the logic of self-government as from the constitutional status of the right and concerns about the legitimacy of judicial review. A constraint on the power of democratically elected institutions of government may seem tolerable only if it can be viewed as a limited but necessary condition of the exercise of legitimate authority by these institutions.

Second, the democratic account's focus sometimes seems to shift from the workings of representative government to the development of wise and public-spirited citizens. While formally concerned with the governing process, the democratic account of freedom of expression sometimes appears to have a deeper concern with the realization of the individual as a 'rational and value-sensitive' agent. Meiklejohn argued that the wisdom and value sensitivity of citizens (and the protection of artistic, scientific, philosophical, and intimate expression) are necessary to democracy. Yet his argument could easily be turned around so that democracy is valued because it is necessary to the development and realization of the individual (Schauer 1982, 41). Do we care about individual wisdom simply because it contributes to democracy? Should we not regard the development of the individual as a more fundamental value that is simply dressed in the language of self-government? However, simply shifting the focus from political process to individual judgment misses something important about the relationship between individual and community.

If democracy involved nothing more than the registration and aggregation of the political preferences of individual members of the community, all that would be required for its operation would be regular elections, interim polling, and communication from competing candidates to the electorate concerning policy alternatives. However, the conception of democracy that underlies the democratic account involves much more than this. Democracy, understood as collective self-determination, requires that 'public action be founded upon a public opinion formed through open and interactive processes of rational deliberation' (Post 1995, 312).[24] Freedom of expression is not just an instrument for advancing the goal of democratic or representative government. In a democracy the responsibility of citizens for the governance of their community is actualized in public discussion and deliberation.[25] The members of a self-governing community seek common understandings and work towards shared goals through the exchange of views. Through participation in public discourse, the individual becomes a citizen capable of understanding, and identifying with, the concerns and opinions of others and oriented towards the public interest, in the sense that she is concerned with the common good and not simply with the satisfaction of personal preferences.[26]

If this is what the democratic argument is about then two of its advantages have disappeared: the definition of a narrow, but absolutely protected, category of protected activity and the justification of judicial review in a democracy. It is impossible to limit the scope of freedom of expression to the discussion of contemporary political issues, something that Meiklejohn came to recognize. It is also clear that the rich and complicated understanding of democracy that underlies this account of the freedom cannot provide a simple or neutral justification for judicial review under the constitution.

4. Autonomy and Self-Realization

There are a variety of arguments for freedom of expression that focus on the interests or well-being of the individual. The most familiar version of this type of argument is that it is a violation of the individual's autonomy, or a failure to show proper respect for the individual, to prevent her from hearing the ideas of others because she might make poor judgments (Scanlon 1977, 162).[27] Human beings are characterized by their ability to reason and judge and should be trusted to assess the messages of others fairly or accurately. A parallel to this 'listener'-focused argument is offered by Ronald Dworkin, who argues that the state fails to show equal concern and respect for the individual 'speaker' when it censors his or her ideas on the grounds that they are wrong or foolish (Dworkin 1985, 386).[28] Other arguments stress the importance of expression to individual self-realization (Weinrib 1990; Baker 1989).[29] The individual realizes his capacities for thought and judgment by expressing his ideas or by listening to and, reflecting upon, the ideas of others.

Sometimes it is argued that expression deserves special protection, beyond that accorded to other human acts, not because it is distinctly valuable but because it is ordinarily a harmless activity (Baker 1989, 56; Haiman 1993, 85).[30] According to this view, the protection of expression follows from our commitment to the harm principle. Individuals should have the liberty to do as they please subject only to the limitation that their actions must not cause harm to others (Mill 1982, 68).[31] While the manner of an individual's expression may sometimes cause harm, as with a loud noise or a disruptive demonstration, the message communicated has only a mental impact and is therefore harmless.

Yet this seems wrong. Individuals express themselves in order to affect attitudes and events in the world. The message, and not just the manner of expression, can sometimes cause harm to others. The message may be hurtful or offensive; it may involve the spread of false ideas; or it may encourage harmful activity by others. Expression 'causes' harm when someone is persuaded by a false idea or persuaded to act in a violent way towards another. It may be true that these harms occur only because the listener consciously accepts the message. But why should this make a difference? If we think that a commitment to freedom of expression means that these harms must be endured or disregarded, we must explain why it is important that individuals be allowed to make judgments for themselves or why expression is so valuable that it should be protected despite the harm it 'causes.'

Generally speaking, those who advance autonomy-based arguments do not claim that freedom of expression is simply an aspect of a more general principle of liberty of action. They assume that the freedom protects a subset of voluntary action, which corresponds more or less with the activity of communication, and that there are distinctive reasons for protecting this type of action. Yet the language of individual respect or autonomy offers few clues as to why communication should have this special status. Why is it disrespectful to silence a speaker when we think that his or her views are wrong, but not disrespectful to criticize those views? Why is it wrong to prevent a listener from hearing certain views, even when we are afraid that he or she might judge unwisely, but not wrong, not a violation of individual autonomy, to prevent the listener from acting on those views? An account of the value of freedom of expression must involve more than a general claim that the restriction of expression is disrespectful to the individual or invades the individual's autonomy. It must provide some explanation of the positive value of the activity of expression (Moon 1985, 342).[32]

Kent Greenawalt suggests that the special connection between expression and autonomy rests on the fact that communication 'is so closely tied to our thoughts and feelings' (Greenawalt 1989, 28). Because of this tie, 'suppression of communication is a more serious impingement on our personalities than other restraints on liberty' (Greenawalt 1989, 38).[33] Yet are not all voluntary acts expressive of the individual and closely tied to his or her thoughts and feelings? The difference is that expression is closely or personally linked to the individual because it is through expression, through conversation with others, that an individual gives shape to his or her ideas and feelings. Expression is not simply an emotional outlet or a vehicle for relaying an individual's existing ideas to another person. An individual's thoughts and feelings, and more generally her identity, are constituted in her expressive activities.

Autonomy- (or self-realization-) based accounts have difficulty explaining the particular value of expression, because they assume that rights, such as freedom of expression, are aspects of the autonomy that the individual retains when he or she enters the social world and that should be insulated from the demands of collective welfare. Within an individualist framework it is impossible to account for the particular value of expression – of communication *between* individuals. Self-expression accounts seem to assume that ideas or meanings originate with the individual, who may decide to relay his or her particular ideas to others. However, the value we attach to freedom of expression makes sense only if we recognize that the creation of meaning (the articulation of ideas and feelings) is a social process, something that takes place between individuals and within a community.

If we can lift the concepts of autonomy and self-realization out of the individualist frame, so that they are no longer simply about freedom from external interference or freedom from others, then they may provide some explanation of the value of freedom of expression (Moon 1985, 345–6). If by autonomy we mean a capacity to think, judge, and give direction to one's life and the ability to participate in collective governance, then freedom of expression may have an important role to play in the realization of autonomy. Similarly, if by self-realization we mean the emergence of the individual as a conscious and feeling person, freedom of expression may be important to self-realization. In both cases, however, the value of freedom of expression rests on the social character of human identity, reason, and judgment. Freedom of expression is central to self-realization and autonomy because individual identity, thought, and feeling emerge in the social realm.

5. Communication and Agency

Whether the emphasis is on democracy, autonomy, or self-expression, each of the established accounts of the value of freedom of expression rests on a recognition that human autonomy/agency is deeply social in its creation and expression. Each recognizes that human judgment, reason, feeling, and identity are realized in communicative interaction with friends, family, co-workers, and other members of the community (Moon 1991, 94).

Speech, or language use, is a social activity 'through which individuals establish and renew relations with one another' (Thompson 1995, 12). In expressing him/herself to others, a speaker employs a language that is created and shaped in discourse. In an important sense language pre-exists the individual user. It is produced intersubjectively and held by the community of speakers. Significantly, language is not a transparent medium, a simple instrument for conveying an individual's ideas and feelings. Speaking involves more than the selection of words that correspond to the communicator's ideas. Using language an individual is able to articulate his ideas and feelings. His ideas and feelings are partly constituted by the language of their expression.[34]

We can never fully dominate the language with which we express ourselves, but nor are we fully dominated by language (Taylor 1985, 232).[35] Mikhail Bakhtin observes that while '[t]he words of language belong to nobody ... the use of words in live speech communication is always individual and contextual in nature' (Bakhtin 1986, 88). In expressing him/herself to others, an individual employs a socially created language that belongs to the larger community of language users. Nevertheless, 'we hear those words only in particular individual utterances, we read them in particular individual works' which must be seen as individual and expressive (Bakhtin 1986, 88).[36] Individuals adapt the symbolic forms of language to their needs in particular communicative contexts and in so doing recreate, extend, alter, and reshape the language (C. Taylor 1995, 97).[37] Recognition that language use is active and creative – that it is 'purposive action[] carried out in [a] structured social context[]' (Thompson 1995, 12) – underlies our view of the individual as a conscious agent, who is capable of reflection and judgment and is not simply the product of social structures.[38]

Language enables us to give form to our feelings and ideas and to 'bring them to fuller and clearer consciousness' (Taylor 1985, 257). An individual's ideas only take shape, only properly exist, when expressed in language, when given symbolic form. When we speak we bring to explicit awareness, to consciousness, that which before we had only an implicit sense (Taylor 1985, 256).[39] In this way our capacity for reflection and our knowledge of self and the world emerge in the public articulation/interpretation of experience. As Clifford Geertz observes, we become individuals, agents capable of particular and intentional action, 'under the guidance of cultural patterns, historically created systems of meaning in terms of which we give form, order, point and direction to our lives' (Geertz 1973, 76).[40]

In giving symbolic form to her ideas and feelings an individual manifests these not simply to him/herself but to others as well. To express something is to enter into dialogue – into a communicative relationship – with other members of the community. When an individual expresses something, not only does she formulate it and put it 'in articulate focus,' she also places it in a public space and joins with others in a common act of focusing on a particular matter (Taylor

1985, 260). The individual reflects upon her ideas and feelings by giving them symbolic form and putting them before herself and others as part of an ongoing discourse. She understands her articulated ideas and feelings in light of the reactions and responses of others.

When an individual speaks, he speaks to someone, whether to a specific person or to a general audience. What he says and how he says it will depend on whom he is addressing and why he is addressing them, on whether, for example, he is engaging in political debate or intimate expression. The speaker seeks from his audience what Bakhtin calls 'an active responsive understanding' which may include agreement, sympathy, elaboration, preparation for action, and disagreement (Bakhtin 1986, 94). Not only is the speaker's expression oriented to an audience and intended to elicit a response, his expression is itself a response, 'a link in the chain of communication' (Bakhtin 1986, 91). The speaker responds to prior acts of expression, drawing on conventional forms of expression and reacting to previously stated views. Every statement an individual makes 'is filled with echoes and reverberations' of the statements of others, which he or she reworks and re-accentuates (Bakhtin 1986, 89).

Effective communication can occur only because the speaker and listener 'share certain conventions for expressing different meanings' (Bruner 1990, 63). As George Steiner notes, 'If a substantial part of all utterances were not public or, more precisely, could not be treated as if they were, chaos and autism would follow' (Steiner 1975, 205). At the same time, however, a particular utterance will be interpreted in light of the listener's distinctive experience – in light of assumptions and expectations that are not necessarily shared by others and that stem from a particular life history.[41]

The creation of meaning is a shared process, something that takes place between speaker and listener.[42] A speaker does not simply convey a meaning that is passively received by an audience. Understanding is an active, creative process in which listeners take hold of, and work over, the symbolic material they receive (Thompson 1995, 39), locating and evaluating this material within their own knowledge or memory (Thompson 1995, 42).[43] Listeners use these symbolic forms 'as a vehicle for reflection and self-reflection, as a basis for thinking about themselves, about others and about the world to which they belong' (Thompson 1995, 42).[44] The views of the listener are reshaped in the process of understanding and reacting to the speaker's words. As Bakhtin observes, the individual's thought 'is born and shaped in the process of articulation and the process of interaction and struggle with others' thought' (Bakhtin 1986, 92).

This intersubjective understanding of agency and identity underlies the claims that freedom of expression contributes to the recognition of truth, the advancement of democracy, and the realization of self. Freedom of expression is valuable because in communicating with others an individual gives shape to his or her ideas and aspirations, becomes capable of reflection and evaluation, and gains greater understanding of her/himself and the world. It is through communicative interaction that an individual develops and emerges as an autonomous agent in the positive sense of being able to consciously direct his or her life and to participate in the direction of his or her community. Through communication an individual creates different kinds of relationships with others and participates in different collective activities, such as self-government and the pursuit of knowledge.

6. The Established Dichotomies: Intrinsic/Instrumental and Listener/Speaker

The established accounts of the value of freedom of expression are described as either instrumental or intrinsic[45] (or as result-oriented or process-oriented (Shiner 1995, 192), or as concerned with the realization of a social goal or with protection of an individual right).[46] Some accounts see freedom of expression as valuable in itself. The freedom is intrinsically valuable because it permits free and rational beings to express their ideas and feelings. Or it must be protected out of respect for the freedom and rationality of individuals. Other accounts see freedom of expression as important because it contributes to a valued state of affairs: freedom of expression is instrumental to the realization of social goods such as public knowledge or democratic government.

Intrinsic accounts assume that freedom of expression, like other rights, is an aspect of the individual's fundamental liberty or autonomy that should be insulated from the demands of collective welfare. Yet any account that regards freedom of expression as a liberty (as a right of the individual to be free from external interference) seems unable to explain the other-regarding or community-oriented character of the protected activity of expression – of individuals speaking and listening to others.

Instrumental accounts of freedom of expression recognize that the freedom protects an other-regarding or social activity and so must be concerned with something more than respect for individual autonomy, something more than individual 'venting' or the exercise of individual reason. They assume that the freedom must be concerned with social goals that are in some way separate from, or beyond, the individual and his or her communicative actions, goals such as truth and democracy. Yet if freedom of expression is an instrumental right, its fundamental character seems less obvious. Its value is contingent on its contribution to the goals of truth and democracy. And there is no shortage of arguments that freedom of expression does not (always) advance these goals.[47]

The value (and potential harm) of expression will remain unclear as long as discussion about freedom of expression is locked into the intrinsic/instrumental dichotomy, in which the freedom is concerned with either the good of the community or the right of the individual. The value of freedom of expression rests on the social nature of individuals and the constitutive character of public discourse. This understanding of the freedom, however, has been inhibited by the individualism that dominates contemporary thinking about rights – its assumptions about the presocial individual and the instrumental value of community life. Once we recognize that individual agency and identity emerge in the social relationship of communication, the traditional split between intrinsic and instrumental accounts (or social and individual accounts) of the value of freedom of expression dissolves (Moon 1995, 470). Expression connects the individual (as speaker or listener) with others and in so doing contributes to her capacity for understanding and judgment, to her engagement in community life, and to her participation in a shared culture and collective governance.

The arguments described as instrumental focus on the contribution of speech to the collective goals of truth and democracy. However, we value truth not as an abstract social achievement but rather as something that is consciously realized by members of the community, individually and collectively, in the process of public discussion. Similarly, freedom of expression is not simply a tool or instrument that contributes to democratic government. We value freedom of expression not simply because it provides individuals with useful political information but more fundamentally because it is the way in which citizens participate in collective self-governance. There is no way to separate the goal from the process or the individual good from the public good.

Attaching the label 'intrinsic' to autonomy or self-realization accounts of the freedom of expression seems also to misdescribe the value at stake. Communication is a joint or public process, in which individual participants realize their human capacities and their individual identities. The individual does not simply gain satisfaction from expressing his pre-existing views on things: an individual's views, and more broadly his judgment and identity, take shape in the communicative process.

Freedom of expression theories are also categorized as either 'listener' or 'speaker' centred (Schauer 1982, 104). Listener-centred theories emphasize the right of the listener to hear and judge expression for herself. The listener's right is protected as a matter of respect for her autonomy as a rational agent or for its contribution to social goals such as the development of truth or the advancement of democratic government. Speaker-centred theories emphasize the value of self-expression. The individual's freedom to express himself is a part of his basic human autonomy or is critical to his ability to direct the development of his own personality. Each of these accounts recognizes the connection between speaking and listening, yet each values one or the other of these activities or, if it values them both, it values them as distinct or independent interests. Freedom of expression is valuable because it advances an important individual interest of the listener (or a more general social interest) and/or an important individual interest of the speaker.

The focus of these accounts on the different interests of the speaker and the listener misses the central dynamic of the freedom, the communicative relationship, in which the interests of speaker and listener are tied (Moon 1985, 352; Moon 1995, 426).[48] The activities of speaking and listening are part of a process and a relationship. This relationship is valuable because individual agency emerges and flourishes in the joint activity of creating meaning.

7. The Scope of Freedom of Expression

In each of the established accounts of the value of freedom of expression, the freedom is seen as protecting acts of communication, in which an individual 'speaker' conveys a message to a 'listener' (*Irwin Toy* 1989, 968; Schauer 1982, 98). This is not a conclusion of theory, but rather an assumption that drives the theoretical arguments. The object of most freedom of expression theory is to explain the special protection of communication and to give a clearer or more precise definition to the scope of this protected activity.

Even though the established accounts define expression in similar terms, each tends to define the core and the margins of the freedom differently. The emphasis on a particular value, such as truth or democracy, or on a particular dimension of the communicative process, will affect the definition of the scope of freedom of expression and the 'balancing' of expression interests against competing values or interests.

Truth-based (or knowledge-based) accounts of the freedom tend to focus on factual claims, which appeal to the audience's autonomous reason and can be described as either true or false. In an account that emphasizes the discovery of truth, the 'word,' and more particularly the printed word, is the paradigm of expression.[49] Words enable individuals to make statements, the truth of which can be debated and judged. They effectively convey ideas and information and support reflection and reasoned judgment on the part of both the 'speaker' and the 'listener.' The printed word, in particular, has the power to reach large audiences, to articulate complex ideas, and to present arguments in a clear, rational, and dispassionate way.[50] While truth-based accounts of freedom of expression sometimes extend protection to more emotive forms of expression, or to art forms such as music, dance, or painting, the inclusion of these forms requires an enlargement of the idea of truth beyond the factual knowledge that individuals and communities use to advance their goals.

The obvious focus of democracy-based accounts of freedom of expression is on communication about the political issues of the day, even if the democratic account is sometimes extended to include protection of scientific and philosophic works. Like truth-based accounts, democracy-based accounts tend to emphasize propositional speech. If the individual is to participate in collective self-government, she must be free to express her views on public issues and to hear the views of others. It is, however, sometimes argued that emotive expression that relates to political issues may be just as important to democratic decision making as calm and rational discussion of the issues. Emotive expression is important because it lets fellow citizens know the depth of the speaker's feelings about a particular issue. I suspect, however, that the increasing emphasis on emotive expression reflects a partial shift in our understanding of democratic participation from informed deliberation and active contribution to public discussion to the manifestation or registration of feelings in polls and elections.

Accounts of the value of freedom of speech that emphasize individual self-realization or autonomy attach significance to both rational and emotive forms (or more correctly dimensions) of expression.[51] Communication is not simply the conveyance of information and ideas, it is also a way of expressing/articulating one's deeply held feelings. As the U.S. Supreme Court recognized in *Cohen* 1971, all acts of expression have both a propositional and an expressive dimension – both rational and emotive force:

> [M]uch linguistic expression serves a dual communicative function: it conveys not only ideas capable of relatively precise, detached explication, but otherwise inexpressible emotions as well. In fact, words are often chosen as much for their emotive as their cognitive force. We cannot sanction the view that the Constitution while solicitous of the cognitive content of individual speech has little or no regard for that emotive function which, practically speaking, may often be the more important element of the overall message sought to be communicated. (*Cohen* 1971, 26)

When self-realization is the guiding value, the paradigm of expression is the spoken word or works of art or other symbolic acts either public or intimate.[52] While the printed word permits the careful articulation and consideration of ideas, oral speech *seems* to involve a more 'direct' and 'immediate' expression of the individual's ideas and feelings. The spoken word is performance-oriented, 'embedded in the human life world, connected with action and struggle' (Ong 1982, 101). Oral communication is more likely to be spontaneous, impulsive, and emotional because it is more closely connected with the immediate context.

In each of the established accounts of the value of freedom of expression, regardless of its particular emphasis, expression is assumed to involve the conveyance of a message to an audience – an engagement of speaker and listener.[53] An act of expression or communication is characterized by the agent's intention to articulate and convey to an audience an idea or feeling. When communicating, the speaker wants the audience to recognize that his or her act is meaningful – that the act is intended to convey to them a message (Moon 1985, 351; Green 1994, 138).[54] The communicative act will be successful only if the audience recognizes the speaker's intention and is able to understand the meaning of the act. As discussed earlier, this characterization of expression or communication as an intentional act does not mean that the act's meaning is simply a matter of the agent's intentions.[55]

An individual may communicate using established symbolic forms, such as spoken or written language, which the audience recognizes as meaningful and intended to convey a message. Or he may use other symbolic forms that have a generally recognized meaning, such as flag burning or certain gestures.[56] The individual may also use less conventionalized forms of expression, such as parking a car, an example used by the Supreme Court of Canada in *Irwin Toy* (1989). While the communicative function of parking may not be very obvious to others, as long as the individual intends by his or her act to convey a message to an audience then that act should be regarded as expression. According to the Supreme Court of Canada, expression can take 'an infinite variety of forms,' including the written and spoken word, the arts and physical gestures (*Irwin Toy* 1989, 607).

There is a way in which everything we do can be seen as expressive of the self, and as telling others something about us. However, the question in every case is whether the actor intends to convey a message to others, and more specifically, whether she intends that others view her act as meaningful.[57] Nevertheless, there is no bright line separating acts intended by the actor to convey a message from other voluntary human acts.

On this view, the creation of a work of art is an act of expression, perhaps even the paradigm case of expression. Even if art is, as Frederick Schauer says, 'a mode of self-expression, or if there is taken to be a necessary gap between what is intended and what is perceived by the observer' (Schauer 1982, 110),[58] art involves the use of conventional forms and is intended by its creator to be viewed as meaningful. Art gives form to human feelings and concerns by making them visible (or audible) and brings them into the public realm for shared contemplation. According to Richard Wollheim, '[t]he value of art ... does not exist exclusively, or even primarily for the artist. It is shared equally between the artist and his [or her] audience' (Wollheim 1980, 86).[59] A work of art materializes 'a way of experiencing' and brings 'a particular cast of mind out into the world of objects, where men [and women] can look at it' (Geertz 1983, 99).[60] It is meant to be viewed as a human creation and as 'the object of an ever-increasing or deepening attention' (Wollheim 1980, 123).

While it is true that we experience art and do not simply interpret it, art is not just human feeling projected onto objects in the world; artistic expression works through signs and depends on a practice or institution. To view something as a work of art is to see it as human expression formulated in and shaped by a particular medium (Gombrich 1963, 11; Wollheim 1980, 124).[61] In calling something a work of art we underline its artificial character. Indeed, according to some contemporary views, the significance of art is that it leads us to recognize the artificial character of communicative codes and the conventional nature of perception and understanding.

If freedom of expression protects communicative relationships, and the joint activity of creating/interpreting meaning, there must be both a 'speaker' and an audience to whom the speaker wishes to communicate a message. Even acts of 'speaking to oneself' bear some resemblance to conventional dialogue. (While such acts may or may not be seen as falling within the scope of freedom of expression they are unlikely to be the subject of state restriction.)[62] A speaker who speaks only to her/himself, when writing a diary for example, employs a language. Although the diarist may not intend to communicate with others, he uses a socially created language to give shape and clarity to his thoughts. The diarist may even be seen as speaking to a future self, recording his ideas and feelings so that they are available to be read and considered at a later time.

It also follows from this view of freedom of expression that the 'speaker' must intend to appeal to his or her audience in a conscious or non-manipulative way.[63] Expression may be confrontational, uncivil, and even insulting and still engage its audience.[64] However, the exclusion by the American courts of 'fighting words' from the protection of the First Amendment is a recognition that at a certain point expression is so uncivil or threatening that it cannot be seen as communicative engagement. More obviously, the relationship of expression is undermined by manipulative expression, in which a speaker seeks to affect audience thought and action while by-passing conscious recognition. Even those accounts of freedom of expression that downplay the relational character of expression find a way to exclude or marginalize manipulative or deceptive expression. They classify (without explanation) deceptive or manipulative expression either as 'action' or 'conduct,' which is denied constitutional recognition, or as 'low value' expression, which is given less weight when balanced against competing interests.[65]

8. Value and Harm

Individualist approaches to freedom of expression have difficulty accounting for both the value and harm of expression. If expression is simply a transparent process in which the individual conveys pre-existing (prelinguistic) ideas and feelings to an audience, then it is unclear why it is different from, and more important than, other human actions. Why should we view freedom of expression as a distinct right rather than simply an aspect of a more general liberty of action?

Expression is valuable because individual identity/agency emerge in communicative interaction; because our ideas and feelings and our understanding of self and the world develop through communication with others.

At the same time, this dependence on expression means that words can sometimes be hurtful or manipulative (Moon 1995, 445–6). While expression sometimes seems to increase knowledge and stimulate reflection, even about our most basic assumptions, at other times it seems to discourage critical thinking, to leave us in 'the deadening grip of disengaged reason' (Taylor 1989a, 377), to deceive and to manipulate. As described in the next chapter, the impact of a particular act of expression will depend not only on its design or form but also on its social and material circumstances.

Chapter Two

The Constitutional Adjudication of Freedom of Expression

1. Introduction: The Canadian Courts' Approach

The Canadian Charter of Rights and Freedoms establishes a two-step process for the adjudication of rights claims. The first step is concerned with whether a Charter right has been breached by a state act. The court must define the protected interest or activity and determine whether it has been interfered with by the state. At this stage, the burden of proof lies with the party claiming a breach of rights. The second step in the adjudicative process is concerned with the justification of limits on Charter rights. Section 1 of the Charter states that the protected rights and freedoms may be limited provided the limits are 'prescribed by law,' 'reasonable,' and 'demonstrably justified in a free and democratic society.' The limitation decision is described by the courts as a balancing of competing interests or values. At this stage, the onus of proof lies with the party seeking to uphold the limitation, usually the state.

The two-step model is built on an understanding of freedom of expression as a right of the individual to be free from external interference. Freedom of expression, however, does not protect liberty/freedom in general. Instead, it protects the individual's freedom to communicate with others, to participate in an activity that is deeply social in character. As well, if participation in the social activity of expression is valuable to the individual and the community, the right to freedom of expression should be concerned not just with preventing state (and other external) interference with the individual's expression but also with ensuring that the individual has real opportunities to communicate with others. The structure of constitutional adjudication, however, tends to suppress the freedom's distributive demands (concern about effective opportunities for expression) and its relational character (recognition/protection of the relationship of communication). This suppression of the social and material character of freedom of expression makes it difficult for the courts to explain the freedom's value and harm and to determine its proper scope and limits.

The Scope of Freedom of Expression

In its elaboration of freedom of expression under section 2(b) of the Charter, the Supreme Court of Canada has made some grand statements about the freedom's value. The court has said that freedom of expression is 'an essential feature of Canadian parliamentary democracy' (*Dolphin Delivery* 1986, 584); that 'a democracy cannot exist without' it (*Edmonton Journal* 1989, 1336); that it is 'one of the fundamental concepts that has formed the basis for the historical development of the political, social and educational institutions of western society' (*Dolphin Delivery* 1986, 583); that it is 'the means by which the individual expresses his or her personal identity and sense of individuality' (*Ford* 1988, 749); that it is an important way of 'seeking and attaining truth' (*Irwin Toy* 1989, 976); and, more generally, that its 'vital importance ... cannot be over-emphasized' (*Edmonton Journal* 1989, 1336). While these statements are general and undeveloped, they are understood by the court to add up to a substantial justification for the constitutional protection of freedom of expression.

The generous tone of these general statements supports a very broad interpretation of the scope of freedom of expression. According to the Supreme Court of Canada, section 2(b) protects any activity that 'conveys or attempts to convey a meaning' (*Irwin Toy* 1989, 968). An act of expression is distinguished from other voluntary human acts by the intention with which it is performed. If the act is intended by the actor to convey a message to someone then it is an act of expression, and prima facie protected under section 2(b). Protection is given 'irrespective of the particular meaning or message sought to be conveyed' (*Keegstra* 1990, 729), because 'in a free, pluralistic and democratic society we prize a diversity of ideas and opinions for their inherent value both to the community and to the individual' (*Irwin Toy* 1989, 968).

Despite the Supreme Court's stated commitment to interpret Charter rights purposively, the court has defined expression without any explicit reference to the values said to underlie freedom of expression.

Indeed, the Supreme Court has said on several occasions that it will not exclude an act of expression from the scope of the freedom simply because it is thought to be without value (*Keegstra* 1990, 760).[1] The underlying values of truth, democracy, and self-realization play an active or explicit role later in the adjudicative process, after the court has defined the category of 'expression' and, most clearly, at the section 1 limitations stage.

In *Irwin Toy* 1989, the Supreme Court of Canada used the example of illegal or unauthorized parking to illustrate the potential breadth of the category of protected expression. The court observed that parking is not ordinarily an expressive act, because it is not ordinarily intended to carry a message. In most cases people park illegally because they cannot find a convenient or available space or because they are unwilling to pay parking charges. According to the court, however, if an individual parks his or her car illegally as a protest against the way that parking spaces are allocated or against some other policy or practice, then the act of illegal parking will fall within the scope of section 2(b) because it is performed for a communicative purpose.[2] In a variety of decisions the court has held that the category of human acts intended to carry a message, and so protected under section 2(b), includes advertising, picketing, hate promotion, soliciting for the purposes of prostitution, and pornography.

There are two exceptions to the court's broad definition of the scope of freedom of expression under section 2(b). First, the court has said that a violent act, even if intended to carry a message, does not fall within the scope of the section: 'While the guarantee of free expression protects all content of expression, certainly violence as a form of expression receives no such protection' (*Irwin Toy* 1989, 970). This exclusion extends only to expression that has a violent *form*. Expression that advocates violence or threatens violence is protected under section 2(b), although subject to limits under section 1.

The court has also narrowed the scope of section 2(b) by drawing a distinction between two different types of state restriction on expressive activity: state acts that have as their purpose the restriction of expression and those which are not designed to restrict expression but nevertheless have this effect.[3] The significance of the purpose/effect distinction, which roughly parallels the distinction in American jurisprudence between content restrictions and time, place, and manner restrictions,[4] is that a law intended to limit expression, and in particular the expression of certain messages, will be found to violate section 2(b) 'automatically,' while a law that simply has the effect of limiting expression will be found to violate section 2(b) only if the person attacking the law can show that the restricted expression advances the values that underlie freedom of expression.[5] In particular, he or she must show that the restricted expression contributes to the realization of truth, participation in social and political decision making, and diversity in the forms of individual self-fulfilment and human flourishing (*Irwin Toy* 1989, 976).

Limits on Freedom of Expression

Once the court has determined that the state has restricted expression protected by section 2(b), it then considers whether the restriction is justified under the terms of section 1 of the Charter. The court asks whether the restriction represents a substantial purpose, advances this purpose rationally, impairs the freedom no more than is necessary, and is proportionate to the impairment of the freedom (*Oakes* 1986, 138–9).

While the Supreme Court of Canada has often said that freedom of expression can only be overridden when its exercise would result in a substantial harm to social or individual interests,[6] it has adopted what it calls a 'contextual approach' to the assessment of limits on the freedom (*Edmonton Journal* 1989, 1356; *Dagenais* 1994, 878).[7] In deciding whether a limit is justified the court will consider the necessity or importance of the restriction but also the extent to which freedom of expression interests are impaired by the restriction.[8] While the court has defined the scope of the freedom under section 2(b) broadly so that it protects all non-violent forms of expression, when assessing limits under section 1 the court distinguishes between core and marginal forms of expression, identifying different instances of expression as more or less valuable and more or less vulnerable to restriction.[9] Political expression, for example, is considered core expression. As such it can be restricted only for the most substantial and compelling reasons. In contrast, pornography and advertising are seen as marginal forms of expression, because they are less directly linked to the values underlying freedom of expression. As a consequence they may be restricted for less substantial reasons. The court has also said that time, place, and manner restrictions may be justified more easily than content-based restrictions.

In practice, the Supreme Court has been prepared to uphold limits on freedom of expression when it is convinced that the exercise of the freedom causes harm to the interests of another, including harm to reputation, business operations, and public order. In most of its freedom of expression cases the court has looked to social science evidence of the link between expression and harm. Yet such evidence is often inconclusive. In many of these cases the court has either fallen back on a 'common sense' recognition of the causal link between a particular form of expression and harmful consequences or deferred to the legislature's judgment that such a link exists, particularly when the restriction is meant to protect a vulnerable group in the community.[10] In a few cases, however, the court has been unwilling to defer to legislative judgment and has struck down the restriction because the link between the restricted expression and the alleged harm was not made out clearly enough.

Critiques of the Approach

There has been some criticism of the way in which the Supreme Court has applied the two-step approach to freedom of expression cases. First, the court has been criticized for failing to maintain the distinction between questions of scope under section 2(b) and questions of limitation under section 1. In particular, there has been criticism of the exclusion of violent expression from the scope of the freedom under section 2(b) (Macklem 1990, 552; Cameron 1989, 268; Cameron 1990, 98; Lepofsky 1993, 52; Anand 1998, 151).[11] It is argued that if the exclusion of violence is really an exception to the protection of expression, and does not simply rest on a judgment that violence is not expression because it does not convey a message, then it is a limitations issue that should be addressed under section 1. The concern is that the violence exclusion involves a premature narrowing of the constitutional understanding of freedom of expression under section 2(b) that may permit limitations on expression that are not properly scrutinized.

Similar concerns have been expressed about the rule that requires a person challenging a law that has the effect (rather than the purpose) of restricting expression, to show that his or her restricted expression advances the values underlying the freedom (Macklem 1990, 553; Lepofsky 1993, 73; Cameron 1990, 125; Cameron 1991, 99; Cameron 1989, 270; Kanter 1992, 493). The concern is that this involves a judgment about the relative value of the restricted expression and/or the importance of the competing claims that support the restriction. It is a limitation issue and should be dealt with under section 1 so that the burden falls on the state, rather than the person challenging the law, to show that the limit is demonstrably justified.

Second, the court has been criticized for taking a deferential approach under section 1 to state restrictions on expression (Cameron 1992, 1151; Cameron 1997, 5; Kramer 1992, 87; Lepofsky 1993, 93; Valois 1992, 423). It is claimed that the court's willingness to defer to the legislature's judgment that a particular form of expression is harmful and should be restricted (along with its unwillingness to accept that social conflict and offence are a necessary cost of freedom of expression) has undermined the constitutional commitment to the freedom. If freedom of expression is a fundamental right, it should be restricted only on the basis of clear and convincing evidence that it causes substantial harm.[12]

The complaint then is that the courts (and in particular the Supreme Court of Canada) have been unfaithful to the established adjudicative structure and as a consequence have eroded the constitutional protection of freedom of expression. I believe, however, that the places where critics see an undermining of the two-step structure are simply points of stress in a structure built on an understanding of freedom of expression as a right of the *individual* to be free from state *interference.*

First, the idea that there is a clear and complete division between questions of scope (breach) and limits (justification) rests on the view that freedom of expression is part of the individual's personal sphere or domain – a sphere that ordinarily should not be interfered with by the state. The issue under section 2(b) is the proper definition of the individual's personal sphere, the activity of expression, while the issue under section 1 is the need or justification for incursions by the state into that sphere. However, if we recognize that freedom of expression is concerned not so much with the protection of an individual's independence from others as with the protection or creation of a relationship of communication between two or more individuals, then the distinction between scope and limits begins to break down.

Many freedom of expression issues involve abuses of the communicative relationship, such as manipulation or deceit. It is unclear whether these should be understood as issues of scope under section 2(b) or limitation issues under section 1. The exclusion of violent acts of expression under section 2(b), as a matter of the freedom's scope rather than its limitation, suggests some recognition by the court that freedom of expression is concerned with the protection of a social relationship. Even though an act of violence may carry a message, it does so in a way that undermines or negates the relationship of communication. Freedom from violence is not simply a competing interest that might justify restriction of expression under section 1 of the Charter.

The distinction between scope and limits also breaks down once we recognize that the freedom has a distributive dimension. The established two-step model is built on an understanding of freedom of expression as a right to be free from external interference, and in particular, government interference. Government interference with the individual's expression will be justified only if necessary to advance a substantial and pressing purpose. In the two-step adjudicative structure it is unclear where concerns about the individual's opportunity (power) to communicate are to be addressed.

The special rule under section 2(b) applied to time, place, and manner restrictions (a law that has the effect, rather than the purpose, of restricting expression will violate section 2(b) only if it is shown that the restricted expression advances the values underlying the freedom) reflects the problems involved in fitting distributive issues into the established framework of freedom of expression adjudication. An assessment of a specific (time, place, and manner) limit on the individual's opportunity to participate in public communication depends not so much on the strength of the state's justification for the limitation as on the alternative spaces available to the individual (or his or her message) in the social distribution of communicative power. Yet the issue of the adequacy of communicative power cuts across the scope/limits divide because it turns on neither the definition of expression nor the identification of a harm substantial enough to override the value of expression.

Finally, I believe that the deferential approach followed by the Supreme Court of Canada in its consideration of limits on freedom of expression under section 1 reflects a basic tension in the court's individualist understanding of the freedom's justification. When defining the scope of the freedom the court sees the individual as free and rational, as a maker of choices, as an autonomous agent capable of giving direction to his or her life. In expressing her/himself, an individual gives voice to her/his thoughts and feelings and provides ideas and information for other individuals to consider, adopt or reject. However, when the court moves from section 2(b) to section 1, it often seems to shift from a discourse of freedom and rationality to a behavioural or causal discourse. Under section 1 (sometimes explicitly and sometimes implicitly) a different image of the individual surfaces, a counter-image to the dominant image of section 2(b). The individual is seen as irrational, manipulable, directed by unchosen preferences, urges, and desires. Expression is seen as a form of action that impacts on the individual, sometimes causing harm or sometimes causing him or her to engage in harmful behaviour.

This shift occurs because the court's initial view of the individual as free and rational, and communication as transparent, makes it difficult to explain the risks or harms of expression. When confronted with issues of manipulation, intimidation, and economic power, the court's faith in the freedom and rationality of the individual collapses. The court recognizes that the expression of others can influence, distort, and sometimes even direct an individual's thoughts and actions. Unable to explain this influence within the discourse of individual freedom and rationality, the court simply shifts to a behavioural or cause/effect discourse that discards the liberal image of the individual and treats him or her as determined, radically situated, and irrational.[13] The individual is viewed as socially determined, subject to the push and pull of external influences. The shift to a behavioural discourse at this second stage of adjudication occurs without any explicit reconsideration of the rationalist assumptions that underlie the court's section 2(b) analysis.

The result in a particular case turns on whether or not the expression at issue can be shown to 'cause' harm to another individual or group by affecting their behaviour or the behaviour of others towards them. The court listens for the crack of the billiard balls. However, the social science evidence of the causal link between expression and harm does not yield a crisp and clear sound. In most cases the court is prepared to defer to the legislature's judgment that a particular form of expression causes harm and should be restricted. Occasionally, however, the court declines to defer to the legislature and instead strikes down the restriction on the ground that the evidence does not establish that the restricted expression causes harm. The difficulty involved in establishing whether an act of expression has 'caused' an individual to act in a certain way, and more significantly the uncertainty about what we mean by causation in the context of human behaviour, means that the result in any particular case turns on whether the court decides to defer to legislative judgment, a decision that rests on unarticulated reasons.

As long as the court operates on the basis of established individualist assumptions about agency, which are reinforced by traditional conceptions of rights and the structure of constitutional adjudication, it will be unable to reconcile a belief in free and rational human agency with a recognition that society influences individual behaviour in significant ways. It will continue to oscillate between a conception of the individual as free and rational and a conception of him or her as socially determined. It will continue to bury any consideration of the real and important conditions of public communication beneath a behavioural discourse.

2. The Relationship of Communication

The culture of rights and the structure of rights adjudication supports an individualist understanding of freedom of expression. Freedom of expression, like other constitutional rights and freedoms, is seen as an important part of the individual's personal sphere that should be protected from external interference, particularly state interference. Most contemporary accounts of the legitimacy of the judicial role in the enforcement of constitutional rights against the state rest on the view that rights are aspects of the individual's basic liberty or autonomy that should be insulated from the ordinary give and take of preference-based politics.

The established justifications for freedom of expression tend to focus on either the interests of the speaker (writer) or those of the listener (reader). Listener-centred theories emphasize the right of the listener to hear and judge expression for him/herself as both intrinsically and instrumentally valuable. The listener's right is protected as a matter of respect for his or her autonomy as a rational agent, but also for its contribution to social goals, such as the development of truth or the advancement of democratic government. Speaker-centred theories emphasize the intrinsic value of self-expression. The individual's freedom to express herself as she chooses is a matter of her fundamental autonomy.

The Supreme Court of Canada, like most contemporary commentators, draws on both listener-centred and speaker-centred accounts of the value of freedom of expression.[14] Added together speaker and listener interests are thought to represent a powerful justification for the constitutional protection of expression. In the Supreme Court's account, while there is an obvious connection between the activities of speaking and listening, each is understood and valued independently. Freedom of expression is valued because it protects an important individual interest of the listener and/or an important individual interest of the speaker.

However, the activities of speaking and listening are interdependent, they are part of a process and a relationship.[15] The interests of the speaker and listener are realized in the joint activity of creating meaning. The court's focus on the individual interests of the speaker and/or the listener misses the central dynamic of freedom of expression: the communicative relationship that joins the interests of speaker and listener. Freedom of expression is concerned not so much with the protection of the individual's personal sphere from external interference as with the protection of (and perhaps even support for) a relationship of communication between two or more persons. There is often a degree of conflict or tension in the communicative relationship: the audience may not always want to hear the message, or the message may seem harsh and even hostile to its audience. Nevertheless, in most of these situations the speaker is still seeking in some sense to engage her or his audience and not simply to deceive or threaten them. It is a cost of freedom of expression that people sometimes have to endure unwanted communication.

The Supreme Court's definition of expression as 'the conveyance of a message' suggests the idea of a communicative relationship. Yet its abstract and formal definition of the freedom's scope allows the court to downplay the relational character of expression (the engagement of speaker and listener) and the constitutive character of expression (the way that speaking and listening shape the speaker's/listener's thoughts and feelings). Indeed, in many cases the court barely acknowledges that the conveyance of a message involves an audience to whom the message is conveyed. Consider, for example, the court's reply in *Butler* 1992, 489–90) to the claim that pornographic films do not convey a message:

> The meaning to be ascribed to the work cannot be measured by the reaction of the audience, which, in some cases, may amount to no more than physical arousal or shock. Rather, the meaning of the work derives from the fact that it has been intentionally created by its author. To use an example, it may very well be said that a blank wall in itself conveys no meaning. However, if one deliberately chooses to capture that image by the medium of film, the work necessarily has some meaning for its author and thereby constitutes expression.

The court seemed to assume that the meaning of an act is simply a matter of the actor's intention and that the conveyance of a message need not involve any engagement with, or attempt to engage, an audience. The court's general definition of expression suppresses the tension between the individualist assumptions that underlie the culture and structure of rights adjudication and the relational character of freedom of expression.

The assumption that a clear distinction can be drawn between issues of scope and issues of limitation rests on an individualist understanding of freedom of expression. In applying the Charter, there are two issues for the court:[16] the scope of the individual activity of expression and the justification for state interference with this activity. However, if freedom of expression is more about human connection than individual independence, scope and limits issues may not be so easy to separate.

Some interests, such as privacy or reputation, may be seen as competing with freedom of expression and as the basis for restriction of the freedom under section 1.[17] Other interests, such as freedom from intimidation, deceit, or manipulation, are less easily viewed in this way. Expression that deceives, intimidates, manipulates, or physically injures its audience involves a significant abuse of the communicative relationship. It is unclear where in the two-step model the courts should deal with these abuses of the relationship, in which the individual interests of speaker and listener diverge. Where in the existing structure should the harm of deceit, for example, be addressed? From one perspective the harm of deceit to the listener seems external to, or separate from, the definition of the individual's freedom of expression. Yet, from another perspective, freedom from deceit can be seen as more than simply a competing interest to be addressed under section 1. It can be viewed as integral to the value and definition of expression.

Generally, when a speaker seeks to deceive, manipulate, or intimidate the listener the court considers that his or her 'expression' falls within the protection of section 2(b) but that the injury to the listener is a possible ground for limitation under section 1. The injury represents a competing interest that should be balanced against the speaker's freedom of expression in a way that takes account of various contextual factors. Yet we may feel uneasy in identifying manipulative or deceitful expression as valuable and protected under section 2(b) and as subject to restriction only because it happens to violate the independent interests of the listener. These harms or abuses seem to undermine freedom of expression values in the most fundamental way.

The Violence Exception

While many commentators have argued that the violence exception represents a failure to apply properly the distinction between scope and limits, I believe that it reflects the problematic nature of the distinction between scope and limits. The Supreme Court has provided very little explanation for the exception, relying simply on our general revulsion to violence. However, its decision to exclude violence from the scope of section 2(b) suggests some recognition that the communicative relationship is central to freedom of expression and that preventing abuse of that relationship is not simply an external competing interest that should be balanced against the freedom under section 1. Chief Justice Dickson in *Keegstra* 1990, 732, referring to the exclusion of violence, stated that 'the extreme repugnance of this form to free expression values justif[ies] such an extraordinary step.' But it is not clear how easily the issue fits here either. There are problems in dealing with violent expression under section 2(b) rather than under section 1. The most obvious is the difficulty in defining the scope of the exclusion, in determining when harmful expression should be excluded under section 2(b) and when it should be addressed under section 1, with the court taking account of all the circumstances.

Irwin Toy 1989: The Violence Exception Introduced

In *Irwin Toy* 1989 the Supreme Court described a potentially significant exception to its definition of 'expression' as the conveyance of meaning. According to the court, expression that takes a violent form falls outside the protection of section 2(b).[18]

This exception may rest simply on a judgment by the court that violent acts are not intended to carry a message and for that reason do not fall within the scope of the freedom. Such a judgment, though, would require a narrower, or at least a clearer, definition of expression than that offered by the court. Indeed, it appears that the court specifically excluded violent acts from the scope of freedom of expression because it recognized that its broad and vague definition of the freedom could be seen as extending protection to many violent acts. Violent acts have 'meaning': they express anger; they assert power. Sometimes an act of violence is described as meaningless, which serves as a reminder that with other such acts the victim (or the larger audience) understands all too well the message that he/she should be afraid or should submit.

Instead of creating an exclusion for violent acts the court might have followed through with its broad understanding of freedom of expression and included these acts within its scope but relied on section 1 to justify their restriction. After all, this has been the court's general approach – to define expression broadly and use section 1 to deal with difficult issues. While a violent act may be expressive, it involves serious harm to others and so its restriction would be easily justified under section 1. Almost certainly the court deviates from its broad and inclusive approach to the scope of freedom of expression, and its reliance on section 1, because it feels uncomfortable treating a violent act as a matter of freedom of expression (the exercise of a fundamental human right) that must give way only when it comes into conflict with another fundamental human interest. The court might reasonably have felt that this gave a small, but undeserved, amount of legitimacy to acts of violence.

The issue of violent expression will not fit comfortably into the existing two-step structure, regardless of how carefully the court may think about the definition of 'expression.' This structure rests on an understanding of freedom of expression as a right of the individual to either speak or listen. Because an act of violence may be seen as expressing the feelings of the actor and even as having meaning or carrying a message, it may be considered expression under section 2(b). But, of course, a violent act represents a crude denial of the listener's interests or rights. This might be seen as a conflict of individual interests that should be resolved through balancing under section 1. Yet the listener's interests are not external to the freedom. Freedom of expression protects the interests of both speaker and listener. Under the established model, when these interests conflict it is unclear which should prevail. More fundamentally, it is unclear whether the interests of the individual listener should be seen as an important aspect of the freedom or as in competition with it. If freedom of expression protects communicative relationships and the combined interests of both speaker and listener, then the issue of violent expression is not simply a matter of balancing separate and competing interests, as the two step-model assumes. Violent 'expression' is an abuse of the communicative process. It attacks or undermines the relationship of communication in a basic way.

Keegstra 1990 : Defining the Scope of the Violence Exception

In *Keegstra* 1990, supporters of the Criminal Code restriction of hate promotion argued that the hateful expression prohibited by the Code fell within the violence exception described in *Irwin Toy* 1989. It was argued that hate propaganda, like other violent forms of expression, is 'inimical' to the values underlying the freedom. More particularly, it was claimed that hate propaganda falls within the exclusion because 'it imperils the ability of target group members themselves to convey thoughts and feelings in non-violent ways without fear of censure' (*Keegstra* 1990, 731). Chief Justice Dickson (for the majority) and Madame Justice McLachlin (for the dissenting minority) confirmed that violent expression was excluded from the protection of section 2(b) but rejected the argument that hate promotion fell within this exclusion.

Chief Justice Dickson drew from the court's previous judgments the principle that 'the content of expression is irrelevant in determining the scope of the Charter provision.' From this he reasoned that the 'violent conduct' exception extends only 'to expression communicated directly through physical harm' (*Keegstra* 1990, 732). In his view, the hateful expression restricted by section 319(2) of the Code is objectionable because of its message, and so is not analogous to violence and does not fall within the exception. Even threats of violence do not fall within the exception, because the harm they cause stems from the audience's understanding of the message.

According to Chief Justice Dickson, when expression has a violent form rather than simply a harmful message, it interferes with the basic values underlying freedom of expression and should not be given protection under section 2(b): 'the extreme repugnance of this form to free expression values justifying such an extraordinary step' (*Keegstra* 1990, 732). However, as Dickson C.J. acknowledged, the distinction between form and content is problematic in a number of ways.[19] First, restriction of a particular form of expression always affects the opportunity to communicate some messages more than others. More fundamentally, though, meaning is inseparable from the form in which it is manifested. A restriction on a particular form of expression must be understood as a restriction on meaning, even if the purpose of the restriction is not to prevent the communication of a particular message. Second, all acts of expression have some sort of direct physical consequences: if not a broken nose, then perhaps broken silence. It is unclear when the physical effects of an expressive act will be considered violent, so that the act falls outside the protection of section 2(b), or when the act will be protected under that section, even though it causes injury to the interests of another – injury such as obstruction or harassment that might justify restriction under section 1. If an act is intended to carry a message, and the reason for its restriction is its harmful effect, then the court must decide whether this effect is such that the expressive conduct should be excluded from the scope of freedom of expression or whether the effect simply justifies restriction under section 1. It is unclear where, or even how, this line is to be drawn.

Madame Justice McLachlin in her dissenting judgment took a broader view of the exclusion, arguing that it should apply to both acts and threats of violence. In her view, threats of violence, like acts of violence, are coercive: they 'tak[e] away free choice and undermin[e] freedom of action' (*Keegstra* 1990, 830). She observed that threats 'undercut one of the essential justifications of free expression – the role of expression in enhancing the freedom to choose between ideas (the argument based on truth) or between courses of conduct (the argument based on democracy). Being antithetical to the values underlying the guarantee of free expression, it is logical and appropriate that violence and threats of violence be excluded from its scope' (*Keegstra* 1990, 830). She did not think that James Keegstra's expression amounted to either a violent act or threat and so she found that the exception did not apply in this case.[20]

The inclusion of threats within the category of violent expression would add to the definitional difficulties. The judgment as to whether harsh and intimidating words should be restricted because they cause fear and upset or because they silence and isolate the listener must take into account a wide range of factors, including the nature of the message and the opportunity for reflection and choice. It is a judgment that cannot rely on any clear divide between acceptable challenge and criticism and unacceptable aggression and antagonism.

Once again the issue of the restriction of acts (or threats) of violence cuts across the scope/limits divide. If the court waits to deal with violent or threatening expression under section 1, it seems to miss the point of freedom of expression and to give legitimacy to unacceptable actions. However, if the court seeks to exclude acts and threats of violence from the protection of section 2(b), it takes on the difficult task of defining the scope of the exclusion. It is unclear when an expressive action should be denied protection under section 2(b) and when it should be protected but subject to restriction under section 1.

Other Abuses of the Relationship

Instead of simply limiting violent expression under section 1, through the process of balancing or accommodating competing interests, the Supreme Court has decided that this form of expression should be excluded entirely from the scope of section 2(b). Yet violence may be seen as expressive of the actor and as advancing (instrumentally) his or her interests, even though it harms the interests of the audience (through physical injury of the victim or intimidation of the larger audience). The established approach to freedom of expression issues would seem to require a choice, even if an easy choice, between the competing interests of speaker and listener, of the sort that is made under section 1 rather than section 2(b).

The court's conclusion that violence undermines the values underlying freedom of expression and should be excluded from the freedom's scope suggests some recognition that freedom of expression is concerned with the protection of a social relationship – that the interests of the speaker and listener are tied. However, in an adjudicative structure and a rights culture that emphasize the protection of individual independence rather than relationship, this recognition can only be partial. In extreme cases, such as physical violence, the court excludes this expression from the scope of section 2(b). In other cases the issue is resolved in the established way under section 1 and is described as a balancing of the speaker's rights against the listener's rights. Sometimes the court even describes this as a balancing of competing freedom of expression values.

The court's decision to exclude violent expression from the scope of section 2(b) rests on a recognition that violence undermines the freedom in a very basic way. Yet this exclusion raises all sorts of definitional problems. How do we define its scope? Why should other instances of harmful expression not be excluded from the scope of freedom of expression? Do we run the risk of excluding harsh but nevertheless valuable expression without proper consideration? Can the line between unpleasant but constitutionally protected expression and unprotected abusive and threatening expression be drawn without taking account of the social, political, economic, and historical context in which the act of expression occurs?[21]

Not surprisingly, the court has decided to define the violence exception narrowly so that it encompasses only those cases in which the action/expression involves serious harm, regardless of the precise circumstances in which it occurs. Other instances of expression, which may cause injury to the listener and may undermine the relationship of communication, are dealt with under section 1. In these cases, the court can consider the larger social context to determine whether the communication should be seen as part of the inevitable 'rough and tumble' of public debate or as an unacceptable instance of abusive or harmful expression.[22]

The relationship of communication can be abused or undermined by means other than physical violence. Manipulation, like violence, might be viewed simply as an abuse or negation of the relationship of communication and not as an interest in competition with freedom of expression. Lying might also be seen as an abuse of the communicative relationship. When a speaker lies, he intends to mislead the listener. He wants the listener to trust him and to treat his words as true.[23] Not only is lying a wrong against the particular listener but, inasmuch as it discourages future trust, it is damaging to the practice of communication and so is a wrong against the larger community. Yet in a shocking passage in the majority judgment in *Zundel* 1992, 262, Madame Justice McLachlin found not only that lying to the general public was protected expression under section 2(b) but that it may sometimes have real value. She offered some examples of valuable lies:

Exaggeration – even clear falsification – may arguably serve useful social purposes linked to the values underlying freedom of expression. A person fighting cruelty to animals may knowingly cite false statistics in pursuit of his or her beliefs and with the purpose of communicating a more fundamental message, e.g. 'cruelty must be stopped.' A doctor, in order to persuade people to be inoculated against a burgeoning epidemic, may exaggerate the number or geographical location of persons potentially infected with the virus. An artist, for artistic purposes, may make a statement that a particular society considers both an assertion of fact and a manifestly deliberate lie; consider the case of Salman Rushdie's *Satanic Verses*, viewed by many Muslim societies as perpetrating deliberate lies against the Prophet. All of this expression arguably has intrinsic value in fostering political participation and individual self-fulfillment. To accept the proposition that deliberate lies can never fall under section 2(b) would be to exclude statements such as the examples above from the possibility of constitutional protection. I cannot accept that such was the intention of the framers of the Constitution. (*Zundel* 1992, 754)[24]

These lies may have seemed valuable to McLachlin J. because she was sympathetic to the ends the liar sought to achieve and because she believed that 'experts' know what is best for the general population. But, as is the case with all lies, these involve an injury to the listener and an undermining of the relationship of communication. Again, this may be seen as an abuse of freedom of expression and not simply as a conflict between the speaker's interests in expressing him/herself and the listener's interests in not being deceived.

While the court has chosen to deal with abuses such as manipulation and deception under section 1, as limitation issues, it has adopted a 'contextual approach' to limitations. Even though all non-violent expression is protected under section 2(b), 'not all expression is equally worthy of protection' (*Rocket* 1990, 78). Some forms of expression can be restricted only if the state shows clear and strong reasons. However, the restriction of other forms of 'expression' will be easier to justify under section 1. In this way 'expression' that undermines the communicative relationship, although covered by section 2(b), may have little or no value when assessed under section 1.

In *Irwin Toy* 1989, for example, while the court was prepared to regard advertising directed at children as expression protected under section 2(b), it had no difficulty finding that the state was justified under section 1 in restricting this expression. The right of an advertiser to express itself was balanced against the right of children to be free from manipulation. However, because the expression was manipulative, it had very little value, perhaps even no value, under section 1.

3. The Distributive Dimension of Freedom of Expression: Interference and Opportunity

The scope/limits divide also comes under pressure when distributive issues are addressed. Traditional accounts of freedom of expression emphasize the importance of protecting the individual's personal sphere from interference by the state. When the state interferes with an individual's expression, a court must decide whether the state has good and strong reasons for its action. Yet, if expression is a valuable activity, we should also be concerned about the real opportunities that individuals have to express themselves and to participate in public discourse. An individual's opportunity to communicate effectively with others depends significantly on the state rules of property, which determine who has a right to use, and to exclude others from using, a particular place or thing. In allocating exclusive control over certain locations, state rules facilitate the communication of some individuals and constrain the communication of others.

Concern about communicative opportunity explains the court's willingness to review the constitutionality not only of government efforts to suppress the expression of certain messages but also government efforts to control 'the physical consequences of certain human activity, regardless of the meaning being conveyed,' including restrictions on the noise volume and location of expression (*Irwin Toy* 1989, 974). Time, place, and manner restrictions, as they are called in the United States, are a concern because they affect the individual's ability to communicate with others, a positively valued activity. However, the courts have applied a less rigorous standard of justification to time, place, and manner restrictions. A time, place, and manner restriction will breach section 2(b) only if the restricted expression advances important values. As well, a time, place, and manner restriction may be justified under section 1 even when it does not represent a substantial and compelling purpose of the kind necessary to justify a content-based restriction.

The special rule that says that a law that has the effect (rather than the purpose) of restricting expression will violate section 2(b) only if it is shown that the restricted expression advances the values underlying the freedom, reflects the problems involved in fitting distributive issues into the established framework of adjudication. On its face, the rule is about ensuring that only valuable expression is protected from time, place, and manner restrictions. However, when examined more closely, the rule seems to involve the introduction into section 2(b) of a lower, or at least a more flexible, standard for justifying this sort of restriction. The introduction of this standard of justification under section 2(b) shows some recognition that the justification of time, place, or manner restrictions does not depend on a simple, one-dimensional balancing of competing interests, the ordinary process under section 1. Instead, it involves an assessment of alternative opportunities for communication, a systemic issue that does not really fit into either of the two steps of adjudication: the definition of the scope of expression or the balancing of competing interests under section 1.

Because the Supreme court of Canada has defined expression broadly to include all acts intended to convey a message, any act is potentially an act of expression. This also means that any law is potentially a time, place, and manner restriction on expression. Understandably, the courts are reluctant to require substantial justification for a law, such as a parking restriction, that would not ordinarily be seen as impeding expressive freedom. In the case of such restrictions, it will almost always be the case that the individual speaker has effective alternatives. In some circumstances, however, where the means of expression seem critical to the effectiveness of the message, the court may choose to exempt the expressive act from the rule's application but not strike down the entire rule.

Irwin Toy 1989: The Purpose/Effect Distinction

The Supreme Court of Canada in *Irwin Toy* 1989 said that a state act that has the effect (and not the purpose) of restricting expression (a time, place, and manner restriction) will violate section 2(b) only if the restricted expression is shown to advance the values underlying the freedom.[25] Yet this additional requirement in the case of time, place, and manner restrictions seemed redundant. Once the court had reached this stage of section 2(b) analysis, it had already decided that the restricted activity was expression prima facie protected under section 2(b). The court's initial decision, that expression included all acts that convey a message, might have been thought to rest on the view that such acts advance the important values associated with freedom of expression. If an act does not advance these values, why should it be considered an act of 'expression' in the first instance?

The court seemed to say that the definition of expression is an issue separate from, and prior to, the assessment of its value – that expression is not defined in a purposive or functional way. It also seemed to assume an instrumental account of the freedom's value – that the expression of ideas and feelings is not valuable in and of itself but is valuable only when it advances truth, democracy, or self-realization. Yet if the first stage of free expression adjudication (the definition of the freedom's scope) does not involve a judgment that the particular act (of expression) advances the values underlying the freedom, why should there be a difference at this next stage between laws that have as their purpose the restriction of expression and laws that simply have this effect? Why should a plaintiff seeking to attack a particular law under section 2(b) have the burden of showing that his or her expression advances the values that underlie the freedom only when the law has the unintended effect of restricting expression. If a law seeks to restrict a particular human act that does not advance the values associated with freedom of expression, why should a court hold that it violates the freedom and go on to assess the law's justification under section 1?

It seems likely that the Supreme Court has taken this approach to laws that simply have a restrictive effect on expression (time, place, and manner restrictions) as a way of avoiding two aspects of section 1 analysis: first, the section 1 requirement that a restriction on the freedom represent a substantial and pressing purpose and second the one-dimensional balancing of competing interests under section 1. Time, place, or manner restrictions, unlike content-based restrictions, do not directly restrict particular messages (although they may be used to conceal the restriction of certain messages or speakers). Ordinarily these restrictions are intended to protect interests such as peace and quiet, privacy, or property use, interests that are sometimes compromised by public expression. The court is prepared to scrutinize these restrictions on expression because it recognizes that a particular restriction, or an accumulation of restrictions, may significantly impair communicative opportunity generally or for certain speakers or messages. However, this will not always be the case. A particular time, place, or manner restriction will not impair the freedom in a significant way when there are other times, places, and manners at/in which the same message may be communicated or the same speaker may speak.[26]

The court wants to uphold time, place, and manner restrictions on the freedom which advance purposes that are worthwhile, but not necessarily substantial and pressing, and that do not significantly impair the freedom, in the sense that they leave a variety of alternative means for public communication. Indeed, the court has begun to do this more explicitly through the introduction of contextual balancing and lower standards of justification for time, place, and manner restrictions under section 1. But what is required in the case of a time, place, and manner restriction is not so much a lower standard of justification as a more flexible standard, one which takes account of the distribution of effective opportunities for communication. When judging the legitimacy of a time, place, and manner restriction, the central issue is not the proper balance between the value of expression and the value of privacy or quiet but whether the individual seeking to express himself is left with adequate alternatives for his communication.

For example, it is not clear that a ban on loud noises in the evening in residential areas would survive section 1 if the state were required to show that the ban represented a substantial and compelling purpose.

Yet a noise by-law of this sort does represent a reasonable state policy and a relatively minor restriction on freedom of expression, since ordinarily it will leave the individual with a variety of other ways to communicate his or her message. The courts may insulate this minor restriction from section 1 and the demand of a substantial and compelling purpose by holding that it does not amount to a violation of section 2(b). In the alternative, the court may uphold the restriction under section 1 by adopting a reduced standard of justification.

If this is the basis for the special rule applied to state acts that have the effect of restricting expression, then the decision that a particular restriction does not violate section 2(b) rests not (or not simply), as the court pretends, on the quality of the restricted expression (whether it advances the values that underlie the freedom) but instead on the degree to which the particular expressive activity is prevented (whether the same message can be communicated in other ways or forums). It is difficult to think of many cases in which a particular time, place, or manner is so ill-suited to public communication that a restriction on expression at/in that time, place, or manner does not constitute at least a minor interference with the speaker's freedom of expression interests.

The court's decision to consider the justification of (some) time, place, and manner restrictions under section 2(b) rather than under section 1, shows some recognition that what is involved is an assessment of the opportunities for communication and not a simple balancing of competing interests of the sort that ordinarily occurs under section 1. The issue of the fairness or adequacy of an individual's opportunity to communicate cuts across the scope/limits distinction. It is an issue that does not really fit into either of the steps of the established structure of constitutional adjudication, the definition of the scope of expression or the balancing of interests under section 1. It does not require the court to determine whether a particular action is expressive or to strike the correct balance between competing values or interests. The court tries to fit this distributive issue into the established model by describing it as an assessment of the value of the restricted expression under section 2(b). However, the special treatment of time, place, and manner restrictions can only really be understood as the introduction of a more flexible standard of protection under section 2(b), a standard that takes account, at least implicitly, of the availability and adequacy of alternative times, places, and manners for/of communication.[27]

4. Limits on Freedom of Expression under Section 1

When the Supreme Court describes the value and scope of freedom of expression under section 2(b) it speaks generously of the freedom's contribution to democracy, truth, and self-realization. At this stage of the court's judgments the tone is one of confidence about what can be achieved through freedom of expression. Yet when the court moves to consider limits on the freedom under section 1, the tone of its judgments often changes: the court becomes sceptical about the value of expression and fearful of its harms. Under section 1 the court is often prepared to defer to legislative judgment and to uphold a wide range of restrictions without clear evidence that the restricted expression 'causes' harm to important individual or social interests.[28]

The change in tone that occurs between section 2(b) and section 1 is obscured to some degree by the abstract language used by the court to describe both scope and limits issues. Some commentators have thought that in many cases the court's section 1 analysis is simply a mistake made possible by the court's abstract approach and that this mistake might be avoided if the court would only keep the underlying justification for the freedom in clearer focus (Cameron 1992, 1151). However, I believe that the shift in tone between section 2(b) and section 1 reflects a basic tension in the court's understanding of the value of freedom of expression and more deeply in its conception of human agency and language/discourse. The court's abstract description of the justification for freedom of expression and the grounds for limiting the freedom simply serves to obscure this tension.

The Supreme Court's approach to freedom of expression under section 2(b) rests on a conception of the individual as a free and rational being, a maker of choices, an autonomous agent capable of giving direction to his or her life. This image underlies the court's account of the different justifications for freedom of expression, including the attainment of truth, democracy, and self-realization, and drives its definition of the freedom's scope. According to the Supreme Court freedom of expression is valuable because truth is more likely to emerge when free and rational individuals are permitted to discuss and consider information and ideas. Democracy is advanced when free and rational individuals are permitted to discuss public issues. Individual autonomy is respected when free and rational individuals are permitted to express their views and to consider the views of others.

At the section 1 stage the court says that its task is to balance competing interests. The court describes this process in a variety of ways, but most often as the balancing of the individual's interest in expression against competing social or collective interests. Yet there is very little explanation in the court's judgments as to how this balancing is to be conducted. Despite routine references to the balancing of competing interests, the key question for the court under section 1 is whether the expression causes a substantial harm. The court looks to social science evidence to establish the causal link between expression and harm, but when this evidence proves inconclusive it is prepared, in many cases at least, to defer to the legislature's judgment that the restricted expression causes harm.

In its section 1 analysis, the court seems to regard freedom of expression not as an important aspect of individual liberty or the common good but simply as an activity or interest that is in competition with other individual or collective interests. Causation is used by the court in an apparently value-neutral way to choose between these competing interests. The right to advance my interests (or my liberty) ends when it interferes with another's interests (or another's liberty). When an act of expression is the active cause of harm to another's interests, its restriction will be justified.

However, this reliance on causation suppresses entirely the idea of free and rational agency that underlies the justification of freedom of expression under section 2(b). The roles of persuasion and judgment are ignored in this cause/effect analysis. As well, cause is not a neutral idea. When a court holds that a particular act of expression should be restricted because it will or may cause injury to another interest, the court is choosing to prefer one claim over another without explaining the grounds for its choice. Furthermore this choice tends to reinforce the social and economic status quo, since the view that expression is the active cause of injury to another interest rests on the perception that the competing (affected) interest is fixed, ordinary, or natural.

At the section 1 stage the court's faith in the free choice and rational judgment of the individual is tempered by, and in many cases gives way to, a fear of manipulation and irrationality. The court's behavioural or cause/effect analysis rests on a very different conception of the individual as irrational, manipulable, and directed by unchosen preferences or desires. The individual does not freely choose who she is or what she wants. She cannot simply remake herself or revise her preferences through free choice. Who she is and what she values or desires is externally determined. She is subject to the push and pull of her environment. She is unable to effectively judge or assess arguments. She is influenced without rational persuasion.

The shift in approach that occurs when the court moves to section 1 is a response to the inability of the traditional concept of freedom of expression, with its underlying conception of the individual as free and rational and expression as transparent, to account for the occurrence or risk of harm. If individuals are free and rational, capable of determining what they will believe and what values they will hold, and if expression is simply transparent, why would freedom of expression ever be harmful? Expression would have no tangible effects; it would simply provide ideas and information that an individual listener might decide to accept or reject. But the court sees that expression can have a significant affect on individuals. Expression is not simply the transmission of transparent ideas and information; sometimes it influences an individual's behaviour in ways in which he or she is not fully conscious. Sometimes it impacts in harmful ways on the individual.

The court deals with the realities of the social world and the limitations of human agency under section 1 by adopting a behavioural approach, which rests on a conception of the individual as determined and irrational. Yet, while this conception of the individual may offer some explanation of the risks of freedom of expression, it seems to undermine the constitutional commitment to the freedom and to support protection of the status quo against collective criticism and action. If individuals do not freely and rationally choose or revise their ideas or purposes, what is the value of free expression? If individuals are easily manipulated, why should freedom of expression be protected constitutionally?

As long as the court views freedom of expression through an individualist lens, it will be unable to account for both the value and the risks of freedom of expression. It will continue to oscillate between a view of the individual as free and rational, which seems to explain the freedom's value, and the opposite view of the individual as determined and irrational or, at least, non-rational, which is offered to explain its risks.

Not only does the conception of the individual as free and rational fail to account for the risks of freedom of expression, it offers only a weak explanation of the freedom's value. If individuals are free and rational, then expression is valuable simply because it provides information and ideas that may help individuals to advance their goals. Similarly, the conception of the individual as socially determined does not account for the value of the freedom and provides only a weak explanation of the harm of expression. If individuals are socially determined then it is hard to see why we would describe expression that influences or directs an individual's thoughts and actions as harmful. We can regard expression as an *external interference* with the individual only if we have some conception of the individual as undetermined – only, that is, if we think that there is an alternative of freedom and rationality, of real agency.

An account of both the value and the harm of expression must recognize that the individual is socially situated but not socially determined. Freedom of expression is valuable because human agency, freedom, and rationality are realized in communicative interaction. However, freedom of expression also carries risks because the meaning of words (and other symbolic forms) is never entirely transparent to either the speaker or the listener. Expression may reinforce or reshape assumptions and attitudes in ways of which we are unaware or uncritical. As well, expression can take place in circumstances that leave the individual without any sense of real choice as to how he or she should respond or react. The difficult task for the courts is to reconcile a commitment to freedom of expression (the right of agents to express their views and consider the views of others) with a recognition of the social shaping of human agency and the social constraints on human choice.

The Supreme Court's oscillation between a conception of the individual as free and rational and a conception of him or her as determined and irrational is illustrated by four early freedom of expression judgments: *Dolphin Delivery* 1986, *British Columbia Government Employees Union* (BCGEU) 1988, *Ford* 1988, and *Irwin Toy* 1989.

Dolphin Delivery 1986: Picketing as Harmful Expression

The first significant freedom of expression case to reach the Supreme Court of Canada, *Dolphin Delivery* 1986, concerned the constitutionality of an injunction against labour picketing. The striking employees of Purolator planned to set up a picket line at the workplace of Dolphin Delivery. They believed that Dolphin Delivery Ltd was doing work for SuperCourier, a company related to Purolator that was carrying on Purolator's British Columbia business during the strike. The Purolator workers hoped that the Dolphin Delivery workers would respect their picket line and that this would put pressure on Dolphin Delivery to stop doing Purolator work, and would indirectly pressure Purolator to settle the contract dispute.

Dolphin Delivery brought an application for an injunction against the Purolator union to prevent it from setting up the picket line. The injunction was granted by the Supreme Court of British Columbia on the grounds that a line by Purolator workers at the site of Dolphin Delivery would be a secondary picket meant to induce Dolphin Delivery to breach its contract with SuperCourier and that this amounted to a common law tort.[29]

The issue that came to the Supreme Court of Canada was whether the injunction violated freedom of expression under the Charter. In deciding whether or not the Charter had been breached it was necessary for the court to decide first, whether or not an injunction issued under the common law rules concerning picketing was subject to review under the Charter; second, whether picketing was a matter of freedom of expression protected by section 2(b); and finally, if picketing was expression, whether or not the restriction of picketing in this case was a justifiable limit under section 1.

Although McIntyre J., writing for the court, decided that the injunction was not government action subject to Charter review, he went on to consider the freedom of expression issue. Mr Justice McIntyre's consideration of the freedom began with a statement of high principle. Drawing on pre-Charter case law he declared that freedom of expression is central to our political democracy. Mr Justice McIntyre used the term 'democracy' in its largest sense, as a social environment in which ideas and information are freely exchanged and participation in community affairs is encouraged. He also invoked values such as truth, autonomy, and self-realization. These values were introduced into the judgment through quotations from J.S. Mill, Milton, Holmes, and others. McIntyre J. made no attempt to connect these values, although presumably they were meant to add up to a powerful justification for the protection of freedom of expression.

Following his brief discussion of the foundation of freedom of expression, McIntyre J. considered the freedom's scope. He quickly pushed beyond the narrow scope accorded to the freedom by the Supreme Court in its pre-Charter decisions. Specifically, he rejected the conclusion reached in the pre-Charter Supreme Court decision of *Dupond* 1978[30] that picketing is not a form of expression. He recognized that '[I]n any form of picketing there is involved at least some element of expression. The picketers would be conveying a message which at a very minimum would be classed as persuasion, aimed at deterring customers and prospective customers from doing business with the respondent' (*Dolphin Delivery* 1986, 586).[31] Picketing is expression and so an injunction against secondary picketing is a limitation on the freedom.

McIntyre J. then considered whether this limitation could be justified under section 1. Although no picket line had ever been established and although no formal evidence was presented to the court about the harm or impact of the proposed line, Justice McIntyre was prepared to uphold the limit under section 1. He said that 'certain elements of the section 1 analysis are obvious or self-evident' and require no evidence (*Dolphin Delivery*, 1986, 590, quoting *Oakes* 1986, 138).

Mr Justice McIntyre first asked whether the limit represents an interest significant enough to justify a restriction on freedom of expression. According to McIntyre J., the establishment of a picket at Dolphin Delivery Ltd, which was intended to discourage Dolphin's employees, customers, and suppliers from entering the premises, would be harmful to Dolphin's interest in unimpeded trade and economic productivity and to the community's interest in social and economic stability: 'The social cost [of labour picketing] is great, man-hours and wages are lost, production and services will be disrupted, and general tensions within the community will be heightened' (*Dolphin Delivery* 1986, 591). He considered both these interests to be 'pressing and substantial.'

Having reached this conclusion, McIntyre J. went on to consider whether the protection of business and community interests was proportionate to the restriction on freedom of expression. He spoke of finding the 'balance between the two competing concerns.' And he appeared to make some sort of judgment about the relative importance of the competing interests of the picketers and the business when he declared that secondary picketing is not necessary to collective bargaining: 'Such industrial conflict [picketing] *may* be tolerated by society but only as an inevitable corollary to the collective bargaining process' (*Dolphin Delivery* 1986, 591) [emphasis added] and '[w]hile picketing is, no doubt, a legislative weapon to be employed in a labour dispute by the employees against their employer, it should not be permitted to harm others' (*Dolphin Delivery* 1986, 591). McIntyre J. considered that it would be unfair for the union to spread the conflict beyond the actual parties to the industrial dispute.

However, the basis for Mr Justice McIntyre's opinion about what is and what is not 'necessary' to collective bargaining was not clearly explained. Despite his many references to balancing, there was little or no indication in his judgment of an actual comparison of the worker's freedom of expression with the company's or the community's competing interests.[32] He thought that secondary picketing unfairly draws innocent parties into the conflict and is not necessary to collective bargaining. He said very little about the harm that might be caused and nothing about the proper balance between expression and economic efficiency interests. Secondary picketing could be restricted because it does not contribute to collective bargaining. There was no mention of its contribution to freedom of expression values. They seem to have played no role in his section 1 analysis.

In the end, Mr Justice McIntyre's decision that the legislature may restrict secondary picketing did not rest on a judgment about the proper balance between expression and business efficiency or even the fair balance of power in a labour dispute. It rested instead on the view that labour picketing causes harm to the interests of other persons. McIntyre J. decided not that the harm to Dolphin Delivery's interests outweighed the importance of the picketers' freedom of expression, but instead that the picketing would cause harm to the interests of Dolphin Delivery and therefore should be restricted. Indeed, his judgment might even be read as saying that if the government were to ban primary picketing the restriction would be justified because such expression causes harm to a business and to the community.

There are some very obvious problems with the causal approach adopted by McIntyre J. First, such an approach seems to run contrary to the court's stated commitment to freedom of expression and its protection of discussion, persuasion, and independent judgment; second, it seems to insulate established economic and social interests from public criticism.

In determining whether or not a restriction on freedom of expression is justified under section 1, is it enough simply to identify an injury or a loss that 'results' from an act of expression? If I picket outside a store, encouraging people not to shop there because it sells goods manufactured in Burma, and if some people listen to my message and decide not to shop at the store, or at least not to buy Burmese goods, am I not harming the store? My expression has had an effect that is contrary to the store's interest in selling goods and making a profit. The more persuasive I am the greater will be the harm.

Human action that causes this sort of harm in this way should be protected by freedom of expression, at least on the theory of the freedom the court seems to rely on at the section 2(b) stage. According to this theory, freedom of expression protects the right of individuals to receive information and ideas and to decide what they will believe and how they should act. It cannot be a ground for limiting the individual's expression that he or she may be successful in convincing others of the correctness of a certain point of view. The audience must be permitted to make (and are capable of making) their own decisions. To say simply that an individual's speech causes harm when people are convinced of the correctness of the speaker's view is to suppress entirely ideas of human agency, choice, judgment – the ideas that lie at the core of the justification for freedom of expression. The speaker has 'caused' 'harm' only by convincing others, who have decided to accept his or her views and to act on them.[33]

Justice McIntyre gave no explanation as to how the picketing would have caused harm to the business interests of Dolphin Delivery. He avoided this question by treating the effect of the picket line on Dolphin Delivery as a finding of fact by the trial judge. The trial judge found that the purpose of the picket line was to injure the plaintiff. He also found that had the picket line been established, some of the employees of Dolphin Delivery and of other companies having business with Dolphin Delivery would not have crossed the line. This would have resulted in considerable disruption to the business interests of Dolphin Delivery.[34] Treating these speculations as findings of fact allowed McIntyre J. to view the harm of the picket line as an inevitable or probable physical effect rather than an (un)predictable consequence of choice by human agents.

Some of the language Justice McIntyre used to describe the picket line evoked the image of a physical barrier. But since the picket line was pre-empted by the injunction there was no evidence of unfair pressure or of any limits on the ability of the Dolphin Delivery employees to make their own judgments about whether to respect or to cross the picket line. In any event, actual physical obstruction or intimidation might have been dealt with under the ordinary law without a complete ban on picketing (for example, a restriction on the number of picketers). The *Oakes* 1986 test specifically provides that a law that advances a legitimate state end, such as the prevention of physical harm, must be narrowly drawn so that it interferes as little as necessary with expressive activity. However, intimidation and obstruction are not explicitly raised as concerns, and so are not directly addressed in the judgment.

By describing the expression as an active cause of harm, the court was able to present itself as a neutral arbiter of conflicting human interests. Expression loses its claim to protection as soon as it causes injury to another. Specifically in this case it lost its claim to protection when it interfered with the right of someone else to carry on his or her business. However, causation is not a neutral standard. When he decided to restrict expression in *Dolphin Delivery* 1986, McIntyre J. gave priority to the activity of operating a business and pursuing profit over the freedom to persuade others not to work for, or buy goods from, the particular business. Not only was McIntyre J. making a choice between competing interests, he was making a choice that favoured established social and economic interests. The attempt by McIntyre J. to resolve conflicts between different interests in a neutral way, using the concept of cause, resulted in the protection of powerful and established interests from public criticism and collective action. Freedom of expression was seen as the active cause of injury only because business efficiency was considered ordinary and market activity was seen as natural.

Finally, the court's approach under section 1 undermined the liberal account of freedom of expression it articulated under section 2(b), an account that rests on a particular understanding of human agency and a particular vision of individual and collective good. Fear of obstruction by picketers and of routine observance of picket lines by workers led the court to swing away from the assumptions about agency that lay beneath its account of the freedom under section 2(b) and to embrace a deterministic view of human conduct. The important arguments that might have been made for or against the restriction of the picket line were suppressed in the court's behavioural discourse. The court failed to consider the reasons Dolphin Delivery employees might have had for respecting or ignoring the picket line, and so avoided important and difficult questions about intimidation, manipulation, and choice in the context of a labour dispute. Choices are always constrained. The question is whether the constraints are so great or so unfair that the individual has 'no real choice.' If choice is constrained to this extent then we may be prepared to say that the expression has 'caused' or 'directed' the individual's actions.[35]

British Columbia Government Employees Union (BCGEU) 1988: The Priority of Access to the Courts

In *BCGEU* 1988, court workers in British Columbia went out on a legal strike and set up picket lines around several courthouses in the province. The workers hoped that those having business in the courts would honour their picket line. However, they recognized that many people who might be sympathetic to their cause would nonetheless feel obliged to cross the line because of their involvement, as litigants, witnesses, or lawyers, in cases being heard in the courts. And so the union set up a pass system, under which an individual who needed to enter a court building could ask the union for permission to cross the line. If the union accepted that the individual had good reason to enter the building, it would provide him or her with a picket pass. Someone who crossed a picket line after obtaining a picket pass would be considered by the union to have honoured the picket line.

After arriving at the central courthouse one morning and crossing the picket line without a pass, Chief Justice McEachern of the Supreme Court of British Columbia issued an injunction against the picketing.[36] The union appealed the injunction, arguing that it violated the freedom of expression of its members and could not be justified under section 1. The court of appeal upheld the injunction as a justified restriction on freedom of expression under section 1. The case was appealed to the Supreme Court of Canada which, in a judgment written by Chief Justice Dickson, also dismissed the appeal.

Chief Justice Dickson followed the court's decision in *Dolphin Delivery* 1986 and found that the picketing in question fell within the scope of section 2(b) but that its restriction was justified under section 1. According to the chief justice, the limitation issue is a matter of the proper balance between 'individual values and the public or societal values' – the freedom to picket balanced against access to the courts (*BCGEU* 1988, 247). He thought that in this case 'the task of striking a balance is not difficult,' because '[a]ssuring unimpeded access to the courts' represents a concern that is 'pressing and substantial' and clearly of 'sufficient importance to warrant overriding a constitutionally protected right or freedom' such as freedom of expression (*BCGEU* 1988, 248): '[W]ithout the public right to have absolute, free and unrestricted access to the courts, the individual and private right to freedom of expression would be lost. The greater public interest must be considered when determining the degree of protection to be accorded to individual interests' (*BCGEU* 1988, 247–8).[37] Despite his many references to 'balancing,' Chief Justice Dickson did not find that access to the courts was just another interest or value that must in some way be balanced against freedom of expression to determine if it 'outweighs' the freedom. In his view, access to the courts is part of the foundation of freedom of expression and the other Charter rights. Without access to the courts there would be no way to ensure that freedom of expression was respected. His decision was based not on the fair or proper accommodation of competing expression and access interests, but rather on the priority of the right of access to the courts over other rights claims.

For Chief Justice Dickson it was obvious that a picket line obstructs access. He thought that there 'can be little doubt as to the correctness' of the finding by the courts below 'that the picketing would inevitably have had the effect of impeding and restricting access to the courts' (*BCGEU* 1988, 231). The picket line was portrayed as a physical obstruction to access. For example, Dickson C.J. said: 'A picket line both in intention and effect, is a barrier. By picketing the courthouses of British Columbia, the appellant Union in effect, set up a barricade which impeded access to the courts by litigants, lawyers, witnesses and the public at large. It is not difficult to imagine the inevitable effects upon the administration of justice' (*BCGEU* 1988, 232).[38] Yet there was no evidence of actual obstruction or harassment. Indeed, the only evidence concerning the impact of the picket line was in the form of an affidavit from a Crown official who said that the 'picket line was orderly and peaceful' and that '[p]ersons appearing to have business inside the Courthouse entered and left the building at will and at no time appeared to be impeded in any way by the picketers' (Glasbeek 1990, 20).

At various points in his judgment, Chief Justice Dickson seemed to recognize that a picket line works not by physically blocking access but rather by persuading individuals not to cross. For example, he said: 'The picketing in the circumstances of the case at bar was peaceful and there were no threats of violence or acts of violence, nor was there any destruction of property. What is at issue is the right of the Union and its members to urge members of the public not to enter the courthouse' (*BCGEU* 1988, 245).[39] Yet he went on to suggest that labour picketing was different from ordinary persuasion and that, at least in British Columbia, the exercise of human agency and freedom of choice stopped when a picket line went up. Dickson C.J. quoted from Paul Weiler's *Reconcilable Differences*: '[A] picket line operates as a signal, telling union members not to cross. Certainly in British Columbia the response is automatic, almost Pavlovian ... The picket line is much more than the simple exercise of a worker's freedom of expression. In a heavily unionized community it is an effective trigger to a work stoppage by a group of employees' (Weiler 1980 quoted in *BCGEU* 1988, 232).[40] The picket line is a barrier because workers respond automatically to it. (Never mind that most of those with business in the courts were not unionized workers (Glasbeek 1990, 24) and that Justice McEachern, who issued the injunction, seemed able to rise above this automatic state.)[41] Thus the picket line 'could only lead to massive interference with the legal and constitutional rights of the citizens of British Columbia' (*BCGEU* 1988, 233).

Yet the court's approach at this stage seemed to run against the view of freedom of expression set out in its section 2(b) analysis. At the section 2(b) stage, the court seemed to view the individual as a rational being capable of autonomous choice. At the limitations stage, however, the court's faith in individual reason and autonomous choice appeared to collapse – at least in the context of a labour dispute. The court seemed unable to articulate a vision of freedom of expression for the real world, where people sometimes act thoughtfully and other times impulsively; where they are subject to different pressures, including economic pressure and threats of ostracism; and where they act for a variety of benevolent and selfish reasons, such as worker solidarity, social justice, fear, ignorance, and conformity.[42] This shift from a discourse of choice and rationality to a discourse of behaviourism, of cause and effect, allowed the court to avoid all difficult questions concerning the social and economic conditions of choice.

Ford v. Attorney-General of Quebec 1988: Language and Community

In *Ford* 1988 and its companion case, *Devine* 1988,[43] the Supreme Court reviewed the constitutionality of the Quebec law that required the use of French on commercial signs and prohibited the use of other languages. The court considered that both the requirement of French and the prohibition of other languages violated section 2(b). However, it concluded that the requirement was justified under section 1 while the prohibition was not justified.[44]

Once again the court described the justification for freedom of expression in broad and general terms. In the court's view, freedom of expression is concerned not only with the operation of democratic government but also with the opportunity/ability of each individual to make informed decisions and to direct his or her life. Once again the court defined the freedom's scope generously. Freedom of expression protects commercial as well as political expression because '[o]ver and above its intrinsic value as expression, commercial expression ... plays a significant role in enabling individuals to make informed economic choices' (*Ford* 1988, 767). In the court's view, a wide range of information, even that provided in the pursuit of economic gain, contributes to the individual's knowledge and to her ability to make judgments that will advance her interests and goals. The freedom protects both the content (the message) and the form (the medium) of expression. In particular, it covers the speaker's choice of language.[45] The court recognized 'that language is not merely a means or a medium of expression; it colours the content and meaning of expression' (*Ford* 1988, 748).[46] In the *Devine* 1988 case the court also held that section 2(b) protects the individual's right not to speak. The state must neither censor the individual's communication nor compel the individual to communicate against his or her will. Freedom of expression, then, is violated not only when an individual is prevented from communicating in the language of her choice, but also when she is compelled to communicate in a particular language.[47]

At the limitations stage the court found that the protection and preservation of the French language in Quebec was 'a serious and legitimate' policy, of sufficient importance to support a limitation on freedom of expression. The court saw a 'rational connection' between this policy and the *requirement* of French on commercial signs. As well, the court considered that the value of maintaining a French 'visage linguistique' in Quebec was proportionate to the interference with individual freedom of expression. A 'visage linguistique' that is predominantly French suggests to anglophone Quebeckers and to non-francophone immigrants that it is necessary to learn 'the majority language'; it also confirms to 'young and ambitious Francophones' that success can be achieved in the French language and that it is not necessary to put aside their language in order to advance in business (*Ford* 1988, 778).

While the court accepted that the requirement of French on commercial signs was rationally connected to the goal of preserving the French language, it doubted that the prohibition of other languages was rationally connected to this goal. In the court's view, the empirical evidence put forward by the Quebec government did not make the case for the exclusion of languages other than French. It did not establish that the prohibition of other languages 'is necessary to the defence and enhancement of the status of the French language in Quebec' (*Ford* 1988, 780).[48] According to the court, even if the prohibition did have some impact, there were other, more effective ways to achieve this goal that were less restrictive of freedom of expression.

Yet none of this really explains the court's conclusion that the compulsion of French was necessary to maintain the *visage linguistique* of Quebec while the exclusion of other languages was not.[49] The court had before it a wide range of studies and statistics that showed the precarious position of the French language in Canada, the result of a declining birth rate and growing non-francophone immigration. The court, however, found that the materials did not demonstrate that the prohibition of other languages was necessary: 'That specific question is simply not addressed by the materials' (*Ford* 1988, 779). Surely, though, the French language would be protected more effectively by the exclusion of other languages from the public realm, and in particular from commercial signs. As long as other languages are used, there will be no need for non-francophones to learn and use French. If the francophone population is exposed to an abundance of English on signs and elsewhere, the French language may be eroded through the incorporation of English expressions.

The court's cause and effect analysis, and its focus on the most efficient way to achieve the goal of preserving the French language, provided no reason for striking down the prohibition of languages other than French. The real explanation for the distinction between the requirement of French, which was justified, and the prohibition of languages other than French, which was not, was hinted at in the court's references to proportionality and fairness, but buried beneath its behavioural analysis.

While the court referred to statistics and predictions about the behaviour of francophones, anglophones, and allophones in Quebec, it may be that the views about free and rational agency that define the court's section 2(b) approach also underlie its section 1 conclusion that the prohibition of other languages is not justified. The prohibition is unjustified not because the exclusion of other languages will contribute little or nothing to the preservation of the French language, but rather because this exclusion is not an acceptable way to protect the French language. If the individual is free and rational and expresses his or her freedom and rationality in public discourse, then a prohibition on the use (commercial or otherwise) of minority languages is not justified, regardless of the statistical evidence. Just as an idea cannot be protected by suppressing competing ideas, it is unacceptable for a majority linguistic group to maintain or strengthen its position by preventing the members of another group from using their language.

This conclusion is reached not by striking the correct balance between the individual's interest in freedom of expression and the linguistic community's competing interest in preservation or by assessing the rationality of the connection between the restrictive means and the goal of preserving the French language. It follows from the view of agency and expression that underlies the established accounts of freedom of expression. Yet, while the court vindicated freedom of expression, it did so, it said, only because of the absence of empirical evidence – only because the Quebec government had not established that English on signs harmed the status of the French language.

At the same time, however, the assumptions about human freedom and rationality that underlie the court's rejection of the Quebec government's language prohibition (and its understanding of freedom of expression) make it difficult to explain why it is acceptable to compel the use of French. The justification for the law requiring French on commercial signs rests on the unequal economic power of different language groups in Quebec. The sign law was a response to the history of economic domination by the anglophone minority and part of a larger scheme that established French as the business language in Quebec. It recognized that the language of business should be determined by the political majority rather than by an economically powerful minority.[50] However, for the court to recognize this as the justification for compelling French on public signs would mean acknowledging the power of wealth to control communication. The court avoided any direct consideration of the question of communicative power/choice by following a behavioural approach and looking to empirical evidence.

The court may have been right that the requirement of French is different from the prohibition of other languages. However, since the court's conclusion rested on statistical evidence, it did not explicitly address the arguments that might have been made in favour of either the requirement of French or the prohibition of other languages in the commercial life of the community. An assessment of these arguments would involve a consideration of the relationship between individual identity and community and the location of freedom of expression within a context of social and economic power. By adopting a behavioural analysis (which asked whether the presence on commercial signs of languages other than French caused harm to the French language in Quebec) the court was able to avoid the real and more complex issue.

Irwin Toy 1989: Advertising and Manipulation

In *Irwin Toy* 1989 the Supreme Court found that a Quebec law prohibiting advertising directed at children restricted freedom of expression but was justified under section 1.

Dickson C.J., for the majority of the court, defined expression as an act that seeks to convey meaning and confirmed that advertising is protected under section 2(b). In his section 1 assessment he found that the restriction satisfied the 'pressing and substantial purpose requirement': 'Broadly speaking the concerns which have motivated both legislative and voluntary regulation in this area are the particular susceptibility of young children to media manipulation, their ability to differentiate between reality and fiction and to grasp the persuasive intention behind the message ...' (*Irwin Toy* 1989, 987). The difficult issue for the court was whether the ban on advertising directed at children up to the age of thirteen was overbroad. There was strong evidence that younger children are susceptible to manipulation in advertising. However, on the susceptibility of older children, seven to thirteen years of age, the evidence was divided. The Quebec Court of Appeal had decided that the evidence only justified a restriction on advertising directed at children under the age of seven.

Dickson C.J. was conscious of the difficulty faced by the legislature in 'mediating between the claims of particular groups' – in this case between advertisers and their audience (*Irwin Toy* 1989, 993). He recognized that the legislature had been forced to 'strike a balance without the benefit of absolute certainty concerning how that balance is best struck' (*Irwin Toy* 1989, 993). Because there was no certainty and because the legislature was a democratic institution, Dickson C.J. thought that the court should show a degree of deference to the legislature's assessment of conflicting evidence and ask only 'whether the government had a reasonable basis, on the evidence tendered, for concluding that the ban on advertising directed at children impaired freedom of expression as little as possible given the government's pressing and substantial objective' (*Irwin Toy* 1989, 949). Dickson C.J. thought that the scientific evidence in this case 'sustains the reasonableness' of the legislature's view that the ban on advertising directed at children under the age of thirteen 'was the minimal impairment of free expression consistent with the pressing and substantial goal of protecting children against manipulation' (*Irwin Toy* 1989, 999).[51]

The justification for the restriction was that advertising directed at children is manipulative – that it influences behaviour while by-passing or discouraging reflection and judgment. However, the model of freedom of expression articulated under section 2(b) cannot really account for this harm. If individuals are free and rational, why would they be vulnerable to manipulation, absent very exceptional circumstances? The court avoided this difficulty by emphasizing the particular susceptibility of children to manipulative or deceptive communication. Children could be viewed as a special case. Freedom of expression doctrine ordinarily requires that a willing audience be permitted to receive and assess ideas and information without interference from the state. However, a group, such as children, whose reasoning capacities are not yet fully developed, may be seen as particularly vulnerable to deception or manipulation.[52] With such an audience special protection by the state may be appropriate, including the restriction of directed advertising.

As noted in the dissenting judgment of Mr Justice McIntyre, it is unlikely that children are entirely exceptional in their vulnerability to manipulation (*Irwin Toy* 1989, 1007).[53] However, because the court's approach to the justification and scope of the freedom was based on a view of the individual as free and rational, the court was unable to offer any account of manipulation, the distortion of free choice, of either children or adults. In place of such an account the court relied on empirical studies, which suggested that advertising has a detrimental or manipulative impact on children. When these studies proved inadequate to make the case for restriction in a clear and decisive way, the court argued for deference to legislative judgment. It was left to the legislature to assess the social science evidence and to judge the harmful impact of advertising on children. This behavioural, or cause and effect, analysis allowed the court to avoid finding a place for manipulation in a theory of freedom of expression that rests upon the basic autonomy and rationality of the individual.

5. The Limits of Judicial Review

When the Supreme Court describes the value of freedom of expression under section 2(b), it adopts a liberal image of the individual. Freedom of expression is valuable because humans are free and rational beings. The goals of democracy and truth are advanced when free and rational individuals are allowed to discuss and debate different issues. As well, freedom of expression allows individuals to exercise or express their freedom and rationality. However, at the section 1 stage of freedom of expression adjudication, concern about the individual's irrationality and susceptibility to the manipulation and pressure of others dominates the court's analysis. The court responds to this concern by adopting a behavioural approach to limitations issues, looking for causes and effects in empirical evidence.

In some cases, the court finds that harm is caused by expression so that the state is justified in imposing a restriction. In these cases the court cites empirical evidence of the connection between expression and harmful behaviour but because this evidence is indeterminate, the court relies on 'common sense' or legislative judgment to complete the connection. In other cases the court finds that the evidence of harm is insufficient to justify restriction under section 1 and declines to defer to legislative judgment. In these cases the court says that freedom of expression is a fundamental right of the individual, which can be limited only on the basis of very clear evidence that it causes substantial harm. Yet, even in these cases, vindication of the commitment to human autonomy and reason is hidden within the behavioural discourse that dominates the court's section 1 analysis. For example, in *Ford* 1988, the court's conclusion that the prohibition of languages other than French is not justified ostensibly rests on the lack of statistical evidence establishing a connection between the prohibition and the prevention of harm to the French language community.[54] It is impossible to predict when the court will defer to the legislature's judgment that the expression causes harm and should be restricted and when it will strike down the law because the causal link has not been clearly established.

However, in two recent cases, *Thomson* 1998 and *K-Mart* 1999, the court declined to support limits on expression under section 1, arguing that a commitment to freedom of expression means treating the individual as 'a rational actor who can ... make independent judgments' (Thomson 1998, 956). These cases may signal a change in the court's approach, the beginning of a movement towards a more civil libertarian approach to freedom of expression in which the court defends the right of the individual to express and hear views regardless of the harms that may be caused. A commitment to freedom of expression means that expression cannot be restricted simply because it persuades its audience to engage in activities that are harmful in some way. We must trust individual reason and respect individual autonomy. This approach involves a downplaying of the potential harms of expression – it may even lead the court to rethink its previous decisions concerning hate promotion, pornography, and other issues.

More likely though, the court is simply using the language of freedom and rationality when it has already decided that the restriction should not be sustained under section 1 because the restricted expression does not cause any noticeable harm (or perhaps because the audience is not operating under any significant constraints). When the court thinks that the restricted expression 'causes' harm, it will uphold the restriction under section 1., and it will frame the justification in causal language. On the other hand, if, in the court's view, no harm is caused or if there is no substantial risk of harm then the court will be prepared to strike down the restriction, in the name of individual freedom and rationality. Under this approach the court continues to oscillate between the incompatible discourses of freedom/rationality and behaviourism, adopting one or the other under section 1 depending on whether it believes the expression at issue causes harm.

The change in discourse that occurs when the judicial analysis moves from section 2(b) to section 1, reflects a deep tension in the established theories of freedom of expression. The two steps of freedom of expression adjudication simply provide a structure for this tension. Established theories, which rest upon a conception of the individual as free and rational, may offer some explanation of the value of expression but they have more difficulty defining the scope of the protected activity and explaining the need for limits. If individuals are free and rational beings, why is the freedom to communicate with others so important? Put in a more positive way, why is the activity of expression more important than the other voluntary actions of free and rational individuals? At the same time, it is unclear how expression causes injury or harm to free and rational individuals. How, for example, does expression manipulate? If individuals are free and rational, why would expression have any kind of tangible impact upon them. When an individual expresses his or her views to an audience, the audience will decide whether to accept or reject those views.

The court oscillates between competing discourses and conflicting conceptions of the individual because the individualism that dominates freedom of expression theory and doctrine blinds the court to the social dimension of human agency. Expression is both valuable and potentially harmful because human agency is socially situated and emerges or develops in communicative interaction – in the creation of meaning. Because individual identity is so dependent on the communicative response/recognition of others, words can be deeply hurtful and can damage self-esteem. Because an individual's reason and judgment are realized in communicative interaction, he or she may be vulnerable to manipulative or deceitful expression.

The individual is not perfectly free and rational, but neither is he or she irrational, driven by fixed and unchangeable preferences. Reflection and judgment are dependent on socially created languages, which give shape to thought and feeling. Language plays neither the innocent role of simply conveying ideas and information to the rational and independent individual nor the oppressive role of interfering with the independence and integrity of the individual.[55] While expression is never fully transparent nor entirely opaque, we have a sense that some forms or instances of expression encourage awareness and insight and others seem to by-pass or discourage reflection. The space available for an individual to critically evaluate what he or she hears or sees can vary dramatically, depending on the social and economic circumstances in which communication takes place.

A recognition by the Supreme Court that freedom of expression is valuable because human agency emerges and develops in public discourse might enable the court to move beyond the current structure of analysis. Difficult questions about the manipulative power of expression and about the role of social and economic power in the communicative process might be addressed and not simply ignored in the rationalism of section 2(b) or buried in the behaviourism of section 1.

However, there are several reasons why a behavioural approach may continue to be attractive to the courts. The courts are not well positioned to address complex questions concerning the social and economic conditions of human reflection and choice. Most contemporary defences of judicial review regard constitutional rights, such as freedom of expression, as aspects of the individual's personal sphere (his or her basic autonomy) that should be insulated from the give and take of ordinary preference-based politics. Yet as the discussion in this chapter makes clear, freedom of expression is not a discrete concern that can be isolated from larger questions of social/economic power. The definition of the scope of freedom of expression and the assessment of its limits involve complex questions that go to the heart of the social/economic order. It is hardly surprising that the Supreme Court of Canada is reluctant to address these issues directly and chooses instead to rely on findings of cause and effect and to defer to the judgment of the elected branches of government. If the court is unwilling or unable to deal with issues of communicative power, its only option may be to treat expression as a cause and agree to the legislative restriction of expression that 'causes' harm.

The courts may be drawn to a causal or behavioural approach because of the difficulties involved in isolating unprotected manipulative expression from the ordinary 'rational' expression that is protected by the freedom. A commitment to freedom of expression means trusting or respecting the free and rational judgment of individuals. In principle, the protection of expression should not depend on approval of the message communicated as good or true. Reconciling this protection with a recognition that human reason is not simply free and transparent and that individuals can sometimes be 'persuaded' by wrong and hurtful views (so that expression sometimes has harmful consequences) must involve some attempt to isolate exceptional conditions – conditions under which free and rational judgment is significantly impaired. In these exceptional circumstances the state may be justified in restricting expression.

The problem, however, is that these circumstances may be difficult to isolate. There is no ideal condition of pure reason and perfect independence and so it is not possible to identify clear deviations from the proper and ordinary conditions of free choice. It will also be difficult to isolate conditions of manipulation if some of the factors that we think may impair autonomy and reason are systemic in character (e.g., racist and sexist cultural assumptions or the corporate/commercial domination of public discourse). Indeed, if some of the constraints on individual reason and choice are difficult to isolate as exceptional, then we may have to acknowledge that freedom of expression rests on less solid ground than we once supposed.

It is easy, then, to understand why the courts are drawn to a behavioural approach and why the key consideration in their analysis is the harm that may result if the message is accepted by the audience. When expression takes place in a context where individual judgment seems distorted or constrained, instead of trying to isolate the exceptional character or circumstances of the expression, it is simpler for a court to label and treat the expression as a form of action that 'impacts' upon the individual. When the constraints on individual judgment do not seem significant the court may find that no harm is caused and that deference to legislative judgment is inappropriate (or perhaps, as in some recent cases, the court may adopt the language of freedom and reason without any explanation as to why it has chosen to use this language over that of causation and behaviour).

Yet if the courts focus on the potential harm of expression without explaining why the judgment of the audience is not to be trusted in the particular circumstance, freedom of expression may no longer be playing a significant role in the courts' judgments. Freedom of expression has little substance if our trust in the 'autonomous' judgment of the individual is the exception – a condition that must be established. It has no substance if it is 'protected' only when we agree with the message or consider the message to be harmless.

A commitment to freedom of expression means defining a reasonably clear space for freedom of expression that does not depend (simply) on our agreement with the message communicated or our judgment that no harm will be caused if the message is accepted. There is no avoiding the difficult task of identifying contextual factors that justify removing an act of expression from the scope of constitutional protection, of isolating situations in which individual 'rationality' is distorted or 'autonomous judgment' is constrained, even if this is a relative judgment that is difficult to make in an adjudicative framework.

Chapter Three

The Regulation of Commercial and Political Advertising

1. Introduction: Manipulation and Domination

Several arguments have been made for excluding commercial advertising from the scope of freedom of expression.[1] The most familiar is that freedom of expression is valued because of its contribution to democratic government and so protects only political expression or expression that contributes to collective deliberation about public issues. According to this argument, commercial advertising does not contribute to the process of self-government and so does not fall within the scope of the freedom (*Klein* 1985, 532; Meiklejohn 1965, 79).

The other notable argument against the protection of commercial advertising is that freedom of expression is valued for its contribution to individual self-expression or self-realization and so does not protect the 'speech' of large commercial institutions, particularly speech designed to persuade consumers to purchase goods or services (Baker 1989, 196).[2] This argument focuses on both the corporate character of the speaker and the profit motive behind the speech. In a large corporation, the separation of management and ownership means that a corporation is represented by agents who do not express themselves personally – who do not engage in *self*-expression – when they communicate on behalf of the corporation in product promotion. As well, because advertising has the exclusive purpose of maximizing business profits, the commercial advertiser is 'bound' to say that which will most effectively achieve this end. Profit-motivated speech is instrumental in character and thus not truly self-*expressive*.

Canadian courts, like their American counterparts, have rejected both these arguments for the exclusion of commercial advertising from the scope of freedom of expression. The courts have rejected the democratic argument for exclusion because they are unwilling to base freedom of expression exclusively on its contribution to democratic government. In the courts' view, the freedom contributes to a variety of ends, including individual self-realization and the public recognition of truth.

The courts have also dismissed the self-expression argument for exclusion because they consider that freedom of expression is based not only on the *speaker*'s interest in expressing him/herself but also on the interests of the *listener*. According to the Supreme Court of Canada, commercial advertising enables individuals 'to make informed economic choices, an important aspect of individual self-fulfillment and personal autonomy' (*Ford* 1988, 767).[3] Indeed, the court in *Ford* 1988, borrowing a line from the U.S. Supreme Court, suggested that the listener's interest in commercial information 'may be as keen, if not keener by far, than his interest in the day's most urgent political debate' (*Ford* 1988, 756).[4]

Even if we thought that freedom of expression was concerned simply with self-realization or self-expression, the claim that commercial or profit-motivated expression is not truly self-expressive rests on a problematic distinction between instrumental expression and self-expression. On the one hand, self-expression is not unconstrained. There are always constraints of different kinds operating on so-called self-expressive speech, guiding and shaping it. When we speak to persuade others to think or act in a particular way, we choose words or adopt a style of expression that we think will be most effective. On the other hand, commercial expression is not wholly determined. While the corporate message may be motivated or directed by a desire to maximize profits, there is no one obvious way to present a product or to persuade consumers of the product's merits. Indeed, it is often difficult to predict or assess the audience impact of an advertisement. The making of an advertisement involves creative choices. Certainly, the public presentation of a product or service by a smaller business (in which owners and managers are the same) will often have a personal character to it. A sole proprietor, such as the plaintiff in *Ford* 1988, a wool shop owner, may regard the public presentation of her business as self-expression important to her identity in the community.[5]

While the Supreme Court of Canada has said that advertising falls within the scope of section 2(b) of the Charter, the court has also said that it does not lie at the core of the freedom and that, in comparison with other forms of expression, its restriction may be easier to justify under section 1. This view is routinely expressed at the beginning of nearly all judicial decisions concerning the regulation of commercial expression. For example, in *Rocket* 1990, Madame Justice McLachlin observed that in the case of commercial expression the motive for imparting information is 'primarily economic' and that 'the loss' that censorship might cause 'is merely loss of profit, and not loss of opportunity to participate in the political process or the "marketplace of ideas," or to realize one's spirited or artistic self-fulfillment' (*Rocket* 1990, 247). For these reasons, said McLachlin J., 'restrictions on expression of this kind might be easier to justify than other infringements of s.2(b)' (*Rocket* 1990, 247).[6]

However, Madame Justice McLachlin recognized that while commercial expression may be 'designed only to increase profits,' it may also play 'an important role in consumer choice' (*Rocket* 1990, 247). Because the interests of the profit-motivated speaker are not significant, any value that profit-motivated (or commercial) expression may have will depend entirely on its contribution to the listener. McLachlin J. in *Rocket* 1990, 247–8, considered that: '[t]hese two opposing factors – that the expression is designed only to increase profit, and that the expression plays an important role in consumer choice – will be present in most if not all cases of commercial expression. Their precise mix, however, will vary greatly ...'[7] For this reason, she thought 'it is inadvisable to create a special and standardized test for restrictions on commercial speech' (*Rocket* 1990, 247).

In the later judgment of *RJR Macdonald* 1995, McLachlin J. argued that profit motive or economic orientation should not lessen the claim of expression to constitutional protection: 'In my view, motivation to profit is irrelevant to the determination of whether the government has established that the law is reasonable or justified as an infringement of freedom of expression' (*RJR Macdonald* 1995, 348). She observed that profit is the motive, in whole or in part, behind a variety of expressive forms, some of which are seen as core to the freedom: 'Book sellers, newspaper owners, toy sellers – are all linked by their shareholder's desire to profit from the corporation's business activity, whether the expression sought to be protected is closely linked to the core values of freedom of expression or not' (*RJR Macdonald* 1995, 348).

It is not clear whether McLachlin J. changed her mind and came to believe that commercial expression is no less valuable than other forms of expression or whether she simply thought that the lesser protection granted to commercial expression rests on something other than its profit motivation. If she was arguing the latter, and still accepted that commercial expression lies outside the core of freedom of expression, she did not say what this lesser value rests on. Despite the remarks made by McLachlin J. in *RJR Macdonald* the Supreme Court of Canada, in other judgments, has stated that 'the fact that the targeted material was expression motivated by economic profit more readily justified the imposition of restrictions' (*Hill* 1995, 1174).

Economic interaction is such a large and important part of the life of both individual and community that it is difficult to dismiss commercial expression as valueless or even as less valuable than other forms of expression (Sharpe 1987, 237). In rejecting the exclusion of 'commercial speech' from the scope of the freedom, the Canadian courts accepted that advertising can convey important ideas and information to consumers and that an individual's identity and sense of worth are tied up with his or her purchasing decisions (and perhaps also with his or her business activities).[8] Indeed, the centrality of economic activity in the life of individual and community makes it very difficult to separate commercial expression from general public discourse and treat it as simply part of the economic marketplace.

The many cross-overs between commercial advertising, cultural expression, and political discourse make it difficult to draw clear lines between these different sorts of expression. The distinction between political and commercial expression is difficult because, as discussed later in this chapter, political expression often makes use of advertising techniques. As well, commercial enterprises, for reasons of profit, often attempt to influence political action through advertising. The distinction between commercial and cultural expression is difficult in a market economy because culture is often treated as a commodity, something that is advertised and sold for profit. Moreover, advertisements often appropriate cultural material for marketing purposes. Modern advertising is less about providing consumers with product information and more about representing products as important cultural/social symbols. According to Leiss et al. 1986: 'Advertising is not just a business expenditure undertaken in the hope of moving some merchandise off store shelves, but is rather an integral part of modern culture. Its creations appropriate and transform a vast range of symbolic ideas; its unsurpassed communicative powers recycle cultural models and references back through the networks of social interactions' (Leiss et al. 1986, 7).

However, the near-complete commercialization of culture underlies a different set of arguments for giving reduced protection to commercial advertising. Despite the court's frequent but very general references to profit motive, two concerns seem to underlie the decision to locate commercial advertising at the margins of freedom of expression. The first is the manipulative or misleading affect that advertising sometimes has on its audience. The other concern is the power of specific advertisements, or advertising in general, to dominate discourse and displace or 'drown out' other messages in the 'market place' of ideas.[9] Profit motive may serve as a sort of proxy for these concerns.[10] Pursuit of profit leads 'speakers' to adopt the most effective means of influencing consumer behaviour, which may be something other than rational persuasion. As well, in a market economy, where 'mass' communication is expensive, profit-motivated speech such as advertising comes 'naturally' to dominate public discourse.

Canadian courts have recognized that, sometimes at least, advertising does not seek to convince the audience of the merits of a particular product but attempts instead to influence audience behaviour without making any sort of reasoned appeal. Yet it is not clear why commercial expression as a general category should be given lesser protection (why it should be relegated to a second tier of constitutional protection) just because, in some instances, it may be manipulative or deceptive. Why should the courts not approach commercial advertising in the same way they approach political or artistic expression: as speech that should be protected unless there are clear and strong grounds for its limitation in a particular case? A specific advertisement should be protected unless it is shown to be manipulative or deceptive.

The decisions of the Supreme Court reveal a deep ambivalence about the constitutional position of commercial advertising. When the court extends protection to advertising under section 2(b) of the Charter, it describes advertising as informative (with the classified ad as the paradigm). Yet when the court declares that advertising deserves a lower level of protection under section 1, it seems to assume that most advertising is non-rational in its audience appeal (with the lifestyle ad as the paradigm). This ambivalence stems from the court's uncertainty as to how to fit manipulation, and manipulative advertising in particular, into its general account of freedom of expression.

Conventional freedom of expression doctrine regards manipulation as an identifiable deviation from ordinary expression. Manipulation is the consequence of the form of the expression and/or the exceptional circumstances in which the expression occurs. When a particular instance of expression, such as an advertisement, makes an irrational appeal or occurs in circumstances that limit the audience's ability to assess its message, state restriction may be justified. Yet the courts' assumption that commercial advertising, as a general category of expression, is less deserving of protection than political or artistic expression and that its restriction is easier to justify under section 1 suggests that manipulation is a systemic problem and not simply a problem affecting particular instances of advertising. It suggests that the 'manipulative' character of a particular advertisement is the consequence not only of its design and immediate context but also of its place in the larger system of commercial expression. In this system, the advertisement that provides clear and useful information and supports reflective consumer choice is the exception.

The commercial domination of public discourse is not specifically identified as a concern in the courts' commercial advertising cases, yet it may be critical to understanding the manipulative or deceptive character of particular ads and may explain the willingness of the courts to set lower standards for the restriction of advertising in general. The overwhelming number of commercial messages that we are confronted with each day reduces the space for critical viewing of particular ads. There are so many ads that it is simply not possible for the audience to reflect on the claims or associations of each. The domination of public discourse by advertising also means that the unnatural images or absurd associations of a particular ad seem unexceptional. Because the principal channels of public discourse are controlled by commercial interests and carry only ads and advertising-funded programming, the underlying message of advertising, that self-realization is achieved through consumption, is an almost unchallengeable cultural assumption.

The commercial domination of public discourse also plays a role in the courts' assumption that the regulation of false advertising raises no freedom of expression concerns. According to conventional freedom of expression thinking, the answer to false or misleading expression is more expression – expression that contradicts the false claims of the other speaker. The audience should be left to choose between competing claims and to decide what they think is true or false, right or wrong. However, as Robert Sharpe notes, this approach has not been followed in the case of commercial expression. The regulation of false and misleading advertising, 'intolerable with regard to other forms of expression, is properly seen as market-place regulation, virtually immune from judicial review' (Sharpe 1987, 259).[11] We do not assume that consumers should be left to determine the accuracy of advertising claims; first, because it may be difficult for non-expert audiences to assess product claims, and second because it is not clear that the 'marketplace of ideas' generates speech contesting the claims of particular advertisements.

Concern that certain messages may dominate discourse and overwhelm or displace other views is more explicit in the debate about the regulation of political or campaign advertising. Election spending limitations, which do not restrict the message or form of expression but only the amount of money that can be spent in support of a particular message, are justified on the ground that unlimited spending will allow the messages of some candidates to 'drown out' those of other candidates. How is it, though, that the message of the better-financed candidate 'drowns out' the message of his or her competitors? The competitors' message can still be heard, even if less often. If greater volume has an impact (if repetition of messages makes a difference) it is because so much contemporary political discourse has adopted the form of commercial advertising, seeking to influence the audience emotionally or non-cognitively.

Manipulation and 'drowning out'/inequality, which are described and responded to as separate problems, are really two aspects or dimensions of the much larger problem of the domination of public discourse by commercial messages and the advertising form. Restrictions aimed at either the manipulative impact of expression or the dominance of particular messages are partial, or symptom, responses to this systemic problem. Inequality in election spending is a problem because of the 'advertising' form of most campaign expression, which is composed of images and slogans with little evaluative content. Commercial advertisements have a manipulative impact only because they so completely dominate public discourse.

It is not surprising that the courts have treated manipulation and inequality as separate problems, each representing a distinct and limited failure in the ordinary operation of public discourse. A commitment to freedom of expression, at least as a judicially protected constitutional right, rests on a belief that, in the absence of special circumstances, individuals should be permitted to express themselves and to assess the expression of others. Manipulation must be viewed as an identifiable deviation from the ordinary conditions of free and rational public discussion and inequality must be viewed as a particular unfairness in electoral competition that can be addressed by setting basic ground rules that level the 'playing field.' Recognition that human reason may be compromised by systemic features of public discourse, such as commercial domination, raises a significant challenge to our commitment to freedom of expression and our faith in constitutional adjudication as a way of advancing or protecting the freedom.

2. Manipulation and the Regulation of Advertising

If an advertisement conveys meaning, then under conventional doctrine it is properly considered expression and should not be denied protection simply because its message is thought to be crass or unimportant, because it originates from commercial interests, or because it may be effective in persuading its audience of the correctness of a particular view. To restrict expression for any of these reasons would interfere with the individual's freedom to make his or her own decisions based on available information and leave little or no communication secure from censorship.

Freedom of expression doctrine, however, has always permitted the restriction of 'manipulative' expression. Expression may be viewed as manipulative (or as incitement) when it takes a form or occurs in conditions that limit the audience's ability to rationally assess the claims made and the implications of acting on those claims. For example, in *On Liberty* (Mill 1982) Mill thought that the authorities would be justified in preventing a fiery speech given near the home of a corn merchant to a crowd of farmers angry about crop prices.[12] A heated speech delivered to a 'mob' appeals to passion and prejudice and might lead to impulsive and harmful actions. The restriction of such a speech in these circumstances represents a legitimate exception to the general protection of freedom of expression.

In American free speech jurisprudence the classic example of a failure in the conditions of ordinary rational discourse comes from a judgment of Mr Justice Holmes, who argued: 'The most stringent protection of free speech would not protect a man in falsely shouting fire in a theatre and causing a panic' (*Schenck* 1919, 52). The false yell of fire in a crowded theatre represents an identifiable and discrete deviation from the conditions of ordinary discourse. The theatre audience in such a case would not have the time to stop and think carefully before acting on the communicated message. The panic that would follow the yell of fire in these circumstances would likely result in injury.

The examples given by Mill and Holmes involve circumstances that limit the audience's ability to carefully or dispassionately assess the communicated message. The assumption is that ordinarily when an individual communicates with others, he or she makes claims that can be described as either true or false and that appeal to the reasoned judgment of the audience. In exceptional circumstances, however, an individual's words (the spoken word more often than the printed) may appeal to passions, prejudices, and fears and may encourage unreflective action. In these circumstances the state is justified in restricting expression. While the line between rational appeal and manipulation may not always be easy to draw, it must, at least, be possible to isolate some of the circumstances or conditions in which reasoned judgment is discouraged, that is, when the time and space for independent judgment are compressed, or when emotions are running so high that individuals are less likely to stop and reflect on the claims being made.

In the theory and doctrine built upon the writing of Mill the 'word,' and more particularly the printed word, is the paradigm of expression (Moon 1991, 85). This follows from Mill's belief that the discovery of truth is the goal of freedom of expression. Words are instruments that enable individuals to make statements, the truth of which can be debated and judged. Whether printed or spoken, words effectively convey ideas and information and encourage reflection and reasoned judgment on the part of both the speaker/author and the listener/reader. In contrast to the spoken word, the printed word is 'easier to verify or refute, and it is invested with an impersonal and objective character ...' (Postman 1986, 21). Because writing 'separates the knower from the known,' it permits 'the conditions for objectivity ... personal disengagement or distancing' (Ong 1982, 46). Communication by print is individualized and distanced from immediate circumstances and so allows space for more thoughtful reflection by the reader and correction by other writers.

Oral communication, however, may not always be oriented simply to the conveyance of ideas and information, to the expression of reason. It is more likely to be spontaneous, impulsive, and emotional because it is more closely connected with the immediate context. It is more likely to involve circumstances that exclude or limit the opportunity for rational reflection and permit an irrational or emotional response. The examples given by Mill and Holmes involve situations in which the audience's 'natural reason' is distorted by the passion and immediacy of the spoken word.

In some of its judgments, most notably *Irwin Toy* 1989, the Supreme Court of Canada identifies manipulation explicitly as a basis for restricting commercial advertising. In other judgments concern about manipulation, although not explicit, seems to underlie the court's decision to uphold a state restriction on advertising. However, even when the court explicitly identifies manipulation as the problem, it does not explain how manipulative expression is to be distinguished from ordinary, non-manipulative communication.

There are good reasons for this avoidance. Since the writing of Mill and Holmes, there has been a dramatic change in the character of public discourse. The visual image, and more specifically the photographic image, has displaced the word as the principal form of public communication. The dominance of visual imagery is so complete that books, magazines, and other forms of print communication have begun to resemble, in both presentation and content, visual forms of expression (Postman 1986, 28). Visual images do not make explicit claims and so the distinction between the rational and the manipulative, which is critical to classical doctrine, may not be so easy to draw in the case of visual expression.

An act is described as manipulative if it is intended to distort or pervert the individual's reasoning process, 'the way the person reaches decisions, forms preferences or adopts goals' (Raz 1986, 377). But what sort of influence counts as manipulation or distortion? When individuals express themselves, they seek to affect the attitudes and actions of others. Freedom of expression is said to be valuable because the free exchange of ideas is necessary to the formation of public opinion and to the realization/creation of individual and group identity. An act of expression cannot be considered manipulative simply because it influences another individual's decision making or shapes his or her ideas. Once we recognize that freedom of expression is valuable because individual feeling and idea are constituted in the social activity of expression it becomes difficult to draw a clear line between rational persuasion and manipulation or distortion (Moon 1991, 105).

While manipulation is described as the consequence of the particular *form* of expression or the immediate context in which the expression takes place, the manipulative force of advertising may be, at least in part, the result of conditions that are systemic and not special and discrete – conditions such as the dominance of contemporary public discourse by commercial messages. If this is so, then 'manipulation' may not be an isolated failure of rational agency. Instead, it may be a general characteristic or condition of commercial discourse.[13] Even if the commercial domination of public discourse is only one of several factors that contribute to the manipulative impact of a particular advertisement, and if advertisements are not invariably manipulative in character (at least to a degree that would justify denial of constitutional protection), the line between rational expression and manipulation will be very difficult to draw and will depend on differences in the form and immediate context of expression that are subtle and difficult to isolate.

Irwin Toy 1989

In *Irwin Toy* 1989 the Supreme Court of Canada decided that a Quebec law restricting television advertising directed at children did not violate the Charter of Rights.[14] The court found that the restricted advertising was protected expression under section 2(b) because it 'attempts to convey meaning.' However, the court held that the restriction was justified under section 1 because it protects children, a particularly susceptible group, from the manipulative influence of advertising.[15]

In its section 1 analysis, the issue of whether the restriction impaired the freedom as little as necessary ('minimal impairment') caused some difficulties for the court. The restriction applied to advertising that is directed at children under thirteen years of age. While the empirical evidence before the court seemed to show that children under the age of seven are susceptible to the manipulative techniques of advertising, it did not show clearly that older children are similarly susceptible. However, the court was prepared to defer to the judgment of the legislature that the social science evidence established that children up to the age of thirteen require protection from the manipulative impact of advertising.

By focusing on children the court was able to uphold the restriction while maintaining an overall commitment to freedom of expression. According to the court, children are 'particularly vulnerable to the techniques of seduction and manipulation abundant in advertising' because their reasoning capacities are not yet fully developed. The court's focus on children, an exceptional group to whom the standard assumptions of rationality and freedom of choice might not apply, prevents any significant erosion of the basic assumptions of freedom of expression.[16] Yet, unless we think that children have no freedom of expression rights, the restriction of advertising directed at children must rest, at least in part, on the character of the 'expression' at issue and not simply on the special circumstances of the audience. What is missing from the court's judgment is an account of the way in which advertising (or children's advertising) is manipulative and so distinguishable from other forms of expression.

RJR Macdonald 1995

In *RJR Macdonald* 1995 a majority of the Supreme Court of Canada decided that two provisions of the federal Tobacco Products Control Act, 1988,[17] a general ban on cigarette advertising and a requirement that packages carry specified health warnings, were contrary to the Canadian Charter of Rights.[18]

The majority judgment of McLachlin J.[19] and the dissenting judgment of LaForest J.[20] agreed that the ban on cigarette advertising was a restriction on the manufacturers' freedom of expression, a breach of section 2(b) of the Charter. Both judgments also accepted that 'prevent[ing] people in Canada from being persuaded by advertising and promotion' to engage in the harmful activity of smoking is a purpose substantial enough to justify restriction of freedom of expression under section 1 of the Charter (*RJR Macdonald* 1995, 335). The judgments diverged, however, in their application of the rational connection and minimal impairment tests under section 1.

In the opinion of McLachlin J., the federal government did not establish that there is a rational connection between a general advertising ban and a decrease in tobacco consumption. She accepted that there is 'a link based on reason' or 'common sense' between lifestyle advertising and tobacco consumption, even though there is no 'direct evidence of a scientific nature showing a causal link' (*RJR Macdonald* 1995, 340–1). However, she saw no basis for thinking that informational advertising (disseminating information concerning product content) and brand-name advertising (promoting one brand over another on the basis of colour design and appearance of packaging) have the effect of increasing or sustaining overall tobacco consumption. At most these forms of advertising support brand loyalty or encourage brand switching. They do not encourage non-smokers to take up the habit. Indeed, in her view, such a ban 'deprives those who lawfully smoke of information relating to price, quality and even health risks associated with different brands' (*RJR Macdonald* 1995, 347).[21] McLachlin J. concluded that because the ban on advertising covered not just lifestyle advertising but also informational and brand-name advertising it was over-inclusive and failed the minimal impairment test.[22]

LaForest J., in dissent, was prepared to uphold the general ban on tobacco advertising. He believed that while cigarette advertising is protected under section 2(b), a lower standard of justification should apply to its limitation under section 1. According to Laforest J., cigarette advertising is not core expression because it is motivated by profit and because it encourages people to engage in an activity that is damaging to their health.[23] He also thought that judicial deference to Parliament's judgment about the proper scope of the ban was appropriate, given the difficulty in establishing the presence or absence of a causal connection between advertising and consumer behaviour.[24] Parliament is in a better position than the courts 'to compile and assess social science evidence, to mediate between competing social interests and to reach out and protect vulnerable groups' (*RJR Macdonald* 1995, 277).

In Mr Justice LaForest's view, Parliament's judgment that a general ban on cigarette advertising is a necessary limit on the freedom to encourage tobacco use is supported by 'common sense' as well as by internal company marketing documents and expert reports.[25] The size of the cigarette companies' advertising budgets suggests that their advertising is concerned not only with maintaining brand loyalty but also with attracting new smokers and inducing existing smokers not to quit.[26] Profits would drop off dramatically unless the companies were able to discourage quitting and find new smokers to replace those who have died prematurely.

The distinction drawn in the majority judgment between lifestyle advertising, which can be restricted by the state, and brand-name and informational advertising, which cannot be restricted, is said to rest on a judgment about the behavioural consequences of each form of advertising. McLachlin J. was prepared to uphold a ban on lifestyle advertising because she accepted that this sort of advertising has the effect of increasing tobacco consumption. However, she concluded that informational and brand-name advertising should not be restricted because these advertising forms do not encourage the smoking habit but simply reinforce brand loyalty or encourage brand switching. She reached this conclusion without offering any explanation as to how an ad can reinforce brand loyalty without reinforcing the smoking habit or how it can encourage brand switching without encouraging smokers not to quit or non-smokers to start.[27]

Is there any real basis for the distinction between lifestyle advertising and informational/brand-name advertising? McLachlin J. said very little in her decision about informational cigarette ads, referring only generally to 'information relating to price, quality and even to health risks associated with different brands' (*RJR Macdonald* 1995, 347). This is hardly surprising. Informational cigarette advertising seems little more than a theoretical possibility. After all, what can the cigarette manufacturers say about their product that is positive and truthful? The example that is always given of an informational ad is one that informs smokers about the tar levels of particular cigarette brands. Yet, as many have pointed out, this sort of advertisement may be seen as deceptive inasmuch as it suggests that smoking lower tar cigarettes is less unhealthy.[28]

Similarly, the distinction between brand-name and lifestyle advertising is unclear. It seems likely that brand-name advertising has an impact on consumer behaviour either because it is in truth a subtle form of lifestyle advertising, associating a brand name with certain lifestyles, values, or feelings, or because it draws on the background of other lifestyle ads that construct an image for the product. Without such a background the simple repetition of a brand name or the use of a particular logo would be unlikely to have much effect on consumer behaviour.

The different conclusions reached by the majority and dissenting judgments indicate the difficulties in predicting the impact of advertising on consumer behaviour. Both the majority and dissenting judgments recognized that identifying a causal connection between advertising and tobacco consumption is not easy. Each judgment relied on a combination of common sense and deference to complete the connection that social science evidence does not establish clearly. McLachlin J., for the majority, found that the connection was sufficiently made out in the case of lifestyle advertising but not in the case of informational and brand-name advertising. However, as her judgment illustrates, it is difficult to know when (and why) the court will defer to legislative judgment or rely on 'common sense' in order to uphold a restriction and when it will decide that the absence of empirical evidence means that the restriction cannot be justified.

The problem of proof lies at the surface of a much deeper problem with the court's approach to limits on freedom of expression. The behavioural approach taken by the court avoids the question of *how* cigarette ads effect human behaviour and ignores the role of human agency in the communication process.[29] Both majority and dissenting judgments seemed to assume that cigarette advertising could be restricted if it was shown to be effective in persuading its audience to smoke but that it could not be banned if it was shown to be ineffective.

McLachlin J. decided that advertisements that provide information to consumers should not be banned. The formal reason offered for this decision was the absence of social science evidence (and common sense) indicating that such ads lead to greater tobacco consumption. On the other hand, she decided that lifestyle advertising could be banned because she believed there is a connection between this form of advertising and overall tobacco consumption. Yet how can it be that the justification for restricting expression is stronger when the expression succeeds in persuading its audience to start or continue smoking? The conventional freedom of expression position is that individuals should be permitted to hear and assess competing views and that we, as a community, must take the risk that they will sometimes make bad decisions. The court's behavioural or causal approach in *RJR Macdonald* 1995 runs contrary to the basic assumptions of freedom and rationality that underlie this conventional understanding of freedom of expression.

The majority's decision to support the restriction of lifestyle advertising rested ostensibly on the existence of evidence showing that such advertising affects individual behaviour, and specifically that it leads to more smoking. However, it may be that we should see behavioural impact as a proxy for concerns about the manipulative form of the advertising at issue.[30] According to this view, the court's decision to uphold the restriction of lifestyle advertising (and not informational and brand-name ads) was based not on behavioural impact, which was something the court had no clear evidence about, but rather on the form of the ad and the nature of its appeal.[31] Lifestyle advertising, in contrast to informational advertising, does not appeal to reasoned judgment. (It is worth recalling that commercial expression is protected under section 2(b) of the Charter because it sometimes provides useful product information to consumers.) Lifestyle ads are designed to influence behaviour in ways that may not deserve constitutional protection. The law is overbroad, then, not because it bans ads that may be ineffective but rather because it bans informational ads, which are not manipulative.

While LaForest J. made occasional references in his judgment to the 'manipulative' character of the advertising, his real focus was on the 'harmful' nature of the activity which the advertising encourages. His judgment has been criticized for failing to separate the activity, which is harmful, from the advocacy of that activity, which, under established freedom of expression doctrine, should be protected (Cameron 1997, 48). Yet perhaps this collapsing of advocacy and activity is justified. The restriction on cigarette advertising could be seen as a partial or indirect restriction on the harmful activity of smoking. Laforest J. recognized that cigarettes would have been banned sometime ago if their harms had been known but that because their use has become so widespread, it would now be difficult to ban them outright. The best alternative is to restrict commercial efforts to persuade individuals to start or continue smoking. Prohibiting the advertisement of this dangerous product represents a sensible middle course.

However, the difficulty with this argument is that if people have a legal right to perform a particular act, such as smoking, it seems wrong to prevent them from hearing expression that supports performance of that act. The ban on cigarette advertising restricts commercial efforts to persuade, or encourage, individuals to engage in a lawful activity. No expression, and certainly no commercial expression, would be safe from restriction, if the state's 'larger' power to restrict an activity included the 'lesser' power to restrict advocacy of that activity. The argument that a restriction on cigarette advertising is justified as an indirect restriction on cigarette smoking only seems plausible because of the character of the advertising – because it is not about rational persuasion.

A commitment to freedom of expression means that the denial of constitutional protection to these ads must rest on something more than their encouragement of a harmful (and still lawful) activity.[32] The emphasis on the harm of the product (and the transfer of that harm to the advertisement) suggests that the restriction is a reasonably narrow exception to the constitutional protection of commercial advertising. However, if we were to accept that expression could be limited whenever it encouraged activity thought to be harmful, we would have removed the principle of freedom of expression completely from the analysis. The only question for the court would be whether or not the expression might persuade individuals to engage in harmful or anti-social behaviour. While Parliament's reason for restricting the advertising of cigarettes, rather than shampoo, is the harmful nature of the product, the denial of constitutional protection to this advertising must rest on the characteristics of the ad or the nature of its appeal and not simply on the product's harmful character. Underlying the focus on harm (and the issue of whether there is a causal connection between the restricted expression and harmful action) is an assumption that this form of advertising has a manipulative impact.[33]

In *RJR Macdonald* 1995, the court did not explicitly address the question of manipulation. This failure may reflect the barren state of contemporary public discourse. Lifestyle ads (and cigarette ads in particular) are an ordinary part of our public discourse and so we may be slow to recognize the absurdity of the cigarette companies' attempt to link their ads to a more idealized form of discourse involving the communication of important information or even the 'exchange' or 'conversation' between company and consumer about a lawful product.[34] Alternatively the Supreme Court's failure to address the question of manipulation may reflect the difficulty in drawing a workable distinction between manipulative and non-manipulative advertising in a culture overwhelmed by repetitive commercial appeals.

3. Lifestyle Advertising and Manipulation

It is sometimes argued that cigarette ads should be restricted because they are 'untruthful' or 'deceptive.' An advertisement that connects cigarettes with the healthy outdoors should be restricted because it makes a false claim that smoking is healthy. Yet cigarette ads are not dishonest in any straightforward sense.[35] They have little or no obvious propositional content and make no explicit claims about their product that might be either accepted or rejected by the audience.[36] The reason is obvious. One brand of cigarettes cannot, at least in an advertisement, be distinguished from another brand on the basis of a characteristic such as taste. Because of the lack of any 'hard' information of a positive nature that can be given about cigarettes, manufacturers use brand images to sell their products. They seek to make their products 'symbols of social standing, representations of personal characteristics of the owner, and ultimately reflections of the person's choices of lifestyle' (Kline 1993, 39). The advertisement's focus is on the characteristics of the consumer rather than the product.

A lifestyle advertisement seeks to give meaning to its product, to differentiate that product from others in the market, by taking a person or object that carries meaning outside the ad, a sign, and linking that sign to the advertised product. The link is made not through argument (that the product is like the object) but through the juxtaposition of the sign and the product within the advertisement (Williamson 1978, 30; Dyer 1982, 116; Leiss et al. 1986, 153). Colour, shape, and other elements of the advertisement's formal structure are used to connect the product with the sign and to encourage the viewer to transfer the sign's meaning to the product. As Leiss et al. 1986 observe: 'Images from quite different contexts can co-exist without contradiction because the message is not being communicated as a "rational argument"; they are meant rather to evoke the realm of "meaning" – and, since the symbols are only "suggestive" (of whatever may occur to the viewer), the ordinary rules of logical inference simply do not apply' (Leiss et al. 1986, 60).[37]

The picture in the familiar Marlboro advertisement is of a cowboy, who may or may not be smoking a cigarette. Cowboys are conventionally associated with masculinity, strength, freedom, and adventure (Dyer 1982, 123). The hope of the advertiser is that the viewer will transfer the values or attributes associated with cowboys to the advertised product. The transfer of meaning from the cowboy to the cigarettes does not depend on argument. The advertisement makes no simple claim that the product has this attribute, or that the product will make you more masculine or more powerful. The viewer of the ad is supposed to see the meaning of the product as already there.[38] The transfer is supported by visual and other links between the product and the symbol. For example, the colours of the western sunset and the cowboy's clothing are matched with the colours of the cigarette packet (Dyer 1982, 120). If this meaning is successfully transferred, the cigarettes will be seen to represent masculinity and freedom. The further implication is that the value transferred to the product will be transferred to the consumer through the act of buying or using it, that use of the product signifies the user's masculinity to others (Williamson 1978, 26).

Lifestyle advertisements do not simply 'cause' the viewer to think or act in a particular way. The audience plays an active role in the construction of the ad's meaning, in identifying the symbolic meaning of the advertised goods. The advertisement is organized according to associative rather than logical relations, and so 'the connections are not made explicitly in the text, but are developed by the viewer' (Leiss et al. 1986, 155).[39] Because the connections are made by the viewer, the ad may be read in different ways by different individuals drawing on their personal experiences and associations. The maker of the advertisement cannot completely determine the ad's meaning, closing down entirely alternative (unintended) readings of the image.[40] This is particularly true when the advertiser seeks to appeal to an audience that is highly diverse.

However, there are a variety of constraints on the individual's reading of a particular lifestyle ad. Because the links between product and lifestyle are associative rather than logical, they are made without critical reflection and take place below the threshold of conscious awareness (Fiske 1987, 101; Leiss et al. 1986, 244).[41] The advertisement is presented as nothing more than a picture of a cowboy smoking a cigarette, as natural and innocent: 'an unmediated picture of external reality' (Fiske 1987, 21). Recognition of the human purpose behind the ad, which is a critical part of the interpretation of communication, is discouraged by the apparent realism or simplicity of the image.[42] The audience is invited to view the images of social relations in ads as natural or as a matter of common sense (Ramsay 1996, 140). Cowboys sometimes smoke cigarettes; it is possible to smoke a cigarette while sitting beside a mountain stream; attractive people sometimes smoke in social settings. While the images may be linked only by association, they 'feel' as if they are connected (Barry 1997, 173; Jamieson 1992, 54).[43]

Television advertising, through the use of cuts, edits, lighting changes, camera changes, changing visual images, music, sound-effects, voice-overs, and so forth, is particularly effective at discouraging critical evaluation of its claims or associations. The 'multimodal nature' of television 'makes analytical processing of rapidly emerging claims' and product associations difficult and unlikely (Jamieson 1992, 10).

Several features of the viewing context are critical to the impact of advertising. Generally speaking, ads are presented in a context that limits the viewer's ability to reflect upon their images or associations. As J. Berger observes: 'The publicity image belongs to the moment. We see it as we turn a page, as we turn the corner as a vehicle passes. Or we see it on a television screen whilst waiting for the commercial break to end' (Berger 1977, 129). The images of advertising stream past us at a speed and in a volume that 'defies rational reflection' (Barry 1997, 171). Indeed, the advertisement is designed to be looked at quickly, in passing, and not as something that requires careful reflection or contemplation.[44]

As well, advertising is part of a system of public discourse that is one-sided or one-directional in character. The ad comes to the individual not as part of an active dialogue or exchange with the advertiser. The structure of public discourse means that the audience has no real opportunity to respond to the ad, except to tune out, or to decline to make a purchase. The audience's power is simply to interpret material that has been presented to it by the advertiser.[45] This material has been carefully selected/constructed using information gained from surveys and focus groups (Schiller 1989, 153). Advertisers draw on textual conventions that rest on common experience, significantly the common experience of watching ads. As well, advertisers have become increasingly sophisticated at directing their ads towards particular audiences. Consider, for example, humorous or satirical ads that seek to co-opt subversive feelings about advertising and consumption, and pitch the particular product to those 'in the know' (Wright 1997, 142).

More significantly, the overwhelming and historically unprecedented volume of advertising to which we are daily exposed makes it difficult for an individual to examine a particular advertisement with any care and so contributes to the unreflective assimilation of the ad's imagery. As Mark Crispin Miller observes, advertisements come at us 'in stupefying numbers, each one overcharged and utterly forgettable, so that we find ourselves lulled into the receptive state of the well hypnotized' (Miller 1988, 31).

Because commercial imagery is so pervasive it forms the background against which particular commercial images are viewed. This background shapes our viewing habits. It develops our ability to assimilate lifestyle and product associations (and dulls our ability to recognize the absurdity of these associations). More generally, the near monopolization of public discourse by commercial expression means that the general value of consumption is unchallenged (Schiller 1989, 156).[46] There is little space for us to question the assumption that our problems can be solved, and our social position elevated, by the appropriate purchase decisions. As Stephen Kline observes: 'However confusing and uncertain our world, the promotional messages that cascade ceaselessly from the media at least adopt a consistent position on the ultimate purpose of a consumer society – that we can always find meaning, comfort and solace in our relationship with goods' (Kline 1993, 11).

It may be possible to neutralize (to some degree) the impact of a lifestyle advertisement by revealing its associative links. Demystification seeks to show that conscious design lies behind the images that appear natural or neutral and that there can be impact without conscious reflection and judgment. Yet, the question of whether 'more speech' might lead to a greater awareness of the impact of advertising seems academic. While ads present a wide range of different (and competing) products, they seldom compare product merits and most certainly do not question the value of consumption. Public discourse is dominated so completely by commercial messages that efforts to counteract or demystify lifestyle ads are exceptional and seem eccentric.

Lifestyle ads do not manipulate through some sort of exceptional trickery, such as sexual images etched into ice cubes (Miller 1988, 31). The manipulative force of a particular advertisement is the consequence not simply of form, the way the ad links product and lifestyle, but also of volume – both the repetition of the particular ad and the domination of public discourse by a form of expression that discourages conscious reflection and critical evaluation. The domination of public discourse by commercial advertising shapes the way we view particular ads and entrenches cultural assumptions about consumption and self-realization.[47]

If the manipulative force of a particular advertisement rests not only on its form but also on the general character of public discourse, it may be difficult to identify a narrow group of ads that is manipulative and undeserving of protection. Some ads are more obviously informative or propositional in character – classified ads, for example. Yet most ads share, to some degree, the lifestyle form and take place within (and are part of) a context that is saturated with commercial messages.

The difficulty involved in distinguishing between manipulative and non-manipulative commercial advertising may explain the courts' decision to treat advertising as low value expression under the Charter. This difficulty may also explain the Supreme Court's behavioural approach in *RJR Macdonald* 1995. The result in that case turned on the question of whether cigarette advertising causes its audience to engage in an activity that is harmful. Yet it is difficult to prove that a particular kind of advertising 'causes' harm. And so it may be that causation is simply a proxy for concerns about the manipulative form and context of particular ads, concerns that are unidentified and unexamined.

4. Election Spending Limits

The Canada Elections Act, 1985, c. E-2[48] imposes expenditure limits on parties, candidates, and independent interests.[49] Under the provisions of the Act, the spending ceiling for parties is tied to the number of names on the voting list in the constituencies where the party has officially nominated a candidate. The limit for a candidate is tied to the number of voters on the voting list in the particular constituency (sections 208–11). 'Third parties' (or independent interests) are permitted to spend no more than $1,000 on advertising that 'directly' promotes or opposes a particular candidate or political party. 'Issue advocacy' by third parties is not subject to spending limits. Other parts of the federal law provide for free-time campaign broadcasts and for the allocation among competing parties of limited paid advertising time on radio and television.[50]

The $1,000 limit on 'third-party' spending in support of a political candidate or party was struck down by the Alberta Court of Appeal in

Somerville 1996.[51] In that case the federal government conceded that the spending ceiling was a restriction on freedom of expression under section 2(b) but sought to justify the limit under section 1. The government argued that significant third-party spending could have an impact on voter behaviour, undermining the integrity of the party and candidate spending ceilings.

Justice Conrad of the Alberta Court of Appeal found no evidence to support the claim that third-party spending affected voter behaviour. However, Conrad J. also said that even if it could be shown that voters were influenced by this spending, the limits would not be justified. The judge observed: 'An important justification for the *Charter* guarantees of free expression and association ... is the need in a democracy for citizens to participate in and affect an election' (*Somerville* 1996, 232). It followed then that expression could not be restricted 'merely because it might have an impact' on the election process (*Somerville* 1996, 232).

In the court's view the restriction at issue was intended to 'silence' non-party or 'independent' voices in the electoral process and to enable official candidates and parties to monopolize campaign expression (*Somerville* 1996, 217). According to the court, this objective 'strikes at the core' of freedom of expression. Voters should have the benefit of 'independent advice and information on candidates and parties' untainted by the 'self-interest involved in candidate and party advertising' (*Somerville* 1996, 236).[52] The court took this view even though the third-party spending limit applied only to direct promotion of a candidate or party and not to 'issue advocacy.'

The decision of the Alberta Court of Appeal in *Somerville* 1996 was not appealed. However, in the case of *Libman* 1997 the Supreme Court of Canada expressed its disagreement with the Alberta court's judgment. *Libman* 1997 involved a challenge to the spending ceilings established by the Quebec law regulating provincial referendum campaigns. The Quebec Referendum Act[53] provided for the financing of two official referendum committees (a 'yes' and a 'no' committee) and imposed limits on the amount each committee could spend. The law also provided that during the referendum period only the authorized agent of an official committee, or his or her delegate, could incur or authorize regulated expenses. An official committee could authorize an affiliated group to spend a certain amount (and according to the court the decision whether or not to permit an affiliated group to spend a portion of the committee's spending allocation must be made in 'a fair and reasonable manner' (*Libman* 1997, 612)). However, an individual or group which chose not to join an official committee nor to participate in the affiliation system would be prohibited from incurring any expenses in support of a position during the referendum campaign.

The Supreme Court accepted that the third-party spending ceilings restricted expression and so violated section 2(b). In the court's view 'freedom of expression includes the right to employ any methods, other than violence, necessary for communication' (*Libman* 1997, 594).[54] However, the court recognized that under section 1 there were substantial and compelling reasons for imposing spending limits, including limits on third-party spending. Spending limits are needed 'to guarantee the democratic nature of referendums by promoting equality between the options' before the public and to promote 'free and informed voting' (*Libman* 1997, 596). Specifically, ceilings are needed to 'prevent the most affluent from monopolizing election discourse and consequently depriving their opponents of a reasonable opportunity to speak and be heard' (*Libman* 1997, 599). Unlimited spending would work against 'informed choice,' allowing some positions to 'bury' others (*Libman* 1997, 596). The court recognized that committee spending limits would be ineffective if third-party spending was not also limited.

However, the court thought that the law under review was overly restrictive. In the court's view the *total* ban on third-party spending during a referendum campaign did not impair freedom of expression, as little as was necessary to protect the integrity of the election process. The court suggested that a less intrusive third-party limit, like the limit in the Canada Elections Act, 1985, c. E-2, which allows third parties to spend up to $1,000 in support of a particular candidate or party, would have enabled third parties to put forward their views without undermining the official committee spending ceilings. The court held that the third-party spending restriction in the Referendum Act 1981 violated the Charter. At the same time, however, the court said that it would have upheld a limit similar to that in the *Canada Elections Act*, 1985, c. E-2. Indeed, the court indicated that had the *Somerville* 1996 case been appealed, it would have overturned the court of appeal decision.

Claims that unlimited spending might enable wealthier candidates to 'drown out' or 'bury' their less wealthy opponents are a familiar part of the case for ceilings. Yet how do the voices of the wealthy 'drown out' or 'bury' the voices of others? The use of metaphors such as 'drowning out' or 'burying,' which suggest physical suppression, cannot hide the fact that in most election campaigns the message of the less well-financed candidate is still expressed, and still heard, albeit less often than that of the wealthy candidate. Indeed, as ceiling opponents often point out, candidates who spend less money sometimes win. If the problem is that a particular candidate does not have enough money to purchase advertising space and get his or her message out, spending ceilings will not help. Ceilings simply limit communicative power; they do not redistribute it. They do not raise the voice of the poor and other marginalized members of the community.[55]

Silencing metaphors (claims about 'drowning out' or 'burying') are used to bolster the argument that substantial inequality in electoral spending is unfair or distorting and to hide some of the argument's difficulties. The first difficulty is that it is unclear what counts as in/equality in communicative power. There are different ways in which individuals may contribute to a campaign (such as volunteer time and creative energy) that are not quantifiable. But even if we focus only on differences in campaign spending, it is unclear when inequality becomes a problem. How great must the spending differential be before it is unfair or before it has a distorting effect on the campaign? Behind this question lies a more fundamental difficulty. It is unclear why unequal spending matters – how unequal spending translates into unequal campaign influence. Why is the voter, who is exposed to competing messages, unable to make a rational and informed choice? Why does it matter that one message is repeated more often than another?

If we regard voters as 'rational and intelligent,' as the Supreme Court of Canada insisted we should in *Thompson* 1998, we should trust them to sift through all the arguments and information and to make reasonable judgments. Concern about 'fair competition' and 'level playing fields' does not quite fit with conventional freedom of expression assumptions about citizen autonomy. For example, in its final report the Royal Commission on Election Spending (Lortie Commission 1991) insisted that campaign expression (including repetitive advertising) provides valuable information to voters, yet went on to argue, somewhat inconsistently, that spending limits are necessary to prevent distortion: 'Recent studies in Canada suggest that many voters, especially those who do not follow politics closely, became aware of issues and party positions and form impressions of the leaders from party advertisements. The attention grabbing and repetitive nature of advertising promotes learning. Most of the 1990 party advertisements, for example, had at least some policy content, and the most effective of them distilled a central policy argument' (Lortie Commission 1991, 1:384–5).

If spending inequality (or advertising volume) is unfair or distorts the democratic process, it is because contemporary campaign communication has increasingly come to resemble commercial advertising

(Moon 1988b, 249).[56] Campaign ads have come to rely on soundbites, slogans, and short visual clips and to emphasize image and impact rather than idea and persuasion. Kathleen Hall Jamieson observes that: 'Like product ads, political spots are brief, usually either thirty or sixty seconds; they assert but do not argue; when they do offer evidence it often assumes the form of the example, although not necessarily the representative example; they both personalize and visualize abstract concepts; because they are brief assertions based in dramatic narrative and/or example and rely on what can be shown, they also favour the simple over the complex' (Jamieson 1992, 150).

Spending differences matter because the largest part of contemporary campaign speech seeks to affect the voter at a visceral level, treating him or her as a consumer of images rather than as a citizen who must make decisions about complex public issues. An appeal for voter support, which is 'undignified by any invitation to reflect,' gains its force through association and repetition (Jamieson 1992, 101). Concern about the form of campaign discourse may account for the intuitive appeal of silencing metaphors, such as 'drowning out,' which suggest behavioural impact and the displacement of reason or the absence of any real engagement.

However, election spending ceilings represent a limited response to the larger problem of the domination of political discourse by the advertising form. The court in *Libman* 1997 seemed to assume that limits would lead to, or at least support, 'informed choice.'[57] Yet inequality is a problem, and ceilings are necessary, precisely because campaign speech is not generally designed to inform. The imposition of expenditure ceilings by the legislature 'levels the playing field' but does not alter the substance of the game. Ceilings may make the competition between images 'fairer,' but they do not bring about a more informed democratic debate and greater exchange or dialogue.

The debate about ceilings has tended to focus on empirical questions, such as whether greater spending has an impact on voting or whether ceilings help incumbents. Yet we are concerned that voters might be predisposed to support the incumbent or might be swayed by the most advertised image because we recognize that self-government should be based on the rational and informed voting of citizens and not on the image and impulse that money sometimes can buy. Election spending ceilings do not directly address this deeper concern. While the underlying problem, or at least a significant part of the problem, may be the dominance of political discourse by the commercial model of expression, this problem is addressed narrowly as simply a matter of spending inequality.

There are obvious reasons for focusing on spending inequality rather than on expressive form (or form plus volume) as the problem. First, any legislative attempt to regulate the form of campaign expression would come too close to state regulation of the content of political debate. Because spending ceilings appear to rest on concerns unrelated to the content of political expression, they may represent a less troubling form of restriction on expression. Second, the dominance of public discourse by commercial advertising is so complete that it is increasingly difficult for us to see the form of campaign speech as a problem that needs to be addressed. As a consequence we tend to view the problem narrowly as an unfair or unbalanced electoral competition.

The commercial domination of public discourse has made it difficult for us to imagine campaign communication that seeks to convince citizens of the wisdom of a particular public policy rather than simply influence their voting behaviour.[58] Ceilings may be accompanied by different devices for encouraging a more open, balanced, and informative campaign debate. These include free-time political broadcasts and organized leaders' debates. Yet the dominance of the commercial model of expression may limit the potential of these devices. Indeed, it appears that free-time broadcasts and leaders' debates, for the most part, have become vehicles for soundbites rather than careful examination of substantive issues.

Ceilings, however, might have an indirect affect on the quality of campaign discourse. Perhaps if there were *significant* restrictions on campaign spending, the character of political discourse would have to change. If the overall volume of campaign speech was reduced, candidates and parties might use their available time and resources differently. Unable to affect voter behaviour using repetitive images or slogans, they might have no choice but to argue policy. Yet, because the commercial model is so dominant, it is difficult to imagine a form of campaign communication that does not rely on the techniques of advertising and does not address us as consumers of political images. As well, severe spending restrictions might simply result in commercial product advertising overwhelming election campaign discourse.

Nevertheless, ceilings may represent the only reasonable means of encouraging more substantive campaign expression and may prevent some of the worst excesses of campaign advertising. Even if we cannot ensure that campaigns run on information, argument, and engagement, it is important that we at least try to limit the impact of wealth on electoral success. While ceilings, as well as public reimbursement and free-time broadcasts, may not transform political debate in any fundamental way, they may at least ensure that the image-based messages of some candidates are not 'swamped,' to use a different metaphor, by the images and slogans of more wealthy candidates.

There is a larger issue lurking in the background here. In the debate about ceilings, campaign speech is assumed to be a special case, distinct from ordinary political discussion. During an election campaign, competing candidates and parties try to affect voter behaviour over a limited time period using a variety of persuasive techniques. More and more, though, we see politicians employing commercial advertising techniques in all their public communication. The distinction between campaign speech and ordinary political speech (by politicians at least) seems entirely unclear. If this is right and politicians are permanently campaigning, then inequality in communicative power should be a more general concern.

While the restriction of commercial advertising is based on the manipulative form of the message, election spending limits are based on the unequal volume of competing messages. Yet just as the impact of lifestyle advertising depends on the domination of public discourse by commercial messages, concern about inequality in election spending, the ability of some candidates or parties to 'drown out' their competitors, depends on the form of contemporary political discourse. The volume/inequality problem is a significant concern because contemporary campaign expression has increasingly come to resemble commercial advertising, with its use of 'soundbites' and short, image-based ads. Election spending ceilings are a different, but again partial, response to the same problem that lies behind the restriction of cigarette and other types of commercial advertising – the domination of public discourse by the advertising form.

5. A Note on Campaign Opinion Polls

In *Thomson* 1998, the Supreme Court of Canada struck down a federal ban on the publication of election campaign polls during the final days of the campaign. According to the federal government, the ban was necessary 'to prevent the potentially distorting affect of public opinion survey results that are released late in the election campaign leaving insufficient time to assess their validity' (*Thomson* 1998, 902).

Bastarache J., for the majority, dismissed this argument. He recognized that polls might contain information useful to voters. Late poll results, in particular, might be useful to those who want to vote strategically, that is, to vote for their second choice, if their first choice seems to have no chance of winning.[59] In any event, argued Bastarache J., it is up to voters to decide what information they want to take into account when deciding how to vote: 'If they feel that their votes are better informed as a result of having this information, then the ban not only interferes with their freedom of expression, but with their perception of the freeness and validity of their vote' (*Thomson* 1998, 972).

We should not, said Bastarache J., underestimate the capacity of voters to assess polls. Voters are exposed to opinion polls throughout the campaign and are likely to spot a single inaccurate poll result.[60] More generally, a commitment to democracy and to freedom of expression means that we must 'presume' that the Canadian voter 'is a rational actor who can learn from experience and make independent judgments about the value of particular sources of electoral information' (*Thomson* 1998, 956). Canadian voters must be 'presumed to have a certain degree of maturity and intelligence' (*Thomson* 1998, 949). We cannot assume that 'Canadians will become so mesmerized by the flurry of polls' in the media that they will forget about the real issues (*Thomson* 1998, 956).[61]

Mr Justice Gonthier dissented. In his view the ban permitted timely discussion and careful scrutiny of all published poll results and so contributed to 'the promotion of an informed vote over a misinformed vote' (*Thomson* 1998, 904). Yet this seems like a fairly weak argument, when put against Mr Justice Bastarache's assertion that our commitment to freedom of expression means that we must treat voters as having the capacity to assess all available information, including up-to-date opinion polls.

However, in the course of his reasons, Gonthier J. suggested a deeper problem – a problem not just with the publication of polls during the final days of the campaign but with the character of campaign reporting generally. He observed that election campaigns have taken 'on an aura of "horse races" and that discussion of issues that concern Canadians [has been] pre-empted' (*Thomson* 1998, 902). Campaign reporting by the media focuses (sometimes almost exclusively) on the strategies adopted by parties and candidates and on the effectiveness of those strategies. The publication of polls is a key part of this 'objective' reporting, in which the important question is who has run a good (mean-

ing effective) campaign rather than who has put forward the best policies for the community. Yet, if we accept the conventional view put
forward by Bastarache J. that voters must be trusted to evaluate the
information provided by the media, then banning certain kinds of reporting, such as the publication of polls, because it diverts attention
from the real issues, may be difficult to reconcile with a commitment to
freedom of expression.

6. Conclusion

Election spending ceilings are concerned with the problem of inequality in campaign discourse. Advertising restrictions are concerned with
the manipulative character of certain ads (in certain contexts). Yet
these two concerns are really two dimensions of a larger systemic problem of the domination of public discourse by the advertising form.
Inequality in campaign spending is a problem significantly because of
the form of so much contemporary political expression. Similarly, the
manipulative force of particular commercial ads rests in part on the
domination of public discourse by commercial messages and the advertising form.

It is understandable that courts have defined these problems narrowly. Freedom of expression rests on a faith in the rational judgment
of individuals and on an image of expression as balanced dialogue or
exchange. Expression can be limited only in exceptional circumstances,
when rational judgment is less likely to prevail because of a combination of the form of expression and the immediate circumstances in
which the expression occurs or when an individual's message is overwhelmed by the sheer volume of competing messages. However, if the
problem is systemic, affecting the rationality and fairness of public discourse generally, the claim to constitutional protection of any instance
of (commercial) expression becomes less powerful. While the courts
address manipulative advertising and unequal election spending as discrete and limited problems, just beneath the surface of these decisions
is a challenge to the assumptions that underlie our commitment to
freedom of expression.

Chapter Four

The Regulation of Pornography

1. Introduction: From Obscenity to Pornography

The public justification for the censorship of sexually explicit representations no longer emphasizes the offensive or immoral character of
such material. Censorship is now justified on the grounds that sexually
explicit representations sometimes have harmful consequences. With
this change in justification has come a shift in the focus of restriction from sexually explicit material in general to sexually explicit
material that depicts violent or degrading activity and a change in the
language used to describe the restricted material from obscenity to
pornography.[1]

The shift from obscenity to pornography is the consequence first of
the rise of the harm principle: the idea that the prevention of harm is
the only legitimate basis for state coercion. This shift has been acceler-
ated by the confrontation of censorship laws with the constitutional
right to freedom of expression and the requirement that any restriction
on expression be 'demonstrably justified.' Second, the shift from obscenity to pornography is the consequence of a growing awareness of
the problems of sexual subordination and violence and a widely held
belief that certain kinds of sexual representation contribute to these
wrongs.

In *Butler* 1992 the Supreme Court of Canada reinterpreted the Criminal Code obscenity prohibition as a ban on *harmful* sexual representation. However, this reinterpretation produced a test for identifying harmful sexual representations that is ambiguous and capable of supporting
the restriction of a wide range of sexual material. The space for a broad

reading/application of the restriction is the consequence of two things. First, it is the consequence of the court's attempt to give a feminist reading to the conservative language and structure of the existing Code restriction. Second, it is the consequence of the court's effort to fit a feminist approach to pornography regulation into the existing framework of freedom of expression adjudication, which is built on liberal or individualist conceptions of language, agency, and harm.

The court in *Butler* 1992 was prepared to uphold the Code restriction on obscene publications on the ground that the restricted material causes harm. Yet the court said very little about how this material causes harm. Significantly, the court did not respond to the conventional argument that expression should not be restricted simply because it might persuade others to think or act in a particular way, even in a harmful way. The court's reluctance to probe into the nature of pornography's harm is understandable. In the feminist critique, pornography causes harm not by persuading its audience to think or act in a particular way but rather by shaping non-cognitively the way the male audience views women. It does not 'cause' discrete acts of violence or discrimination against women; instead, it contributes to a social understanding of gender and sexuality that shapes individual thought and informs individual action. Not only does this understanding of the harm seem difficult to grasp within the conventional freedom of expression analysis, but it also raises hard questions about the scope of the prohibition. Once we accept that the harm of pornography is systemic in character, the category of material that may contribute to that harm becomes very broad and difficult to isolate from ordinary public discourse.

2. A Feminist Reading of a Conservative Provision: The Reinterpretation of Section 163

Before considering the constitutionality of section 163 of the Criminal Code, Sopinka J., writing for the majority of the court,[2] reviewed 'the legislative history of the provision as well as the extensive judicial interpretation and analysis which have infused the bare words of the statute' (*Butler* 1992, 471). In his review of the provision, Sopinka J. continued the judicial reinterpretation of section 163 from a conventional restriction of obscene material that offends the community's sense of decency to a restriction of pornographic material that is degrading and harmful to women.[3]

Under section 163(8) material is obscene if its dominant characteristic is the undue exploitation of sex or the combination of sex with violence, cruelty, crime, or horror. The courts look to 'community standards' when determining if the exploitation of sex is 'undue.' The community standards test was introduced by the Supreme Court of Canada shortly after the enactment of section 163 (*Brodie* 1962) and given its contemporary shape in *Towne Cinema* 1985. In that case Chief Justice Dickson said that 'the task is to determine in an objective way what is tolerable in accordance with the contemporary standards of the Canadian community, and not merely to project one's own personal ideas of what is tolerable' (*Towne Cinema* 1985, 13). The test, he emphasized, is one of tolerance rather than taste. It is concerned not with what Canadians would tolerate being exposed to themselves, but what they would tolerate other Canadians being exposed to. The standard is that of the community as a whole.[4] The judge may hear evidence concerning community standards, usually testimony by an expert witness, but he or she may also draw on his or her own knowledge of those standards.[5]

In *Towne Cinema* 1985 Chief Justice Dickson stressed that 'community standards' is only one of the tests the courts use to determine whether the exploitation of sex is undue. According to Dickson C.J. the courts also consider material to be obscene if it is degrading or dehumanizing in its representation of women, even though the community might be prepared to tolerate this material:[6] 'Even if, at certain times, there is a coincidence between what is not tolerated and what is harmful to society, there is no necessary connection between these two concepts. Thus, a legal definition of "undue" must also encompass publications harmful to members of society and, therefore to society as a whole (*Towne Cinema* 1985, 11, quoted in *Butler* 1992, 467).

However, in *Butler* 1992 Sopinka J. merged the harm test and the community standards test. He considered that the purpose of the obscenity provision is to prevent harm and not simply to vindicate conventional morality. He recognized, however, that there is dispute about the kinds of material that cause harm. In his view the judgment that certain material is harmful should be made by the community. In all cases, said Mr Justice Sopinka, the arbiter for determining what amounts to the undue exploitation of sex – what creates an unacceptable risk of harm to society – should be the community as a whole.[7] If the decision that material is harmful and subject to restriction does not depend on community standards then it will depend on 'the individual tastes of judges' (*Butler* 1992, 484). For Sopinka J. the community standards test provides a way to avoid judicial subjectivity in the application of the prohibition against harmful sexual material.

The task for the courts is to determine 'as best they can what the community would tolerate others being exposed to on the basis of the degree of harm that may flow from such exposure' (*Butler* 1992, 485).[8] 'The stronger the inference of a risk of harm the lesser the likelihood of tolerance' (*Butler* 1992, 485). Something is harmful if 'it predisposes persons to act in an antisocial manner as, for example, the physical or mental mistreatment of women by men ...' (*Butler* 1992, 485). Antisocial conduct 'is conduct which society formally recognizes as incompatible with its proper functioning' (*Butler* 1992, 485).

Applying the community standards test, Sopinka J. decided that the community will not tolerate 'explicit sex with violence.' 'Explicit sex without violence but which subjects people to treatment that is degrading or dehumanizing' 'may' not be tolerated 'if the risk of harm is substantial' (*Butler* 1992, 485).[9] Sopinka J. emphasized that degrading or dehumanizing material fails the community standards test 'not because it offends against morals but because it is perceived by public opinion to be harmful to society, particularly to women' (*Butler* 1992, 479).[10] It is insulting and hurtful to women and it predisposes male consumers to act in a violent or discriminatory way against women. According to Sopinka J. the community standards test does not prohibit a third category of material, 'explicit sex without violence that is neither degrading nor dehumanizing' (*Butler* 1992, 485).[11]

Finally, Sopinka J. observed that the judgment as to whether a particular representation involves the undue exploitation of sex must take account of the larger work within which the representation is located. The court must ask whether 'the undue exploitation of sex is the main object of the work' or whether the portrayal of sex is 'essential to a wider artistic, literary or other similar purpose' (*Butler* 1992, 486). Once again this issue – the dominant theme of the work as a whole – is to be decided on the basis of community standards.

A Conservative Restriction

Mr Justice Sopinka's harm-based rhetoric, which emphasizes the harm of pornographic material to women, fits oddly with the conservative language and structure of section 163. Indeed, the central difficulty for

Sopinka J. in his interpretation of section 163 is to articulate a clear and legitimate purpose for the provision that will withstand Charter review but at the same time not run afoul of the rule against 'shifting purposes.' In *Big M* 1985 the Supreme Court of Canada had stated that '[p]urpose is a function of those who drafted and enacted the legislation at the time' and that a court should not redefine the purpose of the legislation to save it from the charge of unconstitutionality under the Charter (*Big M* 1985, 335).[12] The respondents in *Butler* 1992 argued that a feminist/harm-based reinterpretation of section 163 involved exactly this sort of impermissible shift in purpose.

Sopinka J. answered this argument in two ways. First, he observed that the purpose of the legislation at the time of its enactment in 1959 was the prevention of harm and that this purpose was broad enough to encompass the concerns of 1959 and 1992.[13] Even though the community's awareness and understanding of the harms of pornography have developed since 1959, contemporary concerns about harm to women are continuous with the community's fear in 1959 of the harm of moral corruption. Sopinka J. contrasted this focus on harm prevention with the conservative moralism that characterized the *pre*-1959 obscenity laws. (The view that any deviation from the community's 'particular conception of morality' is 'inherently undesirable, independently of any harm to society' (*Butler* 1992, 492)).[14] Second, Sopinka J. thought that the community standards test gives the provision a general inbuilt flexibility: 'A permissible shift in emphasis was built into the legislation when, as interpreted by the courts, it adopted the community standards test. Community standards as to what is harmful have changed since 1959' (*Butler* 1992, 496).

For Sopinka J. the combination of the harm test and the community standards test gives section 163 both stability and flexibility. The basic purpose of the law has not changed but the law is adaptable to changing circumstances and concerns. But how much stability does this combined test offer? Even if it is accepted that the purpose of the obscenity provision is the prevention of harm (and it is only recently that the courts have explicitly identified this as the purpose), harm is a broad and value-based concept. An activity is harmful if it interferes with, or causes damage to, an important human interest. The purpose of 'harm prevention' is common to the different applications of the obscenity provision because the term 'harm' does not have specific content. 'Harm' is a vessel into which the courts can pour almost anything they choose (Moon 1993, 368).[15]

Sopinka J. recognized that the identification of harmful material is a controversial issue and relied on community standards to fix the content of the ban in a way that did not require *judicial* value choice.[16] (I note that sometimes Sopinka J. seemed to say that the community standards test determines what kind of material causes harm, while other times he seemed to say that the test determines what kind of harm is caused by sexually explicit material.) The community standards test is meant to fill the space at the centre of this law. It is not at all clear, however, that this test can do the work required of it.

The community standards test has been criticized on a number of grounds. These criticisms are of two types. The first questions whether community standards are an appropriate basis for determining whether conduct should be criminalized. Even though the court has said that the purpose of the provision is to prevent harm, community standards are used to determine what is harmful – what causes harm and more fundamentally what counts as harm. Reliance on the community standards test means that an individual will be prevented from publishing material simply because most members of the community think the material is harmful and should be banned. In this way the obscenity provision is different from other Criminal Code provisions, in which Parliament defines more specifically a category of activity that is harmful to a particular human interest. The community standards test seems to collapse the reasons for banning the material (it is harmful) with the reasons for instituting a ban in a democratic political community (the community wants it banned).

Despite the court's attempt to portray the community standards test as neutral in its concern about harm to society, the test has a conservative bias. It has been suggested that the test is 'liberal' relative to its predecessor, the *Hicklin* test,[17] because it draws on the more liberal attitudes of contemporary society about sexual representation.[18] However, the use of community standards seems to rest on a belief that the law should defend the integrity of the community's conventional morality – the community's conception of what is harmful – whatever that may encompass. It appears that the provision is concerned as much with the protection of the moral bonds of society as with the prevention of harm.

A more specific problem with grounding feminist arguments for the restriction of pornography on community standards is that the law's commitment to this understanding of the wrong of pornography is contingent. The law does not seek to prevent harm to women. It seeks to prohibit material that the community considers harmful and is not prepared to tolerate. It may be that at the moment the community is not prepared to tolerate 'degrading' or 'dehumanizing' representations because it thinks that these are harmful to women. Yet, at least in theory, that could change.

The confusing merger of the harm test and the community standards test represents an attempt by the Supreme Court to transform section 163 without violating the shifting purpose rule. But more fundamentally this merger reflects the court's subjectivist understanding of moral judgment (Moon 1993, 369).[19] The court recognized that value-based content must be given to the concept of harm. However, it could see only two possible sources for this content – conventional morality and judicial subjectivity. In the court's view judicial judgment that is not grounded on community standards is simply judicial preference and illegitimate. The court seeks objectivity and legitimacy in the values of the general community.[20]

The second sort of criticism made of the community standards test raises doubts about whether the test can fix the content of the ban on harmful sexual material. There is no shared view in the community about the harm of sexually explicit material and even if there were the courts are ill-equipped to discover what it is. Sopinka J. recognized as much when he observed that there are different views in the community about the sort of material that is harmful or 'degrading and dehumanizing.'[21] A court is not required to hear evidence about community standards. But even if the court does hear evidence, that evidence is bound to be either general and vague or partial and not clearly tied to community values. As many judges have realized, the test is really about what they are prepared to tolerate. The test, then, does not avoid what the Supreme Court wants so badly to avoid – judicial judgment (understood as the expression of judicial preference or taste) about what material should be caught by the prohibition. Judicial subjectivity (value judgment) is simply dressed up in the objective garb of community standards.

This collapse of the objective community standards test may not matter, if we reject the assumption that judicial value judgments are subjective and therefore illegitimate. Yet, even if we take a different view about the legitimacy (and inevitability) of judicial value choice, the choices that judges must make under section 163 seem wide open. (Indeed, the point of the community standards test is to give content to the provision and save it from the criticism that it does not provide sufficient guidance.) More importantly, even if we accept the legitimacy of judicial value choices, the courts have not been prepared to make these choices openly and explicitly. The courts' failure to take responsibility for the law's content – hiding behind the community standards test – leaves the obscenity ban vague and manipulable.

Since community standards do not tie down the content of the ban, the real concern with Mr Justice Sopinka's interpretation of the prohibition is not that its feminist commitment is contingent but instead that the general language used to describe the prohibition's purpose and the material it restricts is open to both feminist and conservative applications by the police, the prosecution, and the judiciary (Moon 1993, 370; Cossman 1997, 108). In seeking to avoid the charge of shifting purpose, Sopinka J. defined the purpose and scope of the prohibition using very general or abstract terms: harm, moral corruption, degradation, and dehumanization. These terms are broad enough to accommodate both conservative and feminist understandings of the wrong of obscenity/pornography. Indeed, they are so vague and so broad that they do not have sufficient content to answer the shifting purpose charge.

Sopinka J. did not recognize that his account of the prohibition is open to a conservative as well as a feminist reading (and lacks substantial content) because he understood only a caricatured version of the conservative argument for the restriction of obscene material. He thought that the current law's focus on the prevention of harm represented a break with the previous conservative restrictions on sexually explicit representations. According to Sopinka J.:

> The obscenity legislation and jurisprudence prior to the enactment of s.163 were evidently concerned with prohibiting the 'immoral influences' of obscene publications and safeguarding the morals of individuals into whose hands such works could fall. The *Hicklin* philosophy posits that explicit sexual depictions, particularly outside the sanctioned contexts of marriage and procreation, threatened the morals or the fabric of society ... In this sense, its dominant, if not exclusive purpose was to advance a particular conception of morality. Any deviation from such morality was considered to be inherently undesirable, independently of any harm to society. (*Butler* 1992, 492)

The conservative position, according to Sopinka J., is that sexually explicit material should be prohibited because it is offensive and because it undermines the moral bonds of the community. It is concerned with the 'prevention of "dirt for dirt's sake"' (*Butler* 1992, 492), with 'moral disapprobation' (*Butler* 1992, 493), and 'with maintaining conventional standards of propriety' rather than with the prevention of harm (*Butler* 1992, 498). It involves the imposition of 'a certain standard of public and sexual morality, solely because it reflects the conventions of a given community' (*Butler* 1992, 492).

Sopinka J. thought that the prevention of harm is distinct from the protection of conventional morality and represents a non-conservative foundation for the restriction of certain kinds of sexually explicit material. This was his view even though he relied on community standards to determine what is harmful. For Sopinka J., section 163 prohibits harmful material and the community standards test is simply the means used by the court to identify the harmful material caught by the prohibition. This, he assumed, is different from enforcing community standards for their own sake.

However, concern about public offence and the erosion of the community's moral standards is not the only way, nor even the most helpful way, to describe the conservative position, which has more substance than Sopinka J. was prepared to acknowledge. It rests on a moral view about the roles of men and women, the importance of the nuclear family, and the nature of sexuality and sexual relations. The conservative position reflects a very different moral outlook from that which underlies the feminist position but it involves more than a simple desire to protect the moral sensibilities of ordinary members of the community (Moon 1993, 371). As Sopinka J. recognized when he linked 'harm' and 'moral corruption,' the language of harm can be used to describe the injury that sexually explicit materials may cause to these conservative 'family values.'[22] More specifically, the language of dehumanization or degradation can be used to describe the devaluation of sexual intimacy, the destabilization of monogamous relationships, or the undermining of traditional gender roles. Certainly Mr Justice Sopinka's description of harm as the predisposition to 'act in an anti-social manner' offers plenty of space for a conservative reading of the provision (*Butler* 1992, 485). Mr Justice Sopinka's example of antisocial conduct was 'the physical or mental mistreatment of women by men' but his definition of the phrase was much broader: 'Antisocial conduct for this purpose is conduct which society recognizes as incompatible with its proper functioning' (*Butler* 1992, 485).

3. Fitting Feminist Arguments into the Established Structure of Freedom of Expression

The other opening for a conservative reading of the *Butler* 1992 decision stems from the court's attempt to fit feminist arguments about the nature and harm of pornography into the existing structure of freedom of expression adjudication. Only by suppressing the issue of causation (how pornography causes harm) was the court able to avoid the tension between its feminist arguments for the restriction of pornography and the assumptions about language, agency, and harm that underlie the existing structure of freedom of expression (Moon 1993, 372). Therefore, added to the uncertainty about the nature of the harm caused by obscenity, which is reflected in the general language of degradation and dehumanization, is an uncertainty about the way obscenity/pornography causes harm and the kind of material that should be restricted because it causes harm.

Sopinka J. followed the pattern of previous Supreme Court judgments by giving little time to the question of whether the obscene material caught by the Code prohibition is expression protected under section 2(b). '[T]here is no doubt,' says Sopinka J., 'that s.163 seeks to prohibit certain types of expressive activity and thereby infringes s.2(b) of the Charter' (*Butler* 1992, 489). He accepted that expression could not be excluded from the freedom's scope on the basis of the content or meaning being conveyed. However, later in his judgment, when he considered proportionality under section 1, Sopinka J. recognized that the restricted expression does not 'directly engage the core of freedom of expression values' and so deserves less weight in the final balance (*Butler* 1992, 500). He also suggested that restriction of 'the targeted material' is more easily justified because it 'is motivated by economic profit' (*Butler* 1992, 501).

Having decided that section 163 restricts expression protected by section 2(b), because it carries a message, Sopinka J. went on to consider whether this restriction is justified under section 1.[23] According to Sopinka J., the substantial and compelling purpose advanced by section 163 is the prevention of harm – and more specifically the prevention of harm to women. Pornographic materials 'place women ... in positions of subordination, servile submission or humiliation' (*Butler* 1992, 479). They portray women 'as objects for sexual exploitation and abuse and have a negative impact on "the individual's sense of self-worth and acceptance"' (*Butler* 1992, 494). Pornography also creates a risk of harm to women because it affects the attitudes of male consumers towards women and sexuality and may lead these consumers to commit acts of violence and discrimination against women. In this way pornography runs against 'the principles of equality and dignity for all persons' (*Butler* 1992, 479).

When Sopinka J. considered the rational connection between the expression restricted by section 163 and the section's substantial and compelling purpose, he contented himself with vague statements about the link between pornography and harm – referring at the same time to the harmful effect that pornography has on its consumers and the harmful acts these consumers commit against women. Sopinka J. observed that pornography 'predisposes' consumers to commit antisocial acts, and in particular acts of violence against women. Exposure to material that degrades the human dimensions of life 'contributes' to the moral desensitization of the male audience, making it more likely that they will act in a violent way (*Butler* 1992, 503). However, he said very little about how this 'predisposition' occurs and how it translates into harmful actions.

In his assessment of the rational connection between the restriction of pornography and the prevention of harm, Sopinka J. considered the empirical evidence concerning the connection between exposure to pornographic imagery and acts of violence against women. Yet, as he admitted, this evidence is far from conclusive: 'the literature of the social sciences remains subject to controversy' (*Butler* 1992, 501). To the doubts raised about this evidence Sopinka J. had two answers.

First, he thought it self-evident that exposure to this sort of material must have an effect on men's attitudes to women, contributing to a predisposition to do violence to women. Sopinka J. was prepared to rely on common sense: 'While a direct link between obscenity and harm to society may be difficult, if not impossible to establish, it is reasonable to presume that exposure to images bears a causal relationship to changes in attitudes and beliefs (*Butler* 1992, 502).[24] According to Sopinka J., this link is recognized by the general community: '[a] substantial body of opinion ... holds that the portrayal of persons being subjected to degrading or dehumanizing sexual treatment results in harm' (*Butler* 1992, 479). However, he did not explain why this self-evident link is not so evident in empirical studies.

Second, Sopinka J. declared that as long as Parliament has a reasonable basis for believing that pornography causes violence against women, the courts should defer to Parliament's judgment. In taking this deferential approach, Sopinka J. followed the earlier decision of *Irwin Toy* 1989, in which the Supreme Court deferred to the judgment of the Quebec legislature that certain kinds of advertising have a manipulative influence on children. The court in *Irwin Toy* 1989 'afforded' the government 'a margin of appreciation to form legitimate objectives based on somewhat inconclusive social science evidence' (*Irwin Toy* 1989, 927; *Butler* 1992, 503). In *Butler* 1992, Sopinka J. thought that 'Parliament was entitled to have a "reasoned apprehension of harm" resulting from the desensitization of individuals exposed to materials which depict violence, cruelty, and dehumanization in sexual relations' (*Butler* 1992, 504).

However, the difficulty with the court's deferential approach is that it is not at all clear what sort of causal judgment Parliament made when it enacted section 163.[25] Even if we accept the court's view that section 163 was intended to prohibit harmful sexual representation, the provision does not fix on a particular conception of harm and does not define a class of material that is thought to be harmful. While the statutory test created by Parliament refers to sex combined with violence, cruelty, and horror, it does not refer specifically to degrading or dehumanizing representations of women. Instead, the provision prohibits representations that unduly exploit sex. In his elaboration of section 163, Sopinka J. held that sexually explicit material is undue if it is harmful, or at least if it creates a risk of harm, and that a decision about what material creates a risk of harm should rest not on the judge's own preferences or feelings but rather on community standards, the perception of the general public. But if community standards determine the link between degrading and dehumanizing material and the unacceptable risk of harm to women, Parliament it seems has not made a causal judgment to which the court can defer. Any deference is to the courts' own application of the community standards test, which determines not only what material causes harm but more importantly what counts as harm. In any event, as discussed in Chapter 2, the court's deferential approach seems inconsistent with the idea that a restriction on freedom of expression can be justified only if a clear and convincing case is made under section 1, that is, only if the restricted material clearly and directly causes harm to important individual or societal interests.

However, the reason for the court's reliance on empirical evidence, common sense, and deference to Parliament is obvious. Sopinka J.

wanted to uphold the obscenity restriction but was unprepared to face the conventional argument that the answer to bad speech is not censorship but instead more and better speech. Ronald Dworkin, for example, opposes the legal restriction of pornography because he sees this restriction as an attempt to silence the expression of a particular viewpoint (Dworkin 1996, 219).[26] (Recall that in its section 2(b) analysis the court considered this material to be expression that was restricted on the basis of its content.) The negative impact of pornography is a matter of audience response – how the audience understands and reacts to the message of the material.[27] For Dworkin any attempt to censor material simply because the larger community does not agree with the view of women it expresses runs contrary to the very idea of freedom of expression. As Alan Borovoy of the Canadian Civil Liberties Union points out: 'If we could suppress material merely because of its detrimental impact on male attitudes towards women, what about other potentially harmful attitudes? Could we suppress Communist propaganda for undermining our attitudes about the value of preserving democracy? Could we suppress certain feminist material because it might arguably create negative attitudes about the institution of marriage' (Borovoy 1988, 63). Individuals must be permitted to assess different points of view. If there is a risk that they may be persuaded by a view that we find objectionable then we should respond to that view and offer what we consider to be the better, and potentially more persuasive, view. Because pornography is 'subjectively' mediated, empirical evidence about its harmful consequences is likely to be indeterminate; more importantly, it is simply irrelevant.

Instead of confronting the argument of civil libertarian opponents of regulation like Dworkin and Borovoy, Sopinka J. offered a behavioural account of the harm of pornography that drops from the analysis the whole question of human reason and judgment. He did not question conventional understandings of harm and expression and so he could avoid civil libertarian conclusions only by suppressing the issue of how the restricted material causes harm to women. A response to the argument that it is illegitimate to censor the viewpoint of the pornographer must move past the basic assumption that the meaning of an individual's act of expression is simply a matter of his prelinguistic ideas and feelings and is always transparent to his audience and the assumption that something causes harm only if it directly interferes with a clearly defined individual interest, such as life, physical integrity, or property.

4. Rethinking the Harm of Pornography

There are a variety of feminist arguments for the restriction of pornography, but, either implicitly or explicitly, all of them seem to reject the understanding of expression, agency, and harm that underlies conventional freedom of expression doctrine. Even when feminist writing seeks to justify the restriction of pornography within the conventional discourse about freedom of expression, it appears to rely on non-conventional assumptions about expression and agency.

Some writers have argued that pornography should be restricted because it undermines the equality rights of women. Kathleen Mahoney, for example, argues that 'Pornographic expression which causes harm to the social status and concrete interests of women negates and limits their equality rights, which ss.15 and 28 affirm as fundamental values of Canadian society' (Mahoney 1991, 167). Freedom of expression should be restricted because it causes harm to the equality rights of women, which have great weight given their important position in the Charter of Rights. Yet in this abstract form the argument does not confront conventional assumptions about communication and agency. It offers no response to the argument that the realization of equality is dependent on freedom of expression – that real equality in the community can only emerge out of free and open debate, including debate about equality rights. The claim that pornographic expression interferes with the right to equality and so may be restricted is incomplete without some recognition of the social and economic constraints on individual autonomy, the non-cognitive character of the pornographic 'message' and the systemic character of the harm of pornography.

Another argument in support of pornography censorship is that the pornographer's expression about women and sexuality should be restricted because it undermines the ability of women to express themselves. Pornography silences women because it undermines their credibility as speakers in the community. Censorship of pornography, then, is justified because it protects or promotes freedom of expression overall. Instead of directly questioning liberal understandings of harm and expression, this approach trades on the general language of silencing and censorship. It joins without argument the 'silencing' that occurs because a speaker is not taken seriously in debate with the silencing of a speaker through 'physical' interference. But these two forms of silencing are very different in character, as opponents of censorship are keen to point out (Dworkin 1996, 232). The silencing argument draws on deeper concerns about the conditions of discourse. It challenges conventional assumptions about the opportunity to communicate and the rationality of expression. In the absence of an explicit consideration of these issues, it will be difficult to decide when expression that questions the credibility of another person should be regarded as a legitimate part of public debate and when it should be suppressed because it undermines that other's freedom/power to communicate.

In two important and related ways feminist arguments in support of pornography regulation involve a rethinking of conventional assumptions about the cause of harm. First, under these arguments, pornography causes harm not by persuading an audience to think or act in a particular way but rather by shaping or constructing non-cognitively the way the male audience views women and experiences sexual desire. Second, the harm of pornography is not simply that it leads to discrete acts of violence or discrimination against women but that it creates or contributes to an understanding of gender and sex as a relationship of sexual domination/subordination that informs individual action.

However, once we understand pornographic harm in this way, it becomes difficult to isolate a clear and discrete category of material for legal restriction. The first difficulty is that there is no clear and simple distinction between sexual expression that encourages reflection and awareness and sexual imagery that affects the viewer at a physical or non-cognitive level. Indeed, if there were such a clear division between rational and non-rational or mental and physical then the courts could simply exclude 'pornographic' material from the scope of freedom of expression on the basis that it has no value as expression. A second difficulty is that a particular sexual image can affect the viewer, or different viewers, in different ways, depending on the circumstances in which the image is viewed. Feminist antipornography arguments are directed principally against mass-produced sexually explicit material that portrays either violence or degradation and is used by consumers as an aid to masturbation. Yet the characteristics or viewing circumstances that make sexual imagery harmful (or pornographic) may be difficult to capture in a legal regulation. The final difficulty in isolating a discrete category of sexual imagery for restriction is that the harm of pornography is systemic. No single image causes the viewer to think or act in a particular way. Instead, sexual imagery throughout the culture contributes, in varying degrees, to the naturalization of sexual domination/subordination.

Pornography is a concern not because of its sexually explicit content but because of the ways in which it organizes images of women – the ways in which women are presented as available and submissive. Ronald

Dworkin and other opponents of regulation assume that the message of pornography is transparent to the viewer and available for reflection and judgment. However, pornography causes harm not because it carries a message that persuades consumers but rather because it presents women and sexuality in a way that does not ask for reflection and judgment. The consumers are not meant to see the image as a meaningful or significant act that should be viewed carefully in order to gain understanding. Pornographic 'expression' does not give reflective form to emotion or idea. Rather, it is a representation of a woman meant for the sexual stimulation of the consumer. This is why some supporters of regulation argue that pornography should be viewed not as speech or expression but rather as a sexual act or an act of sexual oppression.

Pornographic images appear natural. They purport to represent a real event, because photographs 'simply show reality as it is,'[28] and to express a natural impulse because they 'tap a natural response' (Smart 1989, 125). Yet beneath the apparent reality of these images are the highly conventionalized codes or devices by which pornography creates sexual arousal and helps to build in the consumer's mind an association between sexual pleasure and domination. The connection between pleasure and domination is implicit rather than explicit. In the words of Rosalind Coward, the meaning of pornographic photographs arises 'from how various elements are combined, how the picture is framed, what lighting is given, what is connoted by dress and expression, the way these elements are articulated together' (Coward 1982, 11).[29] For example, in most pornographic photos the female model gives 'the look' to the male consumer who is being addressed by the material, her eyes looking up, her mouth open and her lips wet, suggesting submission and desire.

In the image there is no claim, no argument, and so nothing to be accepted or rejected. It is just a picture of a woman meant to sexually arouse the consumer, a natural process. Yet exposure to this material, which is presented and viewed for sexual pleasure, as a sex aid, may help to shape the consumer's 'natural' sexual response. In the words of Frank Michelman, pornography 'operates to affect people's minds at the level of ideological preconception rather than that of critically examinable argumentation'; '[I]t exploits the especially powerful mind-bending potential of sexual stimulus' (Michelman 1989, 299).

Some feminist supporters of restriction, including Helen Longino, argue that pornography should be restricted because its message is hurtful and defamatory. Longino believes that pornography has an explicit message: 'Pornography *lies* when it says that our sexual life is or ought to be subordinate to the service of men, that our pleasure consists in pleasing men and not ourselves, that we are depraved, that we are fit subjects for rape, bondage, torture and murder. Pornography lies explicitly about women's sexuality, and through such lies fosters more lies about our humanity, our dignity, and our personhood' (Longino 1980, 267). The attempt to justify the restriction of pornography by identifying a clear message that is wrong and hurtful plays into the conventional freedom of expression argument that all issues should be open to public debate, that it is wrong to foreclose consideration of a particular social or political argument, and that the answer to bad speech is more and better speech. In this way the position of Longino gives too much ground. For as Catharine Mackinnon points out: 'The fact that pornography, in a feminist view, furthers the idea of the sexual inferiority of women, a political idea, does not make the pornography itself a political idea. That one can express the idea a practice embodies does not make that practice into an idea' (Mackinnon 1987, 154).

This understanding of pornography as something other than expression, as something that affects the viewer without persuading him or her, is based on its form or design but also on its standard use as a sex aid and most importantly on its pervasiveness. Violent sexual attitudes and behaviours are not simply 'caused' by exposure to violent or degrading sexual imagery. The impact of pornography, its shaping of sexual desire, occurs only because the consumer incorporates the image's 'meaning' into his understanding of sex and gender. The meaning or impact of a sexual image is not fixed; rather, it depends on the viewer's values and concerns, on his experiences, and on the circumstances in which he views the image. As Alan Hutchinson observes: 'The same pornographic material will have different effects at different times, in different places and for different people' (Hutchinson 1995b, 128).[30] Significantly, sexual images may sometimes be viewed in ways that give insight into sexuality or dominant patterns of sexual relations or that support alternative visions of sexuality.

While the maker of pornographic imagery cannot control how his or her images are used or determine how they are viewed, the intended and ordinary use of this imagery is as a means of sexual stimulation, an aid to masturbation. This use, in which representations of sexual subordination/domination feed very directly into the emotional and physical experience of sexual arousal, is critical to the fusion of sex and subordination in the consumer's mind. Particular images of sexual violence or degradation are viewed against a larger background of mass-marketed pornography. The power and the invisibility of the pornographic 'message' is greater because the image is repeated so frequently – and it is repeated so frequently because pornography is big business. The volume of pornographic images portraying sex in terms of domination/ subordination or violence makes this portrayal seem normal or natural and reduces the possibility of critical distancing and the likelihood of alternative readings by the consumer.[31]

This understanding of the way pornography affects the consumer points to a very different understanding of its harm. Of central importance in the contemporary censorship debate has been the question of whether there is a discernable link between the consumption of pornography and the commission of acts of violence or discrimination against women. The focus on this question reflects the conventional understanding of harm as an interference with a tangible individual interest, an invasion of the individual's personal sphere. However, the harm of pornography is more encompassing than this.[32]

Pornography causes harm not because a particular story or image leads to a particular violent act against a woman. As Catharine Mackinnon recognizes, the harm 'is not linearly caused in the "John hit Mary" sense' (Mackinnon 1987, 156). The harm of pornography lies in its negative impact on the consumer's/viewer's understanding or perception of gender and sexuality.[33] This understanding, of course, affects the actions of individuals – actions that are sometimes violent: 'Pornography does not just drop out of the sky, go into his head, and stop there. Specifically, men rape, batter, prostitute, molest, and sexually harass women. Under conditions of inequality, they also hire, fire, promote and grade women ...' (Mackinnon 1987, 156).

Yet perhaps Robyn Eckersley is right in saying that 'The important "effects" are not ... the direct ones of violence of the kind focussed on by the anti-pornography campaigns, but rather the way in which everyday viewing is organized' (Eckersley 1987, 164). At the root of men's violent and discriminatory actions is the way men see women (Kappeler 1986, 61).

These actions are not the consequence of exposure to particular images. A particular pornographic representation has an impact only as part of a larger system of pornography or a larger culture of sexual subordination. There are copycat incidents where a man acts out the violence portrayed in a particular pornographic picture, film, or story.[34] But even this sort of imitation depends on the larger context of representation. The particular pornographic piece only gives form or direction to attitudes that are generated in the larger context of pornographic imagery.[35]

Once again the enormous volume of pornographic material contributes to the normalization of sexual subordination. Pornographic images are seen as 'causing' harm because they are so pervasive. Not only are most of these images presented and consumed in a manner that does not encourage reflection or exploration, but, as well, public discourse offers very few alternative visions or images of sexuality that might address or counterbalance the dominant imagery of sexual subordination.

5. The Ambiguity of Cause and Harm

The Supreme Court in *Butler* 1992 looks for direct links between pornography and violence but settles for a common sense recognition that a pornographic work creates a risk of violence. The evidence of a link between pornography and sexual violence is uncertain, first because pornography 'acts' through its human consumers and second because no one piece of pornography 'causes' a particular act of violence.[36]

The court's reluctance to rethink the assumptions of the existing model of freedom of expression and its avoidance of any serious consideration of the way that pornography causes harm to women and to the community results in considerable uncertainty about the scope of the obscenity provision. According to Sopinka J., section 163 restricts material that causes physical and other harm or, at least, creates a risk of such harm. However, it is unclear how harm is caused and so it is difficult to say what material is caught by the prohibition. Not only is there space for a conservative interpretation of the harm that section 163 is intended to prevent but there is also considerable space for conservative concerns to influence a court's judgment about what material causes harm. Indeed, subsequent lower court decisions reveal just how wide open the *Butler* 1992 test is. Most notably, the seizure of gay and lesbian sexual imagery has been upheld on the grounds that it is 'dehumanizing and degrading' or that it supports 'anti-social conduct' (*Glad Day* 1992). As well, the recent *Little Sisters* 1998 case, which is concerned with the targeting of gay and lesbian material by customs officials, is at root about the vagueness of the test for identifying obscenity.[37]

Yet even if the courts were clearer about the harm of pornography and its cause, the possibility of a prohibition with clear parameters seems remote. The law's failure to distinguish clearly between restricted and unrestricted sexual imagery cannot be attributed simply to the inability of lawmakers to agree on what pornography is and why it ought to be restricted. The scope of any pornography prohibition is bound to be unclear because there is no clear dividing line between material that contributes to the public examination or exploration of sexual matters and material that affects the viewer at a physical or non-cognitive level (and contributes to the naturalization of sexual subordination) and because the harm at issue is the consequence of the system of pornographic imagery and not of a single image.

A wide range of images contribute to the view of women as subordinate. Images throughout the culture shape but do not determine attitudes about gender and sexuality. If the problem is systemic, there is no simple way to isolate pornographic material from the larger culture.[38] Images of women in television advertising, film, and fashion magazines often have the same structure as sexually explicit pornography and contribute to the social picture of women as subordinate (Coward 1982, 13). If the impact of representations of sexual violence or degradation does not depend on the nudity of the persons represented, then there is no reason why the restriction should focus on sexually explicit material. The use of sexual explicitness as an essential element in the definition of the category of restricted material suggests that conservative concerns about the pollution of the moral person continue to dominate thinking about obscenity/pornography (Coward 1982, 13).[39]

A harmful pornographic image cannot be identified and isolated from other forms of sexual imagery simply on the basis of formal structure. A variety of contextual factors are critical to the impact of sexual imagery, as either encouraging sexual awareness or reinforcing unreflective attitudes. It matters whether the individual is using the image simply as a sexual aid or whether he or she is viewing the image for other reasons, which may involve a deeper engagement. It matters also whether the image fits with, or runs against the grain of, the individual's assumptions about sexuality. In applying a ban on pornographic imagery a court must make a general judgment about a particular image, even though the line between expression that supports reflection and that which discourages it is unclear and even though no image will have exactly the same impact on, or be viewed in exactly the same way by, different viewers.

Recognition of the breadth of the problem of violent or degrading sexist imagery might support very significant intervention by the state into the way sexuality is represented. The concern, however, is that such intervention would significantly narrow the scope of public discourse about sexual issues, making the state the arbiter of acceptable sexual representation. It would close down any possibility of meaningful freedom of expression in the shaping of collective ideas about sexuality – of alternative readings and uses of sexual imagery. More particularly, such an approach would involve significant risk of repression of non-mainstream sexual expression.

The pervasiveness of pornographic or sexist imagery makes a limited form of censorship difficult, but perhaps necessary. It is often assumed that the focus of any restriction should be on violent sexual imagery, the extreme edge of the flood of mass-marketed material intended for male sexual stimulation. While the impact of violent sexual imagery depends on the larger pornographic culture (and so is only a part of a problem that is systemic), it gives a particularly brutal shape to that culture. Such images may extend the boundaries of the consumer's understanding of 'ordinary' and 'natural' sexual behaviour.[40]

Yet any proposal for censorship must confront a variety of practical enforcement problems. For example, we may wonder whether police officers, prosecutors, and judges are in a good position to decide which images are harmful and should be restricted and which encourage a more critical understanding of sexuality. If the system of pornographic images is harmful because it normalizes sexual subordination, can we feel confident that police officers and judges will be able to stand outside this cultural process? Indeed, we may not be surprised when police and judges see 'unorthodox' sexual activity as antisocial and therefore harmful. In feminist censorship arguments, scepticism about the public's reading of sexually explicit material is awkwardly joined with an optimism about state enforcement and a faith that legal restrictions will catch the right material. Certainly the law as it is presently written and interpreted provides ample opportunity for state authorities to selectively silence different forms of sexual expression.

Chapter Five

The Regulation of
Racist Expression

1. Introduction: The Variety of Hate Speech

Very different kinds of expression are joined under the label 'hate speech.' This label is applied to expression directed at a minority group and intended to be either threatening or insulting to the members of that group. It is also applied to expression directed to members of the majority or dominant group in the community, and meant to persuade them of the undesirable characteristics or activities of minority group members.

Both supporters and opponents of regulation believe that the regulation of hate speech, in its various forms, rests on a single ground, although they disagree about what this single ground is. Supporters of regulation believe that hate speech is justifiably subject to restriction because it 'silences' the members of target groups (or causes harm to their social position within the community). In contrast, opponents of regulation believe that while the restriction of these different forms of hate speech rests on the common ground of 'offence,' this ground is too thin to support the limitation of a fundamental right such as freedom of expression. Since both sides of the regulation debate describe the basis for restriction in such abstract terms there is no real possibility of engagement between them and no recognition by either that the strength of the argument for regulation (and what we mean by silencing or offence) may vary depending on the type of hate speech at issue.

For opponents of regulation, a burning cross, a racist insult, and Holocaust denial literature convey messages that are personally offensive to the members of particular racial/ethnic/religious groups.[1] Yet in the opponents' view, it is obvious that offence is not an acceptable basis for restricting expression; restriction of expression cannot be based on the audience's subjective reaction to the message communicated. For if hate speech can be restricted because the audience experiences offence, why not other forms of expression? All expression would in fact be vulnerable if restriction was justified whenever the audience disliked the message communicated. A commitment to freedom of expression means that individuals and groups must sometimes endure expression they find offensive. Offensive expression may convey deep feelings or it may challenge conventional opinion. Individuals must be permitted to express anger or contempt and to employ strong language or make shocking claims that may shake others from their fixed ideas and assumptions.

Supporters of regulation argue that hate speech, in its various forms, is harmful not because it offends but because it silences the members of target groups or interferes with their right to equal respect and treatment.[2] Hateful remarks are so hurtful that they reduce the target group member to speechlessness or shock him or her into silence. In contrast to offence, 'silencing' seems to offer a more substantial and objective basis for limiting the fundamental right of free expression, a basis that is itself rooted in freedom of expression values. The language of silencing and inequality suggests a greater injury, and a different kind of injury, something more than mere offence or irritation. The term 'offence' does not capture the depth of the injury caused by hate speech, the emotional upset and the fear and insecurity that target group members experience. The description of the injury as 'offence' also ignores the damage hate speech does to the individual's self-esteem and standing in the community.

The silencing argument identifies a harm that is common to all forms of hate speech and equates this harm with state censorship. However, the silencing that results from the expression of hateful views is very different from that which results from direct state censorship. Also, different forms of hate speech may cause, or contribute to, silencing in very different ways, and these differences may matter when deciding the justification of a particular restriction.

Silencing occurs because hate speech is so damaging to the self-esteem of minority group members that they come to feel that they have no useful contribution to make to public discussion. Or it occurs because hate speech convinces members of the larger community that minority group members have nothing worthwhile to say and that their contributions to public debate should not be taken seriously. Hate speech causes silencing and inequality because it affects how the larger community views the members of a target group *and* how target group members view themselves. Either the individual is disinclined to speak because he or she has internalized the message of inferiority *or* the audience is disinclined to listen because they have been convinced that the individual has nothing useful or relevant to say.[3] Understood in this way, the silencing/inequality argument might support the restriction of a wide range of racist statements. Silencing and inequality are the consequence of insults and threats but also (and perhaps more significantly) of statements that are meant to persuade members of the larger community of the undesirable characteristics of a particular racial group.

In the United States, the leading hate speech cases involve threats and insults against racial/ethnic groups. These forms of hate speech give rise to identifiable harms – the fear caused by threats and the harassment of insults. The restriction of racist threats and insults may involve some difficult line drawing, but it is in principle compatible with a commitment to freedom of expression. The issue for the courts is whether the harm caused by these forms of expression is significant enough to justify a restriction on expression. The American courts, however, have described these injuries in the language of 'offence' and have concluded that they are insufficient to support a limitation on free speech.

Under established accounts of freedom of expression racist threats and insults may have some value, inasmuch as they express personal feelings or convey some kind of crude political viewpoint. However, if we think that freedom of expression protects communicative relationships then we might also believe that a certain level of engagement with the audience is required before expression should be protected. The limited value of these acts must be weighed against the intended and significant injury to others. The justification for the restriction of racist threats and insults does not need to be framed in the language of silencing. If words are threatening or harassing, they may be unacceptable whether or not they cause the targeted individual to stop speaking.

The meaning and force of a racist threat depends significantly on the larger background of racist expression and action. A single racist threat or insult can be seen as causing fear or upset to an individual group member, but the depth of the fear or upset is greater because the statement occurs against a larger background of racist expression and action.[4] A burning cross planted in front of the home of the first black family to move into a previously all-white neighbourhood is experienced as threatening because it evokes the history of Klan violence against blacks.[5] Similarly a march with swastikas and SS uniforms in a Jewish neighbourhood is experienced as threatening because it evokes the history of Nazi persecution of Jews.[6] Even if these threats do not seem realistic or immediate to an outside observer they must be viewed from the perspective of a target group member, who experiences them as part of a continuing practice of violence against his or her group. The history and context of violence gives rise to genuine and understandable fear and insecurity. Even if the members of the target group know that the particular demonstration does not represent a realistic threat, the act is so closely linked to a larger practice of violent oppression that it is bound to cause significant anxiety and upset.

The broader context of racist violence provides a basis for distinguishing unacceptable threats from the 'rough and tumble of public debate,' which is sometimes unpleasant and impolite. Even if we accept that the neo-Nazi march manifests some kind of political solidarity among its participants or amounts to a political statement to other members of the community who witness it or hear about it, the march is, in the first instance, a threat against the Jewish residents of the neighbourhood. Any political meaning or significance the march may have stems from its threatening character.

The context of racist violence and discrimination may also provide a basis for treating racist insults differently from other insults.[7] Racist insults are different because they are often a prelude to violent behaviour, but also because the context of violence, discrimination, and oppression adds significantly to their emotional impact. They are intended to injure and do not invite dialogue. As well, a racist insult is not an isolated occurrence. The frequent expression of racial insults (coming from different sources) means that they cannot easily be avoided by individual target group members. Each insult is experienced as part of a practice of harassment that gives rise to a general injury of emotional upset, humiliation, and insecurity.

It is now widely accepted that racist insults should be banned in the workplace, in schools, and in other similar environments. In the workplace or school insults are difficult to avoid. The environment is both closed and hierarchical and so a higher standard of civility may reasonably be expected. However, any ban (and certainly a general ban) on racist insults raises a variety of line-drawing issues, such as the distinction between a racist insult and a claim or argument about race, or the distinction between a derogatory term used against a particular group and the same term used by members of that group to describe themselves. An example of the latter is the self-identification as 'Queer' by many gays and lesbians, in an attempt to neutralize or transform the term's derogatory connotation. The law, of course, does not always deal well with this sort of context-based distinction.

In contrast to the United States, the principal hate speech cases in Canada involve the regulation of racist claims meant to 'persuade' members of the general community, including perhaps members of the target group itself. The concern is that those who hear racist opinions may come to view the target group differently and act towards its members in a discriminatory or violent way. Hate speech, in this form, damages the group's position in the community because it changes or reinforces the way that members of the dominant group think about particular minority groups.

Yet freedom of expression is said to be valuable because the free exchange of ideas is necessary to the formation of public opinion and to the realization/creation of individual and group identity. The individual's thoughts, feelings and, more generally, his identity take shape in public discourse. It is not an invasion of the individual's dignity when others express views about him, even when the views expressed affect how he is regarded by the general community and how he sees himself. The standard freedom of expression position is that ideas cannot be censored simply because we fear that members of the community may find them persuasive or that an individual's self-understanding or self-esteem may be negatively affected. According to this position we should respond to racist claims not with censorship but by offering competing views that make the case for equal respect or by creating more avenues for marginalized groups to express themselves.

The Canadian cases thus involve a fundamental challenge to conventional freedom of expression doctrine. The courts in Canada have tried to reconcile the regulation of racist speech with the constitutional commitment to freedom of expression by isolating a narrow category of hateful or extremist expression that is appropriately subject to restriction. The difficulty, however, is that racist expression must be understood as a systemic problem if we are to account for its harm and justify its restriction. Yet if the problem is systemic, defining a narrow category of harmful/restricted expression and establishing a manageable legal standard may not be possible.

2. The Regulation of Racist Ideas

In Canada, a variety of laws prohibit hateful statements that are intended to reinforce or encourage racist attitudes in others. The expression of racist views is restricted by the Canadian Criminal Code 1985 and by federal and provincial human rights codes. Both forms of regulation have been challenged in the courts and upheld as justified limits on freedom of expression.

The leading case of *Keegstra* 1990 considered the constitutionality of the Criminal Code 1985 ban on the wilful promotion of hatred: section 319(2) of the Code provides that '[e]very person who, by communicating statements, other than in private conversation, wilfully promotes hatred against an identifiable group' commits an offence, punishable for a term of up to two years.[8]

James Keegstra was a teacher in the high school in Eckville, Alberta. For almost ten years he taught his students about an all-encompassing conspiracy on the part of Jews to undermine Christianity and control the world. He told his students that the banking system, the media, Hollywood, the universities, most publishers, most of the churches, and almost all political leaders were agents of this conspiracy. He said that Jews were 'treacherous,' 'subversive,' 'sadistic,' 'money-loving,' 'power hungry,' and 'child killers.' He used the teacher's punishment and reward powers to ensure that his students 'parroted' his theories and ideas (*Keegstra* 1990, 714).[9] Students who did not adopt or acquiesce in his views did poorly in his class. When Mr Keegstra's teaching finally became a public issue he was dismissed from his position. A year later he was charged under section 319(2) of the Criminal Code 1985 with wilfully promoting hatred.

Keegstra challenged the constitutionality of section 319(2), arguing that it violated his freedom of expression under the Canadian Charter of Rights and Freedoms. Chief Justice Dickson, writing for the majority of the Supreme Court of Canada, accepted that section 319(2) of the Criminal Code restricted 'expression,' so that the provision violated 'freedom of expression' under section 2(b) of the Charter. However, he found that the restriction was justified under section 1, the Charter's limitation provision, because it limited 'a special category of expression which strays some distance from the spirit of section 2(b)' (*Keegstra* 1990, 766); it advanced the important goal of preventing the spread of racist ideas; and it advanced this goal rationally and with minimal impairment to the freedom. Madame Justice McLachlin in her dissenting judgment agreed that preventing the spread of hateful ideas was an important end, but doubted that a criminal prohibition would advance this end effectively and at minimal cost to freedom of expression.[10]

Chief Justice Dickson recognized that racist remarks can cause 'very real harm' to the members of the 'target group': 'It is indisputable that the emotional damage caused by words may be of grave psychological and social consequence' (*Keegstra* 1990, 746). The 'derision, hostility and abuse encouraged by hate propaganda ... have a severely negative impact' on an individual target group member because her 'sense of human dignity and belonging to the community at large is closely linked to the concern and respect accorded to the groups to which he or she belongs' (*Keegstra* 1990, 746). Because an individual's identity is partly constituted by her association and interaction with others, she experiences attacks on the groups to which she belongs personally and sometimes very deeply. Because an individual's sense of self is shaped in important ways by the views and actions of others, attacks on her most important associations will cause injury to her self-worth or dignity. Also, if members of the larger community are persuaded by the message of hate speech, they may engage in acts of violence and discrimination, causing 'serious discord' in the community (*Keegstra* 1990, 747).

The majority decision upholding the hate promotion provision of the Criminal Code rests on two important determinations. First, the majority accepted that there is a causal link between the expression of racist views and the spread of hatred in the community. Second, the majority considered that the restriction is narrow in its scope and catches 'only the most intentionally extreme forms of expression' (*Keegstra* 1990, 783). There are, however, problems with both these findings. Most obviously the court's causal or behavioural approach seems incompatible with a commitment to freedom of expression. But even if it makes sense to say that hate speech 'causes' harm, it cannot be the case that any particular hateful statement 'silences' the members of a target group (damages their self-esteem so that they withdraw from public discourse) or leads to their unequal treatment (convinces others that they are undeserving of equal respect). If silencing occurs, it must be the consequence of a system of racist expression and action and not of a narrow category of extreme statements.

In the majority's view the state is justified in restricting the expression of the extreme racist views of hate-mongers such as Keegstra because such views may lead (cause) others to hate the members of the targeted group and to act towards them in a violent or discriminatory way or because these views may be internalized by group members, damaging their self-esteem. The majority accepted that there is a causal link between expression and the spread of hate because it was sceptical about the role of rational agency in the communicative process, at least when racial matters were at issue. According to the majority: 'individuals can be persuaded to believe "almost anything" if information and ideas are communicated using the right technique and in the proper circumstances' (*Keegstra* 1990, 747). Consequently it is important not to 'overplay the view that rationality will overcome all falsehoods in the unregulated marketplace of ideas' (*Keegstra* 1990, 763).

The majority accepted that the hate promotion provision restricts only a narrow category of expression.[11] Merely unpopular or unconventional communications are not caught by the ban. Hatred is an emotion that is 'intense and extreme' in character: 'To promote hatred is to instil detestation, enmity, ill-will and malevolence in another' (*Keegstra* 1990, 777). The majority judgment assumed that only extreme statements would cause these extreme feelings. The majority also noted that the restriction applies only when an individual '*wilfully* promotes hatred.' The speaker must intend to create hatred or he must recognize that hatred is the likely consequence of his expression. This mental element, said the majority, ensures that only the most extreme statements will be caught by the Code provision.[12]

Elsewhere in the majority judgment, however, the 'wilful promotion' test was described in looser terms. The majority acknowledged that the causal link between a particular act of expression and the spread of hatred in the community is difficult to establish.[13] According to the majority, it is enough that the speaker knows or is aware that his or her expression creates a substantial risk that hatred will be spread or that acts of violence will increase. The hate-monger must intend or foresee 'as substantially certain a direct and active stimulation of hatred against an identifiable group' (*Keegstra* 1990, 777).

Dickson C.J., for the majority, said that it is not necessary to prove that a particular act of expression causes hatred, that the link is too difficult to establish. However, it is unclear under his test what sort of connection between speech and hatred must be established before an individual can be said to have violated the provision. The shift in language from cause to risk and from creation of hatred to the 'stimulation' or 'circulation' of hateful feelings suggests some recognition that expression does not cause harm in a simple and mechanical way.[14] The impact of expression is unpredictable, and creates only a risk of harm, because it depends on the reaction of audience members, who bring a wide range of attitudes and assumptions to their assessment of the claims made.

The court assumed that extreme views and acts are caused by extreme statements, by expression that is heated and hateful in tone. The court's emphasis on the (extreme) hatred or prejudice that lies behind particular statements makes sense only if we believe that individual acts of expression create hatred in the community in a discrete and measurable way. Yet once we recognize the problematic character of the causal link between expression and hatred, as the court did in its discussion of the 'wilful promotion' test, the scope of the restriction becomes difficult to contain.

If it is not necessary to show that the accused's purpose was to foster hatred but only that she was aware that hatred would/might be promoted by her expression or that her expression was of a type that might contribute to a climate of racial hatred, then the restriction may cover more than 'extreme' claims. If racist expression does cause hatred in the community, something that is difficult to establish, the responsibility must lie with the system of racist expression rather than with individual acts of expression. No one instance of expression causes hatred but a wide range of racist statements (some extreme and some more temperate and even commonplace) may contribute to racist or hateful attitudes in the community – to the cultural reproduction of racism. The spread of hatred cannot be attributed to individual statements or even to a narrow category of extremist expression.

James Keegstra spoke to persuade his audience that Jews were dishonest and were engaged in a grand conspiracy, something he thought was true. No doubt he could foresee that the result of his expression might be that his audience would become more suspicious of, or more hostile towards, Jews. No doubt he hoped for this result. Yet any expression that is critical of a minority group might have this result, particularly in a community where racial prejudices are so deeply entrenched. Any critical expression, even that which is calmly and 'rationally' expressed, will draw on and contribute to racist or hateful attitudes in the community.[15] Racist views may be harmful even when expressed without obvious anger and animosity. Indeed, their influence (their silencing effect or support for inequality) may be greater when they are presented as thoughtful contributions to public opinion.

3. The Challenge to Freedom of Expression

A commitment to freedom of expression involves protecting the individual's right to express and hear different views. If some individuals are persuaded of certain views, which they then act on, we might say that the expression has 'caused' the action. However, under most accounts of freedom of expression, the state is not justified in restricting expression simply because it 'causes' harm by persuading its audience.[16]

In *Keegstra* 1990 the majority of the Supreme Court of Canada was prepared to treat hate speech as responsible for the spread of hatred and for increases in racist violence, because they doubted that the audience would (always) exercise rational judgment when considering racist claims.[17] Yet faith in human reason underlies most accounts of freedom of expression and cannot simply be cut out and discarded from the analysis. The implications of downplaying this faith in reason are enormous. Upon what is our commitment to freedom of expression based, if not on a belief in human reason and its power to recognize truth? What restrictions on expression are not acceptable once we have lost faith in human reason? If we are unwilling to trust, or give space to, individual judgment and public reason the question of censorship will turn simply on whether the expression at issue conveys a good or bad message or whether we think the public acceptance of the message will have good or bad consequences. But this amounts to a rejection of freedom of expression as a political/constitutional principle. A commitment to freedom of expression means protecting expression for reasons more basic than our agreement with its message, for reasons independent of its content.

If we are to address the harm of hate promotion without undermining the constitutional commitment to freedom of expression, we must isolate a category of hateful or extremist expression from ordinary public discourse because of its irrational appeal or because it occurs in circumstances where rational agency is less likely to prevail. This was suggested by the majority judgment when it claimed that an 'individual can be persuaded to believe almost anything' if the 'right technique' is used in the 'proper circumstance' (*Keegstra* 1990, 747). If a particular instance or form of expression does not engage the audience or contribute to public reflection and judgment but instead 'incites' or 'manipulates' it may not deserve constitutional protection. Yet while the majority judgment in *Keegstra* 1990 assumed that hate promotion (extremist expression) is manipulative or misleading, it did not explain what makes it so or how it is distinguishable from ordinary non-manipulative expression.

The problem of line drawing plays a key role in the argument against the restriction of hate promotion. Indeed, the line-drawing argument often seems to substitute for a more direct claim that the freedom should protect the expression of all viewpoints, no matter how wrong or offensive. Madame Justice McLachlin, in her dissenting judgment, argued against the criminal restriction of hate promotion not by focusing on its value but rather by pointing out how difficult it is to draw a line separating hate promotion from other forms of expression. She was concerned that the line may be drawn in the wrong place so that valuable expression is restricted. As well, she was concerned about the 'chilling effect' of any line that may be drawn. Individuals may be reluctant to publish material, even valuable material, that should not, and probably would not, be restricted because they are unwilling to take the risk that it might fall within a criminal prohibition that does not have a clear and uncontested scope.[18] An individual who is critical of the members of a particular group or who engages in research concerning the different characteristics of racial/ethnic groups will 'think twice' about what she says and may even decide to remain silent, fearing that her expression might fall within this vague prohibition (*Keegstra* 1990, 860).

In support of this concern, Madame Justice McLachlin referred to the 'track record' of section 319(2). She noted that, in the past, the section 'has provoked many questionable actions on the part of the authorities' (*Keegstra* 1990, 859). For example, the novels *The Haj* (Uris 1984) by Leon Uris and *Satanic Verses* (Rushdie 1988) by Salman Rushdie were investigated and/or temporarily interfered with under customs restrictions. Following investigation, the authorities concluded that neither book fell within the particular restriction. However, for McLachlin J. the temporary interference with these books by customs officials illustrated the uncertain application of the restriction and helped to create a climate in which writers have genuine concerns that their work may result in criminal punishment.

The way the line-drawing argument is stated it sounds as if expression that has little or no value must be protected to ensure that valuable expression is also protected. James Keegstra's Holocaust denial and Jewish conspiracy expression must be protected if we are to ensure that Leon Uris is not prevented or discouraged from writing *The Haj* (Uris 1984). But if Keegstra's expression is of little or no value and Uris's expression is clearly valuable, why is it so difficult to draw a line between them? The problem cannot simply be that the judgment of the state (and the courts) is not to be trusted when it comes to drawing lines around the scope of freedom of expression. The definition and limitation of freedom of expression by the courts involves drawing lines. If the line between literature and hate promotion should be avoided, why should we not avoid all the other lines that give freedom of expression its shape? Why is the line that isolates hate promotion more elusive or more dangerous than the others?

I suspect that the line-drawing problem is not, as McLachlin J. suggested, that the line between legitimate and illegitimate expression may be drawn in the wrong place by the legislature or the courts, or that, even if it is drawn in the right place, the line may have a chilling effect on legitimate expression. The problem is rather that the distinction between what in her example is assumed to be legitimate expression and what is assumed to be illegitimate expression is not all that clear. What James Keegstra says is in many ways similar to what Leon Uris writes. This is why it is difficult to draw a line between them and why the censorship of Keegstra's speech puts the writing of Uris at risk.

There are of course differences between the two. Keegstra, in contrast to Uris, makes specific racist claims that are extreme and bizarre. But Uris's writing is most certainly not free of the taint of prejudice. Indeed, it represents a powerful vehicle for the transmission and reinforcement of bigoted attitudes. In *The Haj* (Uris 1984), Leon Uris builds ethnic/racial stereotypes into the characters and events of a fast-paced narrative.[19] The Jewish characters in his book are heroic and honourable while the Arab characters are cowardly and dishonest. Yet because these are merely the attributes of particular characters in a work of historical fiction, they are not explicit claims about Jews and Arabs that are open to consideration and debate by the readers. Uris supports and revitalizes ethnic/racial stereotypes not by argument but simply by weaving them into a 'realistic' narrative that is read by a large audience.

Is the answer simply to exclude both Uris and Keegstra from the protection of freedom of expression? Keegstra makes racist claims that play on the fears and prejudices of some members of the community; Uris's narrative builds on ethnic and religious stereotypes that may be assimilated by the reader without conscious, or at least careful, consideration. The line-drawing problem, however, is not resolved by redrawing the line in another place. The problem is much deeper than the unclear distinction between what Keegstra says and what Uris writes. McLachlin J. has not simply chosen a bad example with *The Haj* (Uris

1984). Racial and other stereotypes are so deeply entrenched in our culture, our language, and our thinking that it is impossible to isolate clearly the offensive claims of Keegstra and the objectionable stereotyping of Uris from ordinary public discourse. A wide range of expression, both extreme and ordinary, conveys racist attitudes and contributes to the spread or reinforcement of racist opinion in the community. This is the real line-drawing problem and it is much deeper than McLachlin J. and the civil libertarian defenders of the constitutional protection of hate propaganda suppose.

It is hardly surprising that civil libertarians emphasize the strategic argument that hate speech must be protected so that truly valuable expression will not be put at risk of censorship. It cannot be easy arguing that hate speech should be protected because it is a valuable part of public discourse. Yet the line-drawing argument is too thin to support the protection of hate speech. If hate speech is itself without value, and even harmful, then it would be both possible and important to draw a line separating it from valuable forms of expression. Ultimately the protection of hate speech must rest on more than its strategic significance. Protection must be based on a belief that hate speech is itself valuable, that it advances freedom of expression values, even though its message is wrong and offensive. Indeed, Madame Justice McLachlin sometimes came close to saying that Keegstra's remarks had some value as part of public discourse.

On this view, the line is difficult to draw because the speech of both Keegstra and Uris contributes to public discourse, even if it is also racist. The argument then is that racist expression should be protected even though it may (sometimes) contribute to racial hatred or intolerance in the community. It should be protected because it expresses the thoughts and feelings of the speaker and provides information and ideas to an audience, who may decide either to accept or to reject what they hear. Keegstra makes specific claims. His most objectionable and offensive claims involve propositions of a kind that can be reflected upon, debated, and judged. The familiar freedom of expression argument is that these claims, absurd and offensive as they may be, should be responded to and not simply censored out of public discourse.

However, a recognition that line drawing is a problem because racial and other stereotypes are pervasive may provide some justification for the restriction of (extreme) racist expression. The line-drawing argument can be turned on its head once we understand why line drawing is so difficult (Moon 1992, 136). Keegstra's hateful expression is difficult to isolate from ordinary public discourse because racist expression and thinking are pervasive. His expression may also be more dangerous because of this pervasiveness.

Keegstra's audience understands and evaluates his claims against a larger background of racist assumptions. Racist claims often play to fears and frustrations (of moral decay or unemployment) in a context where the space for critical reflection is reduced. These claims draw on the social background of bigotry and racial stereotyping of which Leon Uris's novel *The Haj* (Uris 1984) is only a very small part. Against this background, a racist claim is an ordinary part of discourse. Indeed, to some members of the community, even the absurd claims of Keegstra may seem reasonable or plausible. A general audience may be less critical of racist claims, which provide a channel for fear and resentment, and which resonate with widely shared assumptions.[20] Racist claims may resist critical evaluation because they give shape to popular but inchoate assumptions and attitudes.[21] Similarly, the dominance of racist imagery and messages means that members of target groups have little space to 'negotiate' their identity and place in the world.[22]

Nevertheless, restricting hate promotion, whether narrowly or broadly defined, is very different from prohibiting 'the yell of fire in a crowded theatre,' the classic American example of an exception to freedom of expression protection. The 'yell of fire' occurs as an identifiable and discrete deviation from the conditions of ordinary public discourse.[23] The theatre audience does not have the time or space to stop and think carefully before acting on the communicated message. The panic that will follow the yell of fire in these circumstances is likely to result in injury. The court in *Keegstra* 1990, however, based its decision not on any exceptional and temporary circumstances that might distort or limit the audience's ability to rationally assess the message conveyed to them, but rather on a general scepticism about the exercise of human reason in a racist culture. The concern is that certain ways of thinking about race are so deeply embedded in our culture, in its linguistic forms and popular concepts, that racist claims often go unexamined and are difficult to challenge. This scepticism, however, raises questions about the protection of any (negative) claim about race and not just the extreme claims of people like Keegstra.

4. Extreme and Ordinary Racist Expression

Both dissenting and majority judgments in *Keegstra* 1990 focused on the distinction between extremist or racist expression and legitimate political expression. They differed only on the question of how clearly the

line could be drawn between these two categories. The majority judgment of Chief Justice Dickson referred to extremist expression, as if the
parameters of such a category were obvious. The dissent of Madame
Justice McLachlin insisted that it was impossible to define such a category in clear terms.

I have argued, however, that the distinction at issue is really between
the expression of extreme racist opinions and the expression of more
commonplace racist views. In *Keegstra* 1990 the distinction between unprotected and protected expression depends not on whether the opinion expressed is racist or non-racist, harmful or not harmful, but on the
opinion's fit or consistency with popular thinking. An opinion will be
viewed as extreme if it does not seem to rest on conventional standards
of rationality and is removed from popular thinking, which may embrace other (less extreme) forms of racist opinion.

In this way, the expression that the court in *Keegstra* 1990 said is
caught by the criminal ban on hate promotion, although extreme, is
also continuous with ordinary or mainstream expression.[24] Civil libertarians tend to characterize racist speech as marginal, as outside the
mainstream, as the speech of 'eccentrics' or 'cranks' (Dworkin 1996,
237). According to this view, hate speech laws suppress minority or
dissenting views and support the orthodoxy of the majority community.
In contrast, supporters of regulation see racist speech as part of the
dominant discourse of the community. In their view, the harm of racist
speech rests on its systemic presence. Each of these views captures part
of the truth about the extreme racist speech that is sometimes the
subject of legal regulation.

The Supreme Court of Canada in *Keegstra* 1990 interpreted the Criminal Code ban on hate promotion so that it extends only to extremist
expression. In the court's view this narrow ban represents a reasonable
limit on freedom of expression. However, if the spread of hatred is the
consequence of a system of racist expression and action and if the critical examination of particular racist claims is blunted by a larger background of racist assumptions, it may be difficult to justify this narrow
focus on extremist expression.

The court's scepticism about human reason and its concern about
the spread of racist ideas might justify restriction of all forms of racist
expression, from the extreme claims of Keegstra to the more commonplace racial stereotyping of Uris or popular claims about intelligence
and race. Indeed, it may be complained that a partial ban on hate
speech, which focuses only on the most extreme or bizarre racist claims

and leaves 'ordinary' racist expression untouched, suggests that the problem has been dealt with – that what is not regulated is not a concern. Yet less extreme racist claims only seem 'ordinary' because they reflect, or resonate with, common opinion. All racist expression, the extreme and the commonplace, takes place in a larger culture of racist attitudes and assumptions and contributes to the reproduction of this larger culture. Indeed, it is arguable that common forms of racist expression are more harmful because their exposure is greater and their racist message is less obvious.

However, there is another way of looking at the law's distinction between extreme racist expression, which is restricted, and commonplace racist expression, which is not. The distinction can be seen as an attempt to accommodate both a commitment to freedom of expression and a sensitivity to the limits of reason and the risks of harm. While the protection of more commonplace forms of racist expression may rest on a commitment to public debate and discussion of important issues, including race issues, the restriction of extremist expression may rest on a rejection of the naive faith in the harmlessness of expression and the infallibility of human reason that sometimes seems to underlie freedom of expression doctrine.

There are many reasons for *not* restricting 'ordinary' racist expression. Any attempt to exclude all racial prejudice from public discourse would require extraordinary intervention by the state.[25] Because racism is so commonplace, it would be impossible to establish clear and effective legal standards to identify and punish all forms of racist expression, particularly since police, prosecutors, and judges are not unaffected by larger cultural attitudes. Public discussion of racial issues is vital precisely because racist attitudes and assumptions are so pervasive and help to shape individual identity and public opinion.[26] This discussion would be stifled if the state attempted to ban all expression of racist opinion. The community must confront commonly held racist views if it is to rise above them. Public debate makes change possible. Racist attitudes are often spread or reinforced without clear consideration or conscious acceptance and so a key anti-racism strategy is to expose the racist character of commonplace attitudes, to make it more visible and bring it to clearer and, hopefully, more critical consciousness.

However, even if we accept that 'ordinary' or commonplace racist claims should be discussed and addressed and not simply censored out of public discourse, a sensitivity to the limits of reason (particularly in the context of racial matters) and to the significant harm caused by racist ideas and attitudes should lead to a rethinking of the standard laissez-faire approach. Instead of assuming that a 'free market of ideas' will lead to a balanced assessment of racial issues, greater effort should be made by the state and community to ensure that racist views are expressed in a context where they will be challenged and where the likelihood of reasonable assessment by the audience is maximized – where the racist character of certain forms of discourse will be exposed and examined.

A variety of factors may limit our capacity to assess and challenge racist claims. Racist claims are sometimes made to subordinates by individuals in positions of institutional authority, for example, by school teachers to their students. Claims made in this sort of context are less likely to be assessed and challenged and so should be subject to regulation. It may be that in certain contexts the expression of racist views should always be accompanied by a clear and direct response. For example, we might reasonably expect the media not to report claims about racial intelligence without placing such claims in a context that highlights their fundamental flaws or at least sets out a contrary position.

There may be good reasons for protecting 'ordinary' racist expression. However, the case for protecting extreme or bizarre racist assertions is not as strong. Views are 'extreme' precisely because they are removed somewhat from popular opinion. Despite the prevalence of racist expression, it is difficult to imagine that the bizarre views of Keegstra would be taken seriously by anyone who was not already deeply mired in irrational hatred, limited in his or her capacity for reasoned thought, or who was not in a subordinate or vulnerable position in relation to the speaker.[27] It is not a coincidence that two of the leading hate speech cases in Canada concern teachers. One of these teachers, James Keegstra, used his authority to limit the opportunity of his students to critically evaluate his views.[28]

While most members of the community will dismiss the claims of hate-mongers as bizarre and irrational, some individuals, already weighed down by extreme prejudice or susceptible to manipulation or already part of an extremist subculture, will see in these claims a 'plausible' account of their social and economic difficulties. Hate speech offers a focus for their feelings of resentment and frustration. It builds on existing racist attitudes and so leads to more extreme opinions and actions, particularly in times of great insecurity. Its extreme character calls for action against members of the hated group. Any individual who accepts the views presented by Keegstra and other hate-mongers would also have to conclude that radical action was called for.

The restriction of extreme views may also represent community affirmation of, or support for, groups that historically have been the targets of violence and discrimination. While it is impossible for the state to legislate against all forms of racist expression, there may be symbolic value in censoring the expression of extremist claims. (On the other hand, of course, as suggested above, partial restriction may legitimize unrestricted racist expression.) Civil libertarians insist that protection of the individual's freedom to express opinions, including racist opinions, should not be seen as support for the views expressed. However, once we recognize that racism is a systemic problem and that racist views are commonly expressed as part of public discourse then the larger community is in an important way implicated in the problem. It is hardly surprising that (some) target group members view the state's failure to ban racist expression as support for, or acquiescence in, the views expressed, or at least as insensitive to the harm caused by the expression of such views.

Line drawing remains a concern, particularly if the restriction has significant criminal consequences. There is no clear dividing line between the extreme and the ordinary. Yet sensitivity to the limits of reason and the potential harm of racist expression may weaken the force of the line-drawing/chilling-effect argument. Chilling effect may be raised as a concern about a particular legislative provision that gives too much discretion to either a judicial or administrative decision maker, but it should not serve as an all-purpose argument against any form of regulation (and in particular non-criminal regulation) of *extreme* racist expression.

In her dissenting judgment in *Keegstra* 1990, Madame Justice McLachlin expressed concern that a ban on hate promotion, which included the extreme claims of individuals such as Keegstra, might mean that '[s]cientists [would] think twice before researching and publishing results suggesting difference between ethnic or racial groups' (*Keegstra* 1990, 860). But should the state be precluded from restricting extremist expression simply because there is a risk that some of those involved in scientific research might 'think twice' before making damaging claims about racial groups? While I would not want to claim that chilling effect is anything other than a drawback or cost of regulation, it is worth recognizing that if scientists thought twice about researching and publishing such claims, they might think more carefully about their own motives, about the accuracy of their 'findings,' and about the harm that can be caused in a society that is only too ready to receive 'scientific evidence' of racial difference in intelligence. Chilling effect may be less of a concern, if what will be chilled (not banned) most often by a ban on extremist expression is the expression of more commonplace racist views. The scope of any ban on hate promotion may not be clear cut. But the line is often difficult (and likely to have some chilling effect) because it seeks to separate extreme racist claims from the more routine expression of racist attitudes.

5. A Note on Human Rights Code Regulation

Canadian law currently relies on two sorts of legal provision to deal with hate promotion: the criminal prohibition against hate promotion considered in *Keegstra* 1990 and provincial and federal human rights code provisions against racist expression.

Human rights codes are concerned principally with racial and other forms of discrimination in the private sector: in employment, housing, and the provision of services. However, the Canadian Human Rights Act (S.C. 1976–77, c. 33) and several provincial human rights codes also include provisions restricting the expression of racist views.[29] According to the Canadian Human Rights Act, 1976–77 at section 13(1) it is 'a discriminatory practice' contrary to the Act for a person to 'communicate telephonically ... repeatedly ... any matter that is likely to expose a person or persons to hatred or contempt by reason of the fact that that person or those persons are identifiable on the basis of a prohibited ground of discrimination'.[30] The constitutionality of this particular provision was considered by the Supreme Court of Canada in *Taylor* 1990.

According to Dickson C.J., who wrote for the majority in *Taylor* 1990, the aim of human rights statutes, including provisions restricting hate speech, 'is not to bring the full force of the state's power against a blameworthy individual for the purpose of imposing punishment' (*Taylor* 1990, 917). Instead these statutes 'operate in a less confrontational manner, allowing for a conciliatory settlement if possible and, where discrimination exists, gearing remedial responses more towards compensating the victim' (*Taylor* 1990, 917). Dickson C.J. argued that 'the conciliatory nature of the human rights procedure and the absence of criminal sanctions make s.13(1) especially well suited to encourage reform of the communicator of hate propaganda' (*Taylor* 1990, 924).

Human rights laws recognize that individual acts of discrimination are often unconscious in character and part of a systemic practice. The first response to discriminatory behaviour is education and conciliation. Administrative intervention and the imposition of a resolution occurs only when conciliation has failed to bring about a satisfactory solution. A human rights tribunal may make a variety of orders, including a compensation order or an injunction against further wrongful acts. An individual who refuses to obey the tribunal's order may be found in contempt and subjected to criminal punishment.

Chief Justice Dickson in *Taylor* 1990 acknowledged that section 13(1) of the Canadian Human Rights Act, 1976–77 imposes 'a slightly broader limit upon freedom of expression than does s.319(2) of the *Criminal Code*' (the hate promotion provision considered in *Keegstra* 1990) because it does not include a subjective intent requirement, such as 'wilful promotion' (*Taylor* 1990, 928). Nevertheless, he found that 'the conciliatory bent' of the Act made the limit more acceptable than had it been a simple criminal prohibition (*Taylor* 1990, 929). Indeed, Dickson C.J. argued that to read a subjective intent requirement into the Code prohibition would defeat one of the primary goals of antidiscrimination legislation, which is to prevent harmful effects rather than punish wrongdoing (*Taylor* 1990, 931).

However, intervention under federal and provincial human rights legislation is not triggered by everyday racist stereotypes and claims. If these codes purported to regulate the expression of mainstream racist views, they would be seen as far too interventionist, as too restrictive of freedom of expression. The focus of such laws then is on non-mainstream, and perhaps even extreme, racist expression. While conciliation will be effective in some cases, it may be that, in many or most cases of extremist expression, conciliation/education is neither an appropriate nor an effective response. While the procedure under a human rights code begins with an attempt to conciliate between the individuals involved, the process often moves to the tribunal stage and sometimes to a contempt of court hearing. What begins as a conciliation process ends with the imposition of punitive/coercive measures – the exceptional measures of final resort.[31]

In the case of *Taylor* 1990, for example, the Supreme Court of Canada upheld a provision of the Canadian Human Rights Act, 1976–77 that prohibited communication by telephone of 'any matter that is likely to expose a person or persons to hatred or contempt ...' (*Taylor* 1990, 902). The Human Rights Tribunal had granted an injunction against a telephone hate line; the injunction was disobeyed and criminal punishment for contempt was imposed by the Federal Court. None of this should cause surprise. The extremists operating the hate line were unlikely to be brought around through mediation or education to a realization of the wrongfulness of their actions. Reliance on coercive measures, and ultimately punitive measures, became necessary.

6. A General Conclusion

In the United States debate about the appropriate limits on speech revolves around the question of whether or not the speech goes 'too far' and disrupts the security or stability of the community by inciting members of the public to harmful action or deceiving them on an important public matter. Randall P. Bezanson describes the American approach in this way: 'The [critical] distinction between speech and conduct, then, is a quest for a way to free speech and thought without unleashing anarchy – to keep speech in its proper place, so to speak, and to draw distinct and enforceable boundaries between our freedom to think and say what we think, on the one hand, and our impulse to act on our thoughts and words, on the other' (Bezanson 1998, 94). The paradigmatic speaker in American free speech jurisprudence is the lone dissident who confronts or challenges state power or dominant ideologies. She should be free to speak and to challenge convention, unless her words go too far and provoke violence or threaten community security or stability.

In Canada, freedom of expression debate is often framed in similar terms. Yet it may be that an entirely different sort of concern underlies the freedom of expression decisions of the Canadian courts. While the courts describe certain instances of racist, pornographic, or commercial expression as 'going too far' and as appropriately subject to restriction, these forms of expression can only be understood as harmful if we see them as part of a systemic practice. The courts support the restriction of 'extreme' expression or expression that 'goes too far' (ads for dangerous products, violent sexual images, or extreme racist statements). However, the justification for restriction of these 'extreme' statements depends not simply on their form but also on the domination of public discourse by a narrow range of voices and views – the overwhelming presence in our public discourse – the mass marketing – of degrading sexual imagery or racist stereotypes or lifestyle product associations.

The extreme racist remarks of someone like James Keegstra may affect the thinking and behaviour of some members of the public only because racist expression (albeit less extreme) permeates public discourse. As well, ads for harmful products such as cigarettes are effective not simply because of their lifestyle form but also because commercial advertising so completely dominates public discourse. At one level, the issue in these cases is whether a particular instance of expression goes 'too far' and causes harm to important human interests, but at a deeper level the issue is whether certain forms of expression, or certain messages or perspectives, so completely dominate public discourse that the space for critical judgment by the individual is compressed. In such a context, the concern is that (extremist) 'speech' no longer appeals, or contributes, to independent reflection and judgment.

More speech is not always an answer when communicative resources are controlled by a small number of corporations and public discourse operates on marketing 'principles.' Unable or unwilling to respond directly to the larger problem of the imbalance of communicative power and the rise of advertising as the paradigm of public communication, legislatures and courts address the worst and most obvious excesses of public discourse by supporting content restrictions on 'extreme' expression. This response leaves the larger problems with public discourse substantially untouched. At the same time, however, because the line between extreme and ordinary is unclear, a matter of degree, the courts' approach puts the protection of all expression on unstable ground. The challenge for the courts is to maintain a clear and protected space for freedom of expression in a world where reason is imperfect, and often not the object of expression, where individuals sometimes seem pushed and pulled by communicative forces, and where fundamental imbalances in communicative power seem either natural or unchallengeable.

The issue of communicative power lies behind the courts' response to hate promotion, pornography, and advertising. This issue, however, comes nearer to the surface in the next two chapters, which discuss the individual's right of access to public and private property (Chapter 6) and the right of the individual to determine the communicative use of his or her property without state interference (Chapter 7). Yet, even though concerns about communicative power arise more explicitly in the courts' consideration of these issues, this consideration is significantly constrained by the structure of constitutional adjudication.

Chapter Six

Access to State-Owned Property

1. Introduction: The Unavoidable Public Forum Doctrine

Initially, at least, Canadian courts assumed that when dealing with the issue of communicative access to state-owned properties they could avoid the complex 'public forum' doctrine developed by the American courts.[1] The complexity of the American doctrine was attributed to the absence of a limitations provision in the U.S. Bill of Rights. Instead of balancing competing free speech and state interests in individual cases the American courts draw a distinction between two kinds of state-owned property: public forums (state-owned properties, such as parks and streets, that by tradition or designation are open to public communication and not simply to selected speakers) and non-public forums (state-owned properties to which the general public does not ordinarily have access). An individual has a general right to communicate on/in public forums. The state may restrict the content of speech in a public forum only for substantial and compelling reasons and only if the restriction is narrowly drawn. Content-neutral restrictions (time, place, and manner restrictions) will be justified only if they serve an important state interest and leave open alternative channels of communication. However, in the case of a non-public forum, the state may restrict the content of communication provided the restriction is reasonable and not simply based on the state's disagreement with the speaker's viewpoint.[2]

In Canada, it was assumed that because the Charter of Rights and Freedoms contains a limitations provision, the Canadian courts could engage in a direct balancing of competing state and individual interests (the individual's interest in communicative access and the state's interest in exclusion) and would not need to define general categories of property that were either open to, or insulated from, claims of public access. When access was claimed the Canadian courts would consider whether the state had a substantial reason to limit the individual's freedom to express him/herself and whether the particular exclusion advanced the state's purpose rationally and with minimal impairment to the freedom. No claim of access would be rejected a priori on the basis of the state's use of the property or the classification of the property as a non-public forum.

Yet, despite the assumption that complexity could be avoided, the Canadian courts have begun to develop a doctrinal structure for dealing with claims of communicative access to state-owned property that bears a remarkable resemblance to the American public forum doctrine. This development is not surprising. Indeed, some form of public forum doctrine may be unavoidable. The division of state properties into public and non-public forums and the establishment of different standards of justification for the restriction of communicative access to each category is the consequence of the distributive character of the access issue.

The two-step structure of Charter of Rights adjudication rests on an understanding of freedom of expression as a right to be free from state interference. The court first asks whether the state has restricted the individual's expression under section 2(b); if it finds that expression has been restricted, the court then asks whether the restriction is justified under section 1 of the Charter. It is not clear, however, that the access issue can be addressed in this way, as a simple matter of the justification of state interference with expression. When an individual is denied access to state-owned property, it is unclear whether the state has restricted her expression or whether it has simply declined to provide the individual with the resources she may need to communicate her point of view more effectively.

If we take property rights as the baseline, the fixed background against which freedom of expression claims are made, the state does not violate the individual's section 2(b) rights when it denies her/him communicative access to its property. According to this view, the state has not interfered with the individual's freedom of expression; it has simply decided not to lend him the resources needed to get his message out. Yet to say that the state has simply declined to assist the individual, when it prevents him from communicating on its property, ignores the fact that communicative power/opportunity is the consequence of state rules that define and allocate property rights. More importantly, it ignores the fact that public discourse requires common or shared spaces where individuals can exchange ideas and information in a public way. A general denial of access to state property (or an absence of state-created opportunities for communication) would have a dramatic effect on the ability of many individuals to participate in public discussion.[3]

However, if we decide that state denial of access should be seen as a restriction on freedom of expression and not simply as a failure to assist the individual, the onus will then fall on the state to justify every denial of access to its property under section 1 of the Charter. Understandably, the courts will be reluctant to second-guess the state's judgment about the importance of its property use, the incompatibility of communicative access with that use, and the priority that should be given to different speakers or messages when communicative opportunities must be allocated. The courts will also be reluctant to make judgments about the individual's need for communicative access to a particular property. Any assessment of the importance of a particular access claim to the realization of freedom of expression values will turn, in part at least, on the availability and adequacy of alternative forums. Yet, if an individual's constitutional right of access to a particular property depends (at least in part) on whether he or she has a right to communicate on *other* properties, state or private, how is a court to judge the availability and adequacy of alternatives? Will not the right of access to any one of these alternative properties in turn depend, in part, on whether the individual has a right of access to the state property at issue and any other properties?

The public forum doctrine is a response to the distributive character of the access issue. Under the public forum doctrine, the state is not permitted to exclude communication from its property simply on the basis of ownership. However, the doctrine gives a form of priority to state property use (rather than ownership). The distinction between public and non-public forums rests on the ordinary or traditional openness of the property to public expression or on the general compatibility of public expression with the state's property use. The state is not permitted to limit expression on properties to which the public ordinarily has access, except for good and substantial reasons. On properties to which the public is not ordinarily admitted and which perform functions that would be significantly compromised by general communicative access the state is permitted to exclude all access.

The courts avoid an open-ended review of state property use and a systemic assessment of an individual's communicative opportunities by relying on state judgments or practices concerning the general compatibility of public expression with the function or operation of its properties. The classification of a property as a public forum rests on either the state's general practice of allowing access or a general judgment by the courts that access is compatible with the state's property use. This approach allows the courts to avoid, or minimize, second-guessing the state's property use priorities and assessing the compatibility of individual access claims. Even though certain properties, non-public forums, will be insulated from all claims of communicative access, other properties, classified as public forums, will be open to all reasonable access claims.

2. The Dorval Airport Case

The Background

The difficulty in fitting the access issue into the two-step adjudicative structure is illustrated by the Supreme Court's judgment in *Commonwealth of Canada* 1991 and by subsequent applications of that judgment.

In 1984, officials at Dorval airport in Montreal prevented three members of the Committee for the Republic of Canada from communicating their political views to passers-by in the public areas of the airport. The committee members were told that their activities (speaking with passers-by and distributing leaflets) violated a federal airport regulation, which provided that 'no person shall (a) conduct any business or undertaking, commercial or otherwise at an airport; (b) advertise or solicit at an airport on his own behalf or on behalf of any person; or (c) fix, install or place anything at an airport for the purpose of any business or undertaking.'[4]

The committee members brought a motion in the Federal Court seeking a declaration that under the Charter of Rights they had a right to express themselves in the public areas of the airport and that this right had been violated by the airport authorities. Mr Justice Dubé of the Federal Court – Trial Division granted the declaration. He considered that the open area of the airport is a 'public forum' and that the government's ban on soliciting and advertising in such a forum restricted freedom of expression (*Commonwealth of Canada* 1985). He found that this restriction did not advance a substantial and compelling purpose and so could not be justified under section 1 of the Charter.

The case was appealed to the Federal Court of Appeal. Hugessen and MacGuigan JJ. (Pratte J. dissenting) agreed with the trial judge that the airport regulation was an unjustified restriction on freedom of expression (*Commonwealth of Canada* 1987). They did not agree, however, with the trial judge's adoption of the American public forum doctrine. In their view, the restriction of communicative access to *any* state-owned property violates section 2(b) of the Charter and is unconstitutional unless justified under the terms of section 1.

The case was further appealed to the Supreme Court of Canada (*Commonwealth of Canada* 1991).[5] All the members of the court agreed that the airport authorities' interference with the respondents' communication of political views was a restriction on freedom of expression that could not be justified under section 1. However, three different approaches to the issue of communicative access were put forward by the court.

Chief Justice Lamer

Chief Justice Lamer[6] argued that the question of whether an individual has a right to communicate on state-owned property should be resolved under section 2(b) and should depend simply on whether the particular communication is consistent or compatible with the state's use of the property. A restriction that is based on the incompatibility of the particular form of expression with the state's property use does not violate section 2(b) and so does not require special justification under section 1.

Early in his judgment, Chief Justice Lamer described the access issue as an accommodation or balancing of two competing interests. On the one hand, there is the interest of the individual 'wishing to express himself in a place suitable for such expression' (*Commonwealth of Canada* 1991, 153). The individual's interest in access is simply that 'the dissemination of an idea is most effective when there are a large number of listeners' and 'the economic and social structure of our society is such that the largest number of individuals, or potential listeners, is often to be found in places that are state property,' such as parks and roads (*Commonwealth of Canada* 1991, 153). On the other hand, there is the government's interest 'in the effective operation of the place owned by it' (*Commonwealth of Canada* 1991, 152). Communicative access will sometimes interfere with the state's 'public' use of its property.

Lamer C.J. considered that the government's ownership of a particular property 'cannot in itself authorize an infringement of the freedom guaranteed by section 2(b) of the Charter' (*Commonwealth of Canada* 1991, 155). Government ownership is 'quasi-fiduciary' in nature. The government 'owns places for the citizens' benefit and use, unlike a private owner who benefits personally from the places he owns' (*Commonwealth of Canada* 1991, 154). For this reason state property should not be outside the scope of constitutional review and insulated from all claims of access. According to Lamer C.J., limiting freedom of expression 'solely to places owned by the person wishing to communicate ... would certainly deny the very foundation of freedom of expression' (*Commonwealth of Canada* 1991, 155).

Although the chief justice thought that ownership does not give the government an automatic right to exclude communication, and although he often described the restriction of communication on government property as a restriction on freedom of expression, he argued that the reconciliation of the competing government and individual interests should take place under section 2(b), as a matter of the definition of the scope of freedom of expression, rather than under section 1, as a matter of the proper balance between competing values or interests. The chief justice considered that the access issue should be resolved under section 2(b) rather than under section 1 because he thought that the onus of establishing a right of access should remain on the person seeking access and, more significantly, because he thought that the access right should be limited to forms of expression compatible with the state's use of its property. Despite early references to the balancing of interests, when the chief justice articulated the test for determining when access should be permitted, he seemed to give complete priority to the state's interest in protecting the use to which it has dedicated its property.

According to Lamer C.J., 'the individual will only be free to communicate in a place owned by the state if the *form* of the expression he uses is compatible with the principal function or intended purpose of that place' (*Commonwealth of Canada* 1991, 156).[7] A restriction on communicative access (other than a content-based restriction) that protects or advances the state's use of its property will not violate section 2(b) because expression that interferes with the state's use does not fall within the scope of freedom of expression. Restrictions that are not based on the incompatibility of expressive activity with the state's use of the property must still be justified by the state under section 1 of the Charter.[8]

The state does not have unreviewable power to exclude communication from its property, but its property *use* is not subject to review by the courts under the standards of section 1 and need not yield to any claim of access, even access that might contribute to freedom of expression values. In this way Chief Justice Lamer's approach seems to avoid judicial second-guessing of the state's property use and judicial assessment of the background of opportunities for public communication. It either ignores the issue of alternative opportunities for communication or assumes that in the background there are always significant alternatives.

For Lamer C.J. one of the advantages of the compatibility test is its flexibility. The test does not create a category of 'public forums,' where access is virtually guaranteed, subject only to restrictions that advance substantial and compelling state purposes, nor does it insulate a category of property ('private forums') from all access claims. Lamer C.J. rejected 'the nominalistic approach developed by the American courts' in favour of an approach that assesses the compatibility of the specific claim of access with the state's property use (*Commonwealth of Canada* 1991, 152). He illustrated the flexibility of his test using the example of the Library of Parliament:

[N]o one would suggest that an individual could under the aegis of freedom of expression, shout a political message of some kind in the Library of Parliament or some other library. This form of expression in such a context would be incompatible with the fundamental purpose of the place, which essentially requires silence. When an individual undertakes to communicate in a public place, he or she must consider the function which that place must fulfil and adjust his or her means of communicating so that the expression is not an impediment to that function. To refer again to the example of a library, it is likely that wearing a T-shirt bearing a political message would be a form of expression consistent with the intended use of such a place. (*Commonwealth of Canada* 1991, 157)

The chief justice's test does not insulate a particular class of properties from all claims of access, because the test is not whether communication is generally consistent with the state's use of the particular property but rather whether this particular claim of access is compatible with the state's property use.[9]

It is not clear whether Lamer C.J. expects the courts to impose their own views about what is and what is not compatible with the state's use of its property or to show *some* deference to the government's views on the question. Deference to the state's judgment about what is incompatible with the property's use carries the risk that the state will define the exclusion very broadly. Prison authorities, for example, are notorious for taking a broad view of what is necessary to ensure prison security.

In the case before the court, Chief Justice Lamer found that the airport authorities' exclusion of the respondents from the public areas of the terminal building was contrary to section 2(b) because the respondents' political communication was compatible with the use of the property as an airport. In his mind: 'the distribution of pamphlets and discussion with certain members of the public are in no way incompatible with the airport's primary function, that of accommodating the needs of the travelling public. An airport is in many ways a thoroughfare, which in its open areas or waiting areas can accommodate expression without the effectiveness or function of the place being in any way threatened' (*Commonwealth of Canada* 1991, 158).

After he found that the respondents' expression was compatible with the operation of the airport, Lamer C.J. considered the application of section 1 (even though the only arguments the state put forward to justify the restriction were first that its ownership of the airport gave it the right to exclude access and second that access was incompatible with the airport's operation). He found that the airport regulation did not cover the respondents' political expression, so that the limitation on the respondents' freedom of expression 'arose from the action taken by the airport manager ... when he ordered them to cease their activities' (*Commonwealth of Canada* 1991, 164). In the chief justice's opinion this action by the manager, although based on established policy, was not a 'law' and so did not satisfy the section 1 requirement that a limit on the freedom be 'prescribed by law.' Therefore the restriction was not justified under section 1.

McLachlin J.

McLachlin J. adopted what she regarded as the reasonable 'middle ground' on the issue of communicative access to state property, 'between the extremes of the right to expression on all government property and the right to expression on none' (*Commonwealth of Canada* 1991, 242).[10] She thought that if the state had 'the absolute right to prohibit and regulate expression on all property which it owns,' as an incident of its ownership, the purpose of freedom of expression – to permit members of society to communicate their ideas and values to others – would be subverted' (*Commonwealth of Canada* 1991, 230). She also rejected as extreme the position that any denial of communicative access to government-owned property violates freedom of expression and, unless justified under section 1, violates the Charter.[11] Her argument against this 'extreme' position was based on her understanding of the values underlying freedom of expression. She believed that the purposes of freedom of expression do not justify 'conferring on the public a constitutional right to express itself publicly on *all* public property, regardless of its use and function' (*Commonwealth of Canada* 1991, 231).

Adopting the approach set out by the Supreme Court in its earlier judgment of *Irwin Toy* 1989, McLachlin J. said that in reviewing any state restriction on communication (including a restriction on communicative access to state property), a court must ask whether the impugned state act has as its purpose the restriction of expression or whether it has only the effect of restricting expression. If the state act has as its purpose the restriction of expression, then it will violate section 2(b) and, unless it can be justified under the terms of section 1, it will violate the Charter. However, if the state act has simply the effect of restricting expression, it will be found to violate section 2(b) only if those attacking its constitutionality can show that the restricted expression (including its time, place, and manner) advances one of the values underlying the freedom, such as truth, democracy, or self-realization.

According to Madame Justice McLachlin, a restriction on communicative access to state-owned property that is based on the incompatibility of access with the state's use of its property, and not on the content of the communication, will violate section 2(b) only if the restricted communication can be shown to advance the values underlying the constitutional protection of freedom of expression.[12] The court should consider 'whether the forum's relationship with the particular expressive activity invokes any of the values and principles underlying the guarantee' (*Commonwealth of Canada* 1991, 238). The analysis under section 2(b) 'should focus on determining when, as a general proposition, the right to expression on government property arises' (*Commonwealth of Canada* 1991, 236).

If the court decides that access to the particular property would not have advanced the freedom's values, it will find no violation of section 2(b). According to McLachlin J., this threshold test should screen out cases that clearly fall outside the scope of section 2(b). However, 'the threshold should not be so high that persons with legitimate claims are prevented from establishing them' (*Commonwealth of Canada* 1991, 232).

If, on the other hand, the court decides that the restricted access would have advanced the values underlying freedom of expression, the restriction will be found to violate section 2(b). The court must then consider whether the restriction is justified under section 1. In making this judgment the court will weigh and balance the conflicting interests – 'the individual's interest in using the forum in question for his or her expressive purposes against the state's interest in limiting the expression on the particular property' (*Commonwealth of Canada* 1991, 237). In its section 1 analysis, the court should ask the following questions: 'How suitable is the location for the effective communication of the message to the public? Does the property in question have special symbolic significance for the message being communicated? Are there other public arenas in the vicinity in which expression can be disseminated? In short what does the claimant lose by being denied the opportunity to spread his or her message in the form and at the time and place asserted?' (*Commonwealth of Canada* 1991, 250).

According to McLachlin J., constitutional protection of access should extend 'to expression on some but not all government property' (*Commonwealth of Canada* 1991, 236).[13] She thought that communicative access to certain state-owned properties, 'private' state properties such as prison cells, judge's private chambers, private government offices, and publicly owned broadcasting facilities, would not advance the values of democracy, truth, and autonomy. She considered it self-evident that the purposes of freedom of expression would not be served by public expression in these places: 'These are not places of public debate aimed at promoting either the truth or a better understanding of social and political issues. Nor is expression in these places related to the open and welcoming environment essential to the maximization of individual fulfillment and human flourishing' (*Commonwealth of Canada* 1991, 241). A restriction on communicative access to a 'private' state-owned property will not violate section 2(b) and so will not require justification under section 1.

On the other hand, McLachlin J. considered that the purposes of the guarantee of free expression are served by protecting expression in public forums, 'places which have by tradition or designation been dedicated to public expression' (*Commonwealth of Canada* 1991, 241). The use of these places for political, social, or artistic expression 'would clearly seem to be linked to the values underlying the guarantee of free speech' (*Commonwealth of Canada* 1991, 241). A restriction on communicative access to a 'public forum' will violate section 2(b) and so will require justification under section 1.

Madame Justice McLachlin believed that the task at the section 2(b) stage is 'primarily definitional rather than one of balancing' (*Commonwealth of Canada* 1991, 237). The limited scope of the section 2(b) right to communicate on state-owned property is based 'on the values and interests' that underlie freedom of expression and not on the characteristics of particular government properties. Nevertheless, her application of the section 2(b) test seems to yield a categorical distinction between public and private state-owned properties (forums). Her approach results not simply in the exclusion of particular access claims to state-owned property but in the general insulation of a particular, although perhaps very small, set of state properties from all claims of access.[14]

McLachlin J. claimed to derive a public/private forum distinction from an assessment of the freedom of expression value of access to certain properties.[15] And it may be that in many cases, communicative access to prisons, private government offices, and similar state-owned properties will not generate reflection or debate but will simply interfere with the state's use of its property. But we cannot exclude in every case the possibility that communication on/in one of these properties may advance the values of freedom of expression, particularly if we accept that communication is deserving of protection even when it is disruptive or confrontational.[16] The judgment that certain state properties (private forums) should be insulated from all claims of access must rest, at least in part, on the detrimental impact of communicative access on the state's use of these properties – such as the impact on prison security and discipline, prisoner privacy, or the administrative and other costs of compromising the state's absolute control over a publicly owned broadcast facility.

The initial classification of a state property as either public or private rests not simply, as McLachlin J. claimed, on an assessment of the contribution of particular instances of communicative access to the values that underlie the freedom (a vague standard in any event). Rather, it rests on an intuitive understanding of the compatibility of public communication with the state's property use. Moreover, Madame Justice McLachlin's approach does not merely balance the costs and benefits of communicative access. The categorical distinction between public and private state-owned properties seems to give priority to state property use over communicative access claims. As well, the classification of properties as either public or private seems to rest on a judgment about the *general* compatibility of expression with the state use of the property and not on an assessment of the compatibility of access in specific cases. As soon as a property is classified as a private forum (if expression is generally incompatible with the property's use) then no expression need be permitted, including instances of expression that might not significantly disrupt state property use.[17]

L'Heureux-Dubé J.

Madame Justice L'Heureux-Dubé took the view that any time the state restricts expression on its property it violates section 2(b) and must justify the restriction under section 1. She thought that the balancing of competing individual and state interests should take place under section 1. In her view, no other approach fits with the broad construction the Supreme Court has given to section 2(b) in its earlier decisions.[18] Any restriction of expression on state property must satisfy the rationality, minimum impairment, and proportionality standards of section 1. She suggested, however, that these standards should not be applied strictly in access cases.[19]

In the case before the court, L'Heureux-Dubé J. found that the airport's restriction on communication in its public areas violated section 2(b) and was not justified under section 1. In her view the regulation violated section 2(b) because its effect, if not its purpose, was to restrict political expression. She considered that airports had become 'contemporary crossroads,' the functional equivalent of other public thoroughfares, and so should be on the same 'constitutional footing' as streets and parks (*Commonwealth of Canada* 1991, 205).

According to L'Heureux-Dubé J. the restriction could not be justified under section 1. She thought that the restriction was so vague that it did not constitute a limit prescribed by law: an individual reading this regulation would not be able to tell whether his or her conduct was proscribed. Furthermore, she considered that the restriction was too broad to constitute a reasonable limit on freedom of expression. It seemed to cover 'just about any activity' in the airport. A restriction that banned all commercial and political expression in the public areas of the airport had 'no rational connection' with the objectives of security and efficiency put forward by the government (*Commonwealth of Canada* 1991, 223).

When setting out what she believed should be the courts' general approach to communicative access issues, Madame Justice L'Heureux-Dubé called for a flexible balancing of competing state and individual interests under section 1: '[w]hen calibrating the s.1 barometer, the political quality of the stifled expression must be weighed against whatever governmental arguments are raised in opposition. [Section 1] enables us to construct *a contextual rather than a categorical approach*, focusing not only on the scope of the right, but also on the setting in which the freedom of expression claim is made' (*Commonwealth of Canada* 1991, 192)[20] [emphasis added].

L'Heureux-Dubé J. rejected the 'rigid categorization' of the American public forum doctrine. In her view, 'certain government restrictions cannot be automatically excised from the section 2(b) guarantee strictly on the basis that they do not apply to locations traditionally associated with public expression' (*Commonwealth of Canada* 1991, 192). She believed that '[a]n overly rigid characterization focusing exclusively on place would tend to lose sight of the forest for the trees. The First Amendment as well as the Canadian Charter of Rights and Freedoms were designed to protect people not places' (*Commonwealth of Canada* 1991, 202).

However, L'Heureux-Dubé J. also thought that certain state properties could, as a matter of fact, be described as public arenas (a term she used to distinguish her approach from the American public forum doctrine), in the sense that they are generally open to the public and can easily accommodate public communication. She accepted that the public character of these properties was 'relevant when evaluating what is a reasonable restriction on "place" in the review of a time, place, and manner regulation' under section 1 (*Commonwealth of Canada* 1991, 190).[21]

L'Heureux-Dubé J. also believed that a guarantee that encompasses all government property 'is not necessary to fulfill the *Charter*'s purposes, or to avoid a stifling of free expression' (*Commonwealth of Canada* 1991, 198). In her view, 'some but not all, government-owned property is constitutionally open to the public for engaging in expressive activity' (*Commonwealth of Canada* 1991, 198). More specifically, she said that 'the *Charter*'s framers did not intend internal government offices, air traffic control towers, prison cells and Judges' Chambers to be made available for leafleting or demonstrations' (*Commonwealth of Canada* 1991, 198). 'It is evident,' she said, 'that the right to freedom of expression under section 2(b) of the *Charter* does not provide a right of access to all property whether public or private' (*Commonwealth of Canada* 1991, 198).[22]

This sounds very similar to the reasoning that led McLachlin J. to conclude that communication on certain state-owned properties does not fall within the scope of section 2(b). However, according to L'Heureux-Dubé J., the insulation of these 'private' state properties from all access claims is the outcome of 'balancing' under section 1 and not of the definition of the freedom's scope under section 2(b). She thought that '[r]estrictions on expression in particular places will be harder to defend than in others. In some places the justifiability of the restrictions is immediately apparent' (*Commonwealth of Canada* 1991, 198–9).

When determining which properties are 'appropriately open for public expression and bear the earmarks of "public arenas",' L'Heureux-Dubé J. argued that the courts should consider such things as 'the traditional openness of such property for expressive activity'; 'whether the public is ordinarily admitted to the property as of right'; 'the compatibility of the property's purpose with such expressive activities'; 'the impact of the availability of such property for expressive activity on the achievement of section 2(b)'s purpose'; and 'the availability of other public arenas in the vicinity for expressive activities' (*Commonwealth of Canada* 1991, 203).[23]

These factors are to be taken into account when deciding whether a particular state property qualifies as a public arena. Madame Justice L'Heureux-Dubé advocates a flexible balancing of competing interests, yet her approach under section 1 is to divide state properties into two (or more?) categories, public arenas and private state properties (or what I will awkwardly call 'private arenas') by making a general judgment about the compatibility of access with the state's property use. This focus on the general character of different state properties and the division of these properties into two categories seems to limit, and perhaps even to preclude, consideration of specific access claims.

Madame Justice L'Heureux-Dubé insisted that 'the rights and freedoms do not extend to the locations, but rather to the people occupying them' even though 'people's expectations may be affected by where they find themselves' (*Commonwealth of Canada* 1991, 202). Nevertheless, the decision to attach the label public or private arena to a particular property is the critical step in Madame Justice L'Heureux-Dubé's section 1 approach. It matters how a state-owned property is classified, because the two kinds of place seem to attract different standards of review. If a property is classified as a public arena, public communication must be permitted unless the state can show good reasons for restricting it. In the words of L'Heureux-Dubé J., 'those areas tradition- ally associated with, or resembling, sites where all persons have a right to express their views by any means at their disposal, should be vigi- lantly protected from legislative restrictions on speech' (*Commonwealth of Canada* 1991, 225).[24] In the case of properties that are not public arenas, however, restrictions on access will always be justified. It is un- clear whether there is a middle category of properties, in/on which access should be accommodated and state use compromised when nec- essary to ensure communicative opportunity.

Compatibility and the Public/Private Arena Distinction

The judgments of Lamer C.J. and L'Heureux-Dubé and McLachlin JJ. recognized that discussion of public issues would be seriously impeded if private citizens did not have some right to communicate on state- owned property. Thus all three rejected the argument that state-owned property is simply part of the background to Charter review and insu- lated from all claims of access. Yet, at the same time, they were unwill- ing to subject the restriction of communicative access to the ordinary section 1 standard, which provides that a particular restriction will vio- late the Charter unless it is supported by substantial reasons. They were unwilling to regard the constitutional question as simply whether the state's use of its property is important enough to justify a restriction on the basic right of the individual to communicate wherever and when- ever he or she chooses. Instead, the three judgments seemed to give the state's property use priority over the individual's right to communi- cate and to avoid a simple balancing of competing interests in indi- vidual cases. Lamer C.J. gave explicit priority to the state's property use. Under his approach, only expression that is compatible with the state's property use is protected under section 2(b) of the Charter. McLachlin and L'Heureux-Dubé JJ. gave a form of priority to state property use by introducing a version of the public forum doctrine into the standard freedom of expression analysis. McLachlin J. relied on the distinction between public and private forums/arenas when defining the freedom's scope under section 2(b); L'Heureux-Dubé J. relied on the distinction when balancing competing state and expression inter- ests under section 1.

Instead of making a judgment in each case about the compatibility of a particular access claim with the state's property use, McLachlin and

L'Heureux-Dubé JJ. appeared to make a general threshold judgment about the compatibility of communicative access with the state's property use.[25] The classification of a particular property as either a public or private arena (to use the term preferred by L'Heureux-Dubé J.) is based on the property's importance as a forum for communication and the general compatibility of public communication with the state's use of the property. Sometimes the test seems to be whether the property is, by tradition or designation, open to public expression. Other times, it is whether access is generally compatible with the state's use of the property. The first way of putting the test suggests that the courts should defer to established practice or to the judgment of the state that access is either incompatible or compatible with its property use. The second way suggests that the courts must judge the compatibility issue. Different standards of review apply to each of the categories of state-owned property. If a property is classified as a public arena, because communicative access is reasonably compatible with its use by the state, the state may have to make some efforts to accommodate communication, even if this involves some (albeit very minor) compromise of the state's chosen use. On the other hand, those state properties that are considered private arenas, because communicative access is generally incompatible with their use by the state, will be insulated from all claims of access.

All three judges were unwilling to require any significant compromise of the state's property use in order to accommodate communication, and instead required only that the state permit expression that is compatible (either specifically or generally) with its property use. There are a number of reasons that may explain this reluctance.

The members of the court may have been reluctant to treat property ownership as irrelevant or insignificant in the resolution of a dispute involving competing use claims. The system of property rights seems to provide a stable context for individual and collective activity, giving different individuals and groups exclusive control over certain resources and settling the problem of competing claims. More generally, property is such a fundamental part of the social order that it was difficult for the members of the court to give no weight whatsoever to the state's ownership of a particular place or facility. Or, put another way, property is so fundamental that, although the members of the court were not prepared to see it as lying entirely outside the scope of judicial review, they were inclined to regard a judicially defined right of access as a special exception to the exclusive control of the property owner. If communicative access requires the owner to surrender part of his or her established rights, it should be exceptional.

If the courts did not adopt a compatibility standard, they would have to second-guess the state's judgment about the use of its property and make potentially controversial decisions about the importance of particular state policies. For these reasons, the courts may choose not only to adopt a compatibility standard but also to defer to the state's judgment about when expression is compatible with its property use. The court may defer to state claims of incompatibility in a particular case or it may show deference by requiring access only to public arenas, properties that the state has itself opened to public discourse. A judgment about compatibility will rest on a particular understanding of the state's use of the property (a prison or a roadway) and may involve considerations that are complex and technical (the requirements of prison security; the economic and safety costs of accommodating demonstrations on the roads). A court cannot anticipate all the ways in which the state's use of its property will be affected by a decision to allow communication on the property (Post 1995, 262).

However, the principal reason for the judges' reluctance to compromise state property use, and their interest in a public forum approach, stems from the distributive character of the access issue. The access issue is not as Madame Justice L'Heureux-Dubé described it, 'a classic confrontation between the acknowledged value of political expression and legitimate government interests in imposing certain restrictions on expression generally' (*Commonwealth of Canada* 1991, 166). It is instead a confrontation or competition between different uses of state-owned property, a distributive issue that does not fit easily into the established model of rights adjudication.

Under the established model, freedom of expression is understood as a liberty that individuals have unless and until interfered with by the state. The court asks first whether the restricted activity is expression protected under section 2(b) and second, whether the state act that restricts the protected expression represents an interest significant enough to justify the restriction. However, the issue raised by a restriction on access to state-owned property is not simply whether the value of the restriction is substantial enough to justify interference with important expressive activity. The justification of a restriction on access depends significantly on whether the government's use of the property leaves adequate space for public communication or for the public expression of particular views.

The state may be justified in restricting access that interferes in either a large or small way with its property use, provided there are a variety of other forums open to public communication. In such a circumstance, a minor government function, or a less than compelling government purpose, should not be defeated or hindered simply because it involves a restriction on access to a particular property. On the other hand, however, if there are not adequate alternatives, perhaps the state should be required to compromise its property use and permit access.

A balancing of competing property use claims (the state's use of its property versus the importance of the freedom to communicate on/in these properties) should turn in part on whether or not the individual seeking access has other communicative options. It should take account of both the availability and the adequacy of the alternatives for individual speakers and for particular viewpoints. A political protest, for example, may be less powerful if it is held in a park located on the outskirts of the city rather than on the grounds of the City Hall. Of course, access to the park for a political protest may become very important if for some reason the protest cannot take place at the City Hall.

However, the adjudicative process is not suited to the assessment of communicative opportunities/alternatives. Even if the underlying concern of the courts is the adequacy of opportunities for communication in the overall system, the courts' attention is focused on a point in the system, a particular state restriction on access. This focus makes it difficult for the courts to assess the adequacy of the spaces available for public communication and to make the systemic adjustments necessary to achieve a fair compromise between the requirements of public communication and the demands of government policy. How is a court to judge the availability of alternatives to a forum such as Dorval Airport? The right of access to an alternative forum will depend, in part, on whether the individual has a right of access to the Dorval Airport (the very question before the court) and to other properties (a question not directly before the court).

A judgment about alternatives in a particular case can only be made if there is a reasonably stable background of communication rights and restrictions, perhaps in the form of recognized public and private forums, classified on the basis of either the state's practice of allowing or prohibiting communication on the property or the courts' judgment that communication is generally compatible or incompatible with the ordinary state use of the property. Any approach that tries to be open and flexible and to judge the importance of access to a particular property (taking account of the available alternatives) seems inevitably to rely on assumptions about the background of communicative alternatives and ultimately to evolve into a version of the public forum doctrine, which sets different review standards for different classes of property.

The requirement that the state accommodate expression on/in a public forum/arena rests on a general conclusion that compelling access for communication will not (significantly) impair the state's use of the property and on an assumption that the property is an important forum for communication. The complete insulation of a private forum/arena from access claims rests on a general conclusion that public communication will interfere significantly with the state's property use and on an assumption that as long as communication is permitted on/ in other properties, which are considered public forums/arenas, there will be adequate space for public communication.

The Instability of the Different Tests

All three judgments in the *Commonwealth of Canada* 1991 sought to make the access issue manageable within the adjudicative structure – to contain the distributive dimension of the issue – by giving priority to state use (but not ownership) of its property. Lamer C.J. did this with a compatibility test, which asks whether a particular claim of access is compatible with the state's property use. In contrast, McLachlin and L'Heureux-Dubé JJ., relying on a public/private arena distinction, judged compatibility as a general matter: is expression generally compatible with the state use of the property or is the property generally open to the public for expression? However, the tests put forward in each judgment are ambiguous and sometimes contradictory. All three judgments are characterized by a tension between a commitment to ensuring that there is adequate space for public discourse and a reluctance to engage in an open-ended and potentially unmanageable assessment of the adequacy of communicative opportunities.

(a) The instability of the public/private distinction. The division of state property into public and private forums/arenas represents an unstable compromise between competing institutional concerns: on the one hand,

a commitment to a broad-based freedom of expression protected by the courts and, on the other hand, a reluctance to second-guess legislative judgment about what is necessary to the effective operation of its property and a desire to contain the open-ended character of the access decision. The line between public arenas (and the accommodation of public expression) and private arenas (and the exclusion of public expression) will be pulled in one direction by the demands of freedom of expression to protect a wider range of opportunities for public discourse in general and to protect specific instances of compatible expression that may be excluded in the general assessment of compatibility. The pull will be greater when the unstated assumptions about alternative forums do not seem to hold. The dividing line will be pushed in the opposite direction by the desire to contain the judicial assessment of communicative opportunity and judicial second-guessing of state claims that access is incompatible with its property use.

According to McLachlin J., her test 'offers sufficient flexibility to permit development of a legal doctrine sensitive to emerging concerns and new situations' (*Commonwealth of Canada* 1991, 242). However, the use of the public arena/private arena categories is meant to limit some of this flexibility and to avoid ad hoc balancing. In the case of some of the properties described by McLachlin and L'Heureux-Dubé JJ. as private arenas, the detrimental impact of communicative access on the state's use might be significant enough to outweigh the value of every access claim, particularly if we assume a reasonably stable background of alternative opportunities to communicate in public arenas such as streets and parks. But with other properties that might be classed as private arenas there may be certain kinds of expression that will not interfere significantly with the state's use (e.g., Lamer C.J.'s example of the silent protest in the Parliamentary Library or perhaps even controlled access to a prison).

More significantly, there may be times when access is so important that the state should be required to accommodate communication even if this involves compromising its property use. Sometimes there may be no adequate alternative location for the communication of a particular message. While the need to ensure safety and security at a prison will justify the restriction of most claims of access, there may be some claims of access that should be permitted. For example, there will be little opportunity for the public to supervise the operation of the prison system if the press and representatives of public interest groups are denied any form of access. It is unclear whether the tests suggested by McLachlin and L'Heureux-Dubé JJ. will accommodate exceptional access claims.

The distinction between public and private arenas, relied on by L'Heureux-Dubé and McLachlin JJ., rests on a general conclusion about the compatibility of public communication with the state's use of the particular property. However, the location of the line separating public arenas (the accommodation of access) and private arenas (the giving of priority to the state's property use) will depend on the decision makers' assumptions about the need for space for public discourse. The public arena category will be broadly defined by the courts, with little deference to the state (and some degree of compromise demanded of it), if courts believe that public discourse requires greater space. I note that Madame Justice McLachlin insisted that 'the threshold should not be set so high that persons with legitimate claims are prevented from establishing them' (*Commonwealth of Canada* 1991, 232). Again, it is unclear from the judgments of L'Heureux-Dubé and McLachlin JJ. whether there might also be a middle category, a category of state properties that are neither public nor private arenas, and, if there is such a category, how large it might be.

The court's definition of the shape or scope of a particular public or private arena will also be affected by concerns about effective alternatives.[26] Forums/arenas do not come neatly packaged with clear and fixed parameters. A private arena may be narrowly defined, carved from a larger arena – a judge's chambers rather than a courthouse or a prison cell rather than a prison. The narrow definition of a private arena may rest on a recognition that if the state is permitted to restrict all instances of expression throughout the courthouse or the prison, important communication, for which there is no alternative outlet, will be silenced.

The line separating public and private arenas is bound to be unstable. There is simply no correct or obvious place to draw the line between those properties that are generally compatible with expression and must be open to public communication, unless the state can show good and strong reasons for restricting the particular form of communication, and those which are generally incompatible with public communication and are insulated from all claims of access, regardless of the merits of the specific claim. If the courts take seriously the Charter's commitment to freedom of expression, they will define the category of private arenas narrowly. However, if the courts feel uncomfortable with the task of reviewing the state's property use, the category will be broadly defined.

(b) The instability of the compatibility test. Chief Justice Lamer gave priority to the state's use of its property by limiting the protection of section 2(b) to expression that is compatible with the state's property use. This approach no doubt rests on an assumption that there are adequate alternatives for individual communication so that it is not necessary for the state to compromise its property use.

A compatibility standard may be applied strictly so that the access right is limited significantly. It is almost always possible to find that a particular act of communication is incompatible or inconsistent, to some degree, with the state's property use because it causes some disruption or inconvenience. For example, it might be argued that communication by religious and other groups on street corners is 'incompatible' with the ordinary use of the streets because it impedes the flow of pedestrian or automobile traffic.[27] Chief Justice Lamer sought to avoid this possibility by narrowing the test under section 2(b) to incompatibility with the *fundamental* purpose, or the *very* or *principal* function, of the place.[28] But what is the principal function of the place and how will the courts distinguish it from minor aspects of the state's use of the property? By what standards should the courts measure the trade-off between minor uses of the property and competing communicative access claims? Will a minor interference with the principal function of the state property always be excluded from the protection of section 2(b)?[29]

Because compatibility is a relative idea, there is every reason to think that other factors will enter into the analysis, affecting the strictness/flexibility of the test. The application of the compatibility standard is easily influenced by a desire to accommodate important access claims. The chief justice's standard of incompatibility may also apply differently depending on the 'public' or 'private' character of the property. The state may be required to suffer a degree of inconvenience or disruption when access is sought to a property that has traditionally been open to the public. However, in the case of a property that has not been open to the public, the state may not be required to compromise its use in any way.

Any attempt to define the compatibility test so that it does not result in broad findings of incompatibility opens the door to some balancing of competing interests. When important access claims are made, the courts may insist on a tighter connection between the state's use of the property and the exclusion of communication and they may push the state to accommodate some communication and to suffer a degree of interference with its use of the property. Although formally excluded under a compatibility test, the demands of freedom of expression re-enter the analysis, affecting the shape and standard of the compatibility requirement. Of course, the balancing of competing state and individual interests occurs under section 2(b) rather than under section 1 and is hidden behind the vague language of compatibility.

Conclusion

The judgments of Lamer C.J. and McLachlin and L'Heureux-Dubé JJ. in *Commonwealth of Canada* 1991 present different approaches to the issue of public communication on state-owned property. Each approach represents an attempt to fit the access issue into the established model of freedom of expression adjudication. (Indeed, all three judgments claimed to follow the adjudicative steps set out by the court in *Irwin Toy* 1989.) All three judgments held that the state cannot without reason exclude communication from its property. But none of the judgments was prepared to engage in an open-ended review of state property use and require the state to justify every restriction on communicative access under the terms of section 1.

With all three approaches, the effort to contain the scope of review is unstable. Chief Justice Lamer put forward a test of consistency or compatibility of communicative access with the state's property use. However, the compatibility standard is vague and malleable. In applying this standard the courts are bound to draw on a variety of considerations, such as the importance of the access claimed and the availability of alternative forums. The chief justice's formal test, which seeks to avoid the second-guessing of government property use and the assessment of alternative forums, may be eroded to an uncertain degree by a recognition that access to state-owned property is vital to the exercise of freedom of expression and that opportunities for public communication, generally, or for the communication of a particular viewpoint, may be inadequate.

With the approaches of McLachlin and L'Heureux-Dubé JJ. much turns on whether the property is classified as a public arena/forum or a private arena/forum. Yet it is difficult to know when these labels will be attached. The insulation of certain properties from all claims of access rests on a desire to limit judicial review of the state's property use. However, working against this is a wish to ensure adequate space for public discourse in all its forms.

Subsequent cases confirm the court's uncertainty as to how the access issue should be fitted into an adjudicative framework. In *Ramsden* 1993, for example, the Supreme Court of Canada struck down a municipal by-law that prohibited the posting of notices on public property, including telephone poles. Mr Justice Iacobucci for the court declined to commit to a single approach to the access issue. Instead, he applied all three of the approaches set out in *Commonwealth of Canada* 1991 and found the ban on notices to be unconstitutional under each. The court's unwillingness to settle on a single approach to the issue is not surprising. Each of the approaches taken in *Commonwealth of Canada* 1991 claims to be faithful to the general structure of Charter adjudication. However, the access issue cannot be made to fit neatly into this structure. Each approach represents an unstable compromise between an open-ended and flexible assessment of communicative opportunity and a manageable standard of review.

3. Access to Private Property

Perhaps too much time is spent worrying about the right of access to state property. Public meeting places, the places where individuals gather and interact, are increasingly owned by private corporations (Bakan 1997, 68; Moon 1988a, 362). Individuals interact in shopping malls and office buildings. More significantly, the scale of political community has grown to such an extent that meaningful public expression is no longer conducted face-to-face, by speaking at community meetings or handing out leaflets on the street corner (or in the shopping mall).[30] Public discourse is instead 'mediated.' It takes place in the pages of privately owned daily newspapers or in the programs of privately owned television and radio stations. Members of the community rely on these media to provide them with information and ideas and are inclined to view the ideas expressed in leaflets or from soapboxes as eccentric. The assumption is that if it is not in the newspaper or on the television then it cannot be a serious or important opinion.[31] Communicative access to the streets matters not because influential public debate takes place there but because the streets may be the only forum for those unable to gain access to the media. As well, access to state property, such as the front steps of the legislative building, is sometimes important to an individual or group because it enables them to conduct a public show/demonstration that is then reported by the media to a larger audience.

In *Commonwealth of Canada* 1991, L'Heureux-Dubé J. 'left for another day' the issue of communicative access to private property (*Commonwealth of Canada* 1991, 197). McLachlin J., however, thought that it was 'clear that section 2(b) confers no right to use private property as a forum for expression' (*Commonwealth of Canada* 1991, 228).[32] It is true that constitutional claims of access to privately owned property do not have much promise, given the court's commitment to a 'government action' doctrine. In a series of cases, the Supreme Court of Canada has said that the Charter applies only to government action that interferes with an individual's Charter rights.[33] Private action that interferes with an individual's freedom of expression may be prohibited by provincial or federal law, but it is not subject to review under the Charter.[34]

There are, however, two significant stress points in the government action doctrine, either of which may provide a possible entry for limited communicative access rights to 'privately owned' property (Moon 1988a, 357). Both stem from the fact that private actors can act as they do only because laws permit or empower them to do so. The first point of stress in the government action doctrine is the issue of when the state is responsible under the Charter for the actions that it has empowered private parties to perform. The second is the issue of when an individual or organization can be considered a state actor because it exercises powers that have been delegated to it by the state.

If private power depends on state authority, the state may be seen as bearing some responsibility for the wrongs committed by private actors. For example, when it enforces a privately negotiated restrictive covenant (which prohibits the future sale of a property to the members of a particular racial or religious group) the state may be seen as participating in an act of discrimination (*Shelley* 1948). Along the same lines, because it has empowered property owners to exclude expression from their property, the state might be seen as ultimately responsible for the owners' exclusion decisions.

Yet this may involve too great an erosion of the government action doctrine. All private action can be traced back to some form of state action. Unless we are willing to discard the doctrine entirely, we cannot hold the state responsible for a private wrong simply because it has permitted a private actor to control a particular resource or exercise a particular power. If the state has not actively supported or encouraged the private wrong but has simply empowered private parties to control their property as they choose, what wrong can we attribute to the state? The state has not itself excluded anyone from the property; it has simply established a system of ownership rights that permit exclusion by private actors. The focus of any review by the courts would not be on the acceptability of the private owner's decision to exclude another from his or her property but would instead be on the legitimacy of the state-created system of property rights (Moon 1988b, 367). While we may have real concerns about the state's allocation of communicative resources/opportunities in the community, it is very doubtful that this sort of distributive injustice can be identified and remedied in an adjudicative structure.

The other stress point in the government action doctrine also rests on the recognition that private power derives from government action; however, it takes this recognition in another direction. When the state delegates power to an otherwise private actor, that actor may be viewed as exercising state power and as clothed with state authority. However, not just any delegation of power by the state will be sufficient to make the actor a 'state' agent – otherwise all private parties would be considered state actors (extensions of the state) and all private action would be considered government action, subject to Charter review. The question is what kind or degree of power delegation is sufficient to turn a private actor into a reviewable state actor? One answer is that an otherwise 'private' actor becomes a state actor when the state delegates to him or her the power to perform a public function. The category of state actors would then include entities that perform important functions traditionally associated with the state.

The courts in the United States adopted an approach of this sort in *Marsh* 1946, where it was held that the decision of a company-owned town to exclude communication from its streets was subject to constitutional review. The court held that the company's decision to exclude communication from its property (and its use of the State of Alabama's trespass law) to enforce that decision was subject to review under the First Amendment because the town was 'operated primarily to benefit the public' and its operation was 'essentially a public function' (*Marsh* 1946, 506). According to the court, the streets and parks of the company town were the 'functional equivalents' of state properties. The State of Alabama had permitted the company to 'use its property as a town, operate a "business block" in the town and a street and sidewalk on that block' (*Marsh* 1946, 507).

In *Marsh* 1946, the constitutional wrong was said to be the application of the state trespass law, rather than the company's decision to exclude expression. However, since the state could be said to permit any and every exercise of 'private' power, it was the 'public' character of the role played by the company that made the application of the trespass law different in this case. And so even if Alabama was the subject of the claim (being prevented from enforcing its trespass law) the focus of the claim was on the public function performed by the company and the company's decision not to permit communication on its property.

In *Logan Valley* 1968, the U.S. Supreme Court applied the reasoning in *Marsh* 1946 to shopping malls. A group of individuals wanted to picket a non-union store in the mall but were denied access to the mall property by its owner. Mr Justice Marshall for the majority of the court held that 'because the shopping mall serves as the community business block and is freely accessible and open to people in the area and those passing through [*Marsh* 1946] ... the State may not delegate the power through the use of its trespass law, wholly to exclude those members of the public wishing to exercise their First Amendment rights on the premises in a manner and for a purpose generally consonant with the use to which the property is actually put' (*Logan Valley* 1968, 319). However, *Logan Valley* 1968 was overturned by the U.S. Supreme Court in *Hudgens* 1976. The Court in *Hudgens* 1976 recognized that once the public function rule was applied to shopping malls, it became difficult to contain the rule and maintain a commitment to the 'state action' doctrine.

In Canada the extension of access rights to privately owned properties that perform a 'public function' may be difficult, in light of some of the Supreme Court's statements about the application of the Charter of Rights. In cases concerning the applicability of the Charter to hospitals and universities, the Supreme Court has said that the key question is not whether the institution performs a public function but whether the institution is effectively under the direction of government (*McKinney* 1990, 273–4).[35] If an institution, such as a university, has significant autonomy in the governance of its affairs, it will not be subject to Charter review, even though it may perform an important public function.[36]

Even if the Canadian courts were to extend access rights to private properties that resemble traditional public forums, the significance of such an extension should not be overstated.[37] Significant public discourse takes place in the media and it seems very unlikely that any court will be prepared to treat a daily newspaper or television broadcast station as a 'public forum' that must be opened up to diverse views under the Charter (Moon 1988a, 374; *Trieger* 1988; *Reform Party* 1995).[38] Access rights to the media may be too complex for constitutional definition. What we should hope for from the courts, however, is that they not interfere with legislative efforts to open the media up to a wider range of voices and views.[39] As discussed in the next chapter, the courts have been prepared in some cases to hold that legislative efforts to open up privately owned communicative forums, such as newspapers, to different viewpoints violates the property owner's freedom of expression.

4. A Note on State Support for Expression

The Canadian courts have not been prepared to impose on the state a general obligation to support expression. This reluctance is understandable. It is difficult to imagine what shape a constitutional obligation to support expression could take. At what point would we say that the communicative opportunities of some or all members of the community are so inadequate or that public discourse is so narrow in its scope that the state has a constitutional obligation to support communication?

More controversially, the Canadian courts have also been unwilling to impose on the state a limited obligation to ensure that any support program it establishes is operated in an even-handed way.[40] Yet, for the same reasons that it is difficult to define a general state obligation to support communicative opportunity, it may also be difficult to determine when a state-created program, such as an arts subsidy, violates constitutional standards of fairness (other than those relating to the right to equality under section 15 of the Charter).

When the state supports or subsidizes expression it makes choices between different speakers or different messages, giving support to some and refusing support to others. Unless we believe that state allocation decisions should be entirely random, the decision to give or deny support must rest on state views (or the views of state-appointed decision makers) about the relative value of different forms or instances of expression. In the case of an arts subsidy program, for example, the state chooses among different applicants on grounds such as aesthetic merit or artistic medium. If an applicant is unsuccessful because her work has been judged aesthetically inferior to that of other applicants, we do not ordinarily consider that the state has violated her freedom of expression rights. It is also generally accepted that the government is entitled to express, or lend its support to, particular views, such as national unity, the protection of Canadian culture, or the need for greater crime control.

Yet sometimes when the state declines to give support to a speaker, or decides to withdraw support from him or her, we view the state decision not as a failure to support the speaker, which involves no constitutional wrong, but instead as a wrongful attempt to suppress or marginalize the speaker's viewpoint.[41] Whether we view a state allocation decision as support for speech or as suppression of speech will depend on our understanding of the purpose, scope, and stability of the particular support program. Certain state programs of support for expression are so well established, so broad in scope, and so much a part of the public sphere that a decision by the state to withhold support from a particular speaker or group of speakers, or from a particular viewpoint, seems much like state censorship.

The most obvious example of such a 'program' is the dedication of certain state properties, such as streets and parks, to public interaction. Some state-owned properties, 'public forums,' have become important parts of the public sphere. To deny an individual communicative access to such a property would seem deeply unfair and might have a significant impact on his or her communicative opportunity relative to others. In *Commonwealth of Canada* 1991, the Supreme Court of Canada recognized that if it treated state property as simply part of the background against which individuals exercise their freedom of expression rights, the scope or significance of those rights would be severely reduced. Instead, the court treated exclusion of communication from some or all state properties as a limitation on expression rights under the Charter, and not as a refusal by the state to actively support individual expression.

Similarly, if the state were to deny a controversial newspaper access to the postal service, or if it were to remove from that paper a postal rate subsidy that was available to other newspapers, it would be seen as suppressing or censoring the excluded newspaper (Kreimer 1984, 1318).[42] The postal subsidy is a general support for newspapers (and for public discourse) that newspapers have come to rely on. In this context, the selective removal of such a subsidy would be seen not simply as support for the views of the subsidized papers but as suppression of the views of the excluded paper.

Any time the state denies a general social benefit to an individual because it disagrees with his or her viewpoint, the denial may be seen as censorship. Consider the familiar example of the police officer who declines to protect a speaker from an angry mob because he or she also objects to the message being communicated. The failure to enforce ordinary assault laws in such a case would be experienced by the speaker as state censorship or, at least, as state support for censorship. The individual reasonably expects the state to protect her from unlawful interference with her expression. Assault laws are part of the basic framework within which public discourse takes place. Furthermore, protection from assault rests on concerns or values that are unrelated to the speaker's viewpoint. For these reasons, a state decision not to protect an individual speaker from assault would be viewed as suppression of expression and not simply as a failure to support or protect expression.

Similarly, if the state were to refuse welfare to an individual who expressed views critical of the government, we would consider that the state had interfered with his or her freedom of expression rights. We would view the denial as censorship because the provision of welfare is assumed to rest on criteria unrelated to the character or value of one's contribution to public discourse. Even in the case of an arts subsidy program, where choices must be made between different speakers on the basis of the character or quality of their expression, the state may be precluded from using certain expression-related criteria. The state may grant or deny support on the basis of the artist's medium or the aesthetic quality of his work. It will not, however, be permitted to base its allocation decisions on the artist's political affiliation, his history of political activity, his political message, or any other criteria unrelated to the apparent objectives of an arts subsidy program. Of course, selective subsidy cases will seldom be this straightforward. In most cases the allocation criteria will not so obviously be irrelevant to the legitimate objectives of the subsidy program.

In *Haig* 1993, a case concerned with the right to vote in a referendum, the Supreme Court of Canada suggested that in exceptional situations it might be prepared to hold that the state has not provided support in a manner consistent with freedom of expression. However, the court gave little clue as to how it would go about judging the fairness of criteria adopted by the state for allocating communicative support.

In 1992 the federal government conducted a referendum on a set of proposed amendments to the Canadian Constitution (The 'Charlottetown Accord'). The federal referendum was held in all provinces and territories except Quebec. In Quebec, the provincial government held a separate referendum on the same day and on the same question. The Quebec referendum, however, was conducted in accordance with provincial legislation that varied in certain respects from the federal referendum law. Under the Quebec law, an individual was eligible to vote only if he or she had resided in the province for more than six months prior to the referendum. In contrast, the federal law required only that the individual be ordinarily resident in a particular province on the enumeration date. The plaintiff, Mr Haig, had moved from Ontario to Quebec before the enumeration date. Because he was ordinarily resident in Quebec at the time of enumeration, he was not eligible under federal law to vote in Ontario. Yet, because he had not resided in Quebec for the six-month period required under the provincial law, he was not eligible to vote in Quebec either. Mr Haig argued that his freedom of expression under the Charter was infringed because he was denied the right to vote in the referendum.

Madame Justice L'Heureux-Dubé, on behalf of the court, agreed that the 'casting of a ballot in a referendum is undoubtably a means of expression' (*Haig* 1993, 1034). However, she was not prepared to see the federal government's failure to give Mr Haig a referendum vote as state interference with his freedom of expression. She noted that freedom of expression is generally thought to create 'negative rather than positive entitlements' (*Haig* 1993, 1034). The government is not ordinarily required to provide a 'particular platform to facilitate expression' (*Haig* 1993, 1035). Or, in more colloquial terms, the freedom 'prohibits gags, but does not compel the distribution of megaphones' (*Haig* 1993, 1035).

Yet Madame Justice L'Heureux-Dubé accepted that a 'non-interference' approach may not always ensure the efficient operation of the 'marketplace of ideas.' She suggested that 'positive government action' may sometimes be required to make freedom of expression meaningful (Haig 1993, 1039). She had in mind two kinds of state action: state action to prevent private censorship, for example, police intervention to stop a crowd from silencing a speaker; and state provision of information to the public to ensure 'open government.'[43] If the state fails to act in these ways, it may be found to have violated the individual's constitutional right to free expression.

In any event, L'Heureux-Dubé J. did not think that the case before the court involved one of these exceptional circumstances when state action or intervention is required to ensure freedom of expression. According to L'Heureux-Dubé J., the state is not required to consult its citizens through the particular mechanism of a referendum; to put it another way, citizens have no right to express their views in a referendum. The decision to conduct a referendum is a matter for the legislature. The government 'is under no obligation to extend this platform of expression to anyone, let alone to everyone' (*Haig* 1993, 1041). The argument of L'Heureux-Dubé J. seems to be that if the state is not constitutionally required to provide a particular form of support for expression then it cannot be constitutionally required to allocate support in any particular way.

Yet even if the government is under no obligation to conduct a referendum, once it decides to consult the public in this manner it assumes an obligation to ensure that all citizens are able to participate in a fair way. The government in this case sought reaction to its constitutional proposals not through focus groups or opinion polls, which involve input from a selected (but hopefully representative) group of individuals. A referendum is a process for gauging public reaction to a state initiative but also for gaining democratic legitimacy for that initiative. The significance of a referendum depends on its being broadly democratic. While the government may not have excluded Mr Haig because it disagreed with his political views, his exclusion from voting was arbitrary and unfair. Mr Haig was denied an expressive opportunity (or at least an opportunity to participate in a collective expression of opinion) that was available to other citizens. It is hardly surprising that he experienced this denial as an interference with his freedom of expression.

A year later, in *NWAC* 1994, the Supreme Court of Canada reiterated its view that freedom of expression does not generally give rise to positive claims against the state. Once again the issue involved the constitutional reform process. The federal government had provided funds to four national Aboriginal organizations, the Assembly of First Nations, the Inuit Tapirisat of Canada, the Native Council of Canada, and the Métis Council of Canada to assist their participation in the consultation process that eventually led to the Charlottetown Accord.[44] The Native Women's Association of Canada (NWAC) claimed that their exclusion from direct funding and from direct participation in the consultation process meant that the interests of Aboriginal women were not properly taken into account. The NWAC argued that it had a right under the Charter to be provided with a forum for expression equal to that of the other national Aboriginal organizations, which the NWAC saw as male-dominated and insensitive to the interests of Aboriginal women.

Sopinka J., who wrote for a majority of the Supreme Court of Canada, held that the government decision not to grant equal participation and funding to the NWAC did not violate section 2(b). Sopinka J. took from *Haig* 1993 'the principle that generally the government is under no obligation to fund or provide a specific platform of expression to an individual or group' (*NWAC* 1994, 655).[45] However, Sopinka J. observed that *Haig* 1993 left open 'the possibility that in certain circumstances, positive governmental action may be required in order to make the freedom of expression meaningful' (*NWAC* 1994, 655). He was clear, though, that any government obligation to facilitate expression, or to ensure that its support is provided in an evenhanded way, is very limited: '[I]t cannot be said that every time the Government of Canada chooses to fund or consult a certain group, thereby providing a platform upon which to convey certain views, that the Government is also required to fund a group purporting to represent the opposite point of view. Otherwise the implications of this proposition would be untenable' (*NWAC* 1994, 656).

Sopinka J. could not see how the provision of funding and the invitation to participate in constitutional discussions granted to several national Aboriginal organizations could be understood as stifling expression: 'It did not stifle expression'; rather, it 'facilitated and enhanced the expression of Aboriginal groups' (*NWAC* 1994, 657). 'It will be very rare,' said Sopinka J., 'that the provision of a platform or funding to one or several organizations will have the effect of suppressing another's freedom of expression' (*NWAC* 1994, 657). Indeed, if the issue is framed in this way, it is difficult to imagine any successful claim to support. How could a grant of support to one organization ever be seen as suppressing the expression of another unfunded organization?

Denial of support is experienced as censorship when it occurs as an exclusion from a general program of support and is based on criteria unrelated to the legitimate aims of the program. The claim made by the NWAC was difficult not because the federal government was under no obligation to fund or consult; indeed, the government has an obligation to consult with Aboriginal people before making certain changes to the constitution. It was difficult because consultation (in contrast to a referendum) involves selection. The government must choose which groups or organizations it will consult. In this case, the government chose to consult with four organizations that it saw as broadly representative of the Aboriginal community in Canada. The NWAC argued that the selected organizations did not adequately represent Aboriginal women. The court, however, found no evidence that any of these groups were male dominated and not representative of Aboriginal women or their particular perspective. According to the court, the funded organizations were all 'bona fide' national representatives of Aboriginal people.

Perhaps the court would have been prepared to declare as unconstitutional a government decision that granted funds to an organization with an exclusively male membership but denied funds to a female organization. It would be quite another matter, however, for the court to decide that the four national organizations did not effectively represent the interests of women or any segment of the Aboriginal community. Not only is there a wide range of Aboriginal perspectives and interests that must be 'represented' by the national organizations, there is also a wide range of Aboriginal women's perspectives. It is difficult to imagine a workable constitutional standard for determining whether the full range (the potentially unlimited range) of Aboriginal perspectives has been fairly or adequately represented. (I note that there were many who argued that the NWAC itself did not reflect the views of most Aboriginal women.) The court in *NWAC* 1994 was understandably reluctant to second-guess the government's judgment that the four national Aboriginal organizations adequately represented the interests of all Aboriginal people.[46]

Chapter Seven

Compelled Expression and Freedom of the Press

1. Introduction: The Right to Speak and Not to Speak

Not only is it wrong for the state to prevent an individual from communicating with others, it is also wrong for the state to compel an individual to communicate against his or her will. According to Mr Justice Beetz in *National Bank* (1984), 296: 'The freedoms [freedom of thought, belief, opinion and expression] guarantee to every person the right to express the opinions he may have: afortiori they must prohibit compelling anyone to utter opinions that are not his own.'[1] In this description, the right not to express oneself ('not to speak') is simply the other side of the freedom of expression coin.[2] Whether an individual chooses to speak or not to speak, his or her choice is deserving of respect and protection.

Does it follow, though, that freedom of expression must encompass both a right to speak and a right not to speak? The Charter of Rights does not protect every choice or liberty. Rather, it protects the choice or liberty to engage in activities that are thought to be fundamentally important to the individual and community, activities such as expression or religious worship. Leaving aside those occasions when silence is itself expressive (the most obvious example being a moment of silence), it is not at all clear that silence (non-speech) is as valuable as expression.[3] The right *not* to speak is constitutionally protected because the activity of expression is vitally important to the individual's identity and place in the community and not because silence is as valuable to the individual as expression. The articulation of her thoughts and feelings is so important to the individual that it is a serious affront to have to speak words, to express views, that are not her own.

This understanding of the right not to speak has two important consequences for the definition of its scope. First, if compelled expression is objectionable because it is experienced by the individual as a personal invasion, or as an interference with his or her 'freedom of mind,' then a large and artificial entity such as a corporation cannot have the same claim to freedom from compulsion to communicate. As well, it is unclear to what extent the 'right not to speak' should protect the individual's (or the corporation's) exclusive communicative use of her or his property against state-required access. Certain properties, like clothing, cars, and homes, may be seen as closely connected to the individual and to her or his ability to communicate with others. A state requirement that one of these 'personal' properties be made available for the communicative use of others might well be experienced by the owner as an invasion of his or her personal sphere. However, this would not apply to properties that have no personal significance to the owner. Notably, it would not apply to the property of a large corporation that is held as an investment.

Second, while it is wrong for the state to compel an individual to communicate with others, it does not follow that freedom of expression should support or protect silence in the same way that it supports or protects expression. The constitutional right to freedom of expression is understood principally as a prohibition against direct state censorship. However, because expression is a valuable activity, the freedom also supports or protects some of the conditions necessary for effective expression. For example, freedom of expression is generally thought to protect the individual's right to contribute and spend money in support of expression. But if this protection of spending rests on the positive value of expressive activity, it does not follow that the freedom is violated when the state requires an individual to contribute financially to the expression by others of views with which he or she disagrees.

2. Invasion of the Individual's Sphere of Intellect and Spirit

In the United States the right against compelled speech first appeared in the U.S. Supreme Court judgment of *Barnette* 1943. The case involved the suspension from school of children who, for religious reasons, refused to salute the flag as required by a school board resolution.[4] The U.S. Supreme Court held that the resolution was contrary to the First Amendment. In the court's opinion, the flag salute was an expression of loyalty that individuals should not be compelled to make. Mr Justice Jackson declared:

> If there is a fixed star in our constitutional constellation, it is that no official, high or petty can prescribe what shall be orthodox in politics, nationalism, religion, or other matters of opinion or force citizens to confess by word or act their faith therein ... We think the action of the local authorities in compelling the flag salute and pledge transcends constitutional limitations on their power and invades the sphere of intellect and spirit which it is the purpose of the First Amendment to our Constitution to reserve from all official control. (*Barnette* 1943, 642)

Here was a clear attempt by the state to impose ideological conformity, which could not be rationalized as a reconciliation of competing individual rights.[5] The 'invasion' seemed significant in this case because of the very personal character of an expression of national pride and loyalty. The invasion was greater perhaps because the children had chosen not to salute the flag for religious reasons.[6] The school board may have hoped that the daily collective flag salute would somehow generate greater national pride among the students and even alter the views of the dissenting children. More likely though, the board simply thought that if an American child did not voluntarily show appropriate respect for the flag, he or she should be forced to do so.[7]

If the children in this case had given way and agreed to participate in the flag salute, the teachers and students witnessing the salute would have known that it was not done voluntarily. Mr Justice Frankfurter, in his dissenting judgment, pointed out that the children and their parents were not restricted in their opportunity to 'disavow as publicly as they choose to do so the meaning that others attach to the gesture of salute' (*Barnette* 1943, 664).[8] The school board's resolution was objectionable not because people might think that the flag salute by these students was a voluntary act reflecting sincere belief but because it required an individual to present him/herself publicly in a way that was not true to his or her personal beliefs. The wrong was the indignity of having to affirm publicly views that were not one's own.

The standard instrumental arguments for freedom of expression (its contribution to the realization of truth and democracy) cannot adequately account for the view that compelling an individual to express views that are not his own violates his fundamental right to free expression. Indeed, it can plausibly be argued that the goals of truth and democracy might sometimes be advanced by expression that is not voluntary. As long as what is said contributes new or different ideas to public discussion, ideas that must be addressed and accepted or rejected, it may not matter who said them or whether they were the actual views of the speaker. Sometimes, of course, state authorities might seek to narrow the range of views expressed on a particular issue by combining a compulsion to express the official view with censorship of other views. However, in such a case, it could be argued that it is the censorship rather than the compulsion that limits debate and violates freedom of expression.

It is true that an audience's assessment of an idea may be affected by who has expressed it or how many people have expressed it. For example, certain views might carry more weight if expressed by someone thought to have expertise in a particular area. It is possible then that compelled expression might work against the search for truth if the audience is unaware that an individual's contribution to public discussion has been compelled by the state and is not the outcome of his or her judgment. Compelled expression will also work against truth and democracy inasmuch as it erodes people's confidence that what an individual says is his or her genuine view.

Generally, however, when an individual is compelled to express him/herself, the audience is aware that the message has been compelled and is not the individual's own. Thus, in most cases, the problem with compelled expression is not that the audience might believe the views expressed to be genuine, or even that the audience cannot be certain whether an individual's speech represents his or her actual view. Compelled expression is wrong because an individual's communication (what she says or writes) is closely linked to her sense of self and to her place in the community. Our ideas, feelings and, more broadly, our identity, take shape in public expression, when we give them symbolic form and make them accessible to others, who respond or react to them in different ways. Because public articulation of ideas and feelings is so critical to the individual's identity, any interference with his or her expression, whether in the form of censorship or compulsion, is experienced as an invasion of the self. Compelled expression is invasive even though, in many or most cases, the audience is aware that the views expressed are not the actual views of the speaker, or, at least, are not views the speaker has him/herself chosen to express.

There are many other wrongs that resemble compelled expression but are objectionable for slightly different reasons. For example, when the state compels an individual or organization to reveal membership lists, self-incriminating facts, sources for a newspaper story, or information confided to him or her as counsellor or confessor, the concern is not so much, or not simply, that the individual has been compelled to communicate but rather that the particular information she/he has been compelled to disclose should remain confidential for reasons of either personal dignity or public policy.

If a government official were to claim that an individual had said something that he or she had not said (for example, if an official released a statement under the name of another individual) the individual would not suffer the indignity of having to utter words that did not reflect his or her real beliefs or feelings. However, the official's claim could distort the public perception of the individual. While this might be experienced by the individual as an interference with his or her public personality, it is a wrong that seems more closely related to defamation than to compelled expression.[9] Since the public generally knows when expression has been compelled by the state, the principal objection to compelled expression is not that others might mistakenly believe that the views expressed by the individual under compulsion reflect her or his actual thinking but is, rather, the indignity suffered by the individual when forced to express views that do not necessarily reflect his or her thinking.

3. Compelled Corporate/Commercial Expression

In *Ford* 1988, and its companion case, *Devine* 1988, the Supreme Court of Canada considered the constitutionality of the Quebec law that compelled the use of French on commercial signs and prohibited the use of other languages. According to the court, section 2(b) was violated by both the prohibition on other languages and the compulsion to use French.

At the limitations stage of its analysis, the court held that the prohibition of other languages is not rationally connected to the important goal of protecting and preserving the French language in Quebec.[10] In the court's view, the empirical evidence put forward by the Quebec government did not establish that the prohibition of other languages is an effective way to protect French. Even if the prohibition has some impact, said the court, there are other and better ways to achieve this goal that are less restrictive of the freedom. In contrast, the court saw a 'rational connection' between the goal of preserving the French language and the requirement of French on commercial signs. Further, it considered that the requirement of French, which maintains a French visage linguistique in Quebec, is proportionate to the interference with individual freedom of expression.[11]

The justification for the requirement of French on commercial signs lies in the unequal economic power of the different language groups in Quebec. The sign law is a response to the historic domination of the Quebec economy by the anglophone minority. It seeks to ensure that the members of the majority francophone community are able to participate fully in the commercial life of the province. In the past, members of the majority French language community had to speak English if they wanted to move from the shop floor into management or if they wanted to engage in different sorts of commercial transactions. The sign law rests on a belief that the language of business should be determined by the political majority rather than by an economically powerful minority.

In *Slaight* 1989, the Supreme Court of Canada reviewed an order by an adjudicator compelling an employer to provide a letter of recommendation for a wrongfully dismissed employee. The adjudicator had decided that an employee of radio station Q107 in Toronto had been wrongfully dismissed from his job and had ordered the station to pay monetary compensation and to provide the employee with a letter of recommendation. The letter was to state matters of fact, such as the employee's sales figures for each of the three years of his employment, as well as the adjudicator's finding that the employee had been wrongfully dismissed. The adjudicator also ordered that 'any communication to Q107 ... from any person or company inquiring about Mr. Ron Davidson's employment at Q107, shall be answered exclusively by sending or delivering a copy of the ... letter of recommendation' (*Slaight* 1989, 1047).

Chief Justice Dickson, for the majority of the court, held that both parts of the order (the requirement that the station provide the specified letter and the requirement that it respond to any requests for information only with a copy of this letter) violated the station's freedom of expression but that these violations were justified under section 1. Central to the court's section 1 assessment is a recognition of the 'unequal balance of power that normally exists between an employer and employee' (*Slaight* 1989, 1051). The adjudicator believed that the representatives of the station had not been honest about Mr Davidson's work record and was concerned that they would respond to any requests from prospective employers for information about Mr Davidson in a way that was both dishonest and damaging. This is why he thought it necessary to set out what the employer was to say and do in response to any requests for information. Chief Justice Dickson shared the adjudicator's concern: 'The inequality in one employment relationship would be continued even after its termination with the result that the worker looking for a new job would be placed in an even more unequal bargaining position vis-à-vis prospective employers than is normally the case. On the facts of this case, constitutionally protecting freedom of expression would be tantamount to condoning the continuation of an abuse of an already unequal relationship' (*Slaight* 1989, 1052).

Beetz J. dissented on the ground that the adjudicator's order 'forces the employer to write, as if they were his own, statements of fact in which, rightly or wrongly, he may not believe ...' (*Slaight* 1989, 1059). Lamer J. dissented in part. He did not object to the part of the order that required the employer to send a specified letter in response to any requests for a reference concerning Mr Davidson, but he thought that the employer should not have been forbidden to add its own views. His concern was that if an employer is prevented from stating its own views, readers might assume that the letter represents the employer's opinion. In Mr Justice Lamer's view, while the state may sometimes be justified in compelling expression, it must permit the person under compulsion to indicate that the views expressed are not his or her own. The difficulty with this position is that if the employer is permitted to state that the letter does not reflect its opinion (or if the employer contests the assertions in the letter), the value of the letter may be undermined. The employer's power to damage the employment prospects of its former employee would remain.

In both *Ford* 1989 and *Slaight* 1989, the Supreme Court of Canada found that the compulsion to speak violated section 2(b) but was justified under section 1. It may be significant that in one case the required expression was commercial in character and in the other case it related to business operations. If compelled expression is objectionable because it invades the individual's personal sphere, there may be less concern when commercial expression is compelled, or when a large corporation is compelled to communicate in order to ensure a more open or balanced flow of information. The concerns about individual dignity that underlie the decision in *Barnette* 1943 do not arise in the same way when a large and artificial legal entity is compelled to speak.

As well, the significant control that economically powerful actors sometimes have over information or important channels of communication may justify compelled expression in some situations. For example, government regulations requiring manufacturers to list the ingredients on product packaging are routine and unquestioned because consumers have neither the time nor the expertise to investigate product attributes or verify manufacturers' claims. More controversial, it seems, is the requirement that cigarette manufacturers place warnings on cigarette packages about the health hazards of smoking.

In *RJR Macdonald* 1995, a majority of the Supreme Court of Canada held that a federal requirement that manufacturers include specified health warnings on cigarette packaging violates the Charter.[12] McLachlin J., for the majority, held that the requirement violates section 2(b) because it compels the manufacturers 'to say what they do not wish to say' and 'in a way that associates them with the opinions in question' (*RJR Macdonald* 1995, 348). She accepted that the reasons for requiring manufacturers to include these warnings are substantial enough to justify limitation under section 1 of their 'right not to speak.' However, she believed that because the warnings are not attributed to the government (and the manufacturer is prohibited from displaying any message on the package other than brand name, trade mark, and health warning), some consumers might mistakenly think that they are voluntary statements made by the cigarette companies: 'some may draw [the inference] that it is the corporations themselves who are warning of the danger' (*RJR Macdonald* 1995, 348). Since, in her view, a warning attributed to the government would be no less effective than an unattributed warning, the requirement is more intrusive than necessary and so could not be justified under section 1 as a minimal impairment on the freedom.

But is attribution really the issue? In his dissenting judgment, LaForest J. observed that everyone who reads these packages will know that the warnings are compelled by legislation and are not voluntary statements by the manufacturers.[13] As suggested earlier, in most cases of compelled expression the audience is aware that the statements are not made voluntarily. The central objection to compelled expression is not that the individual will be identified with views that are not her own but rather that she will suffer the indignity of having to express such views. If the problem were simply mistaken association, it could always be corrected by striking down the censoring part of the law, which prohibited the company from expressing its actual views on the issue.

If we see any sense in the claim that mandatory health warnings amount to compelled expression, it is only because we are in the habit of treating the corporation as an entity with a mind and will and hence a dignity interest. We forget that a corporation is itself a property owned by individual and/or corporate shareholders. Requiring a large corporation (characterized by a separation of ownership and management) to 'communicate' someone else's message does not amount to compelling an individual to express her/himself, but is simply a limitation on the shareholders' control over their property. The owners and managers will not be printing or distributing the packages themselves. At most the requirement that health warnings be included on the cigarette packages is an expropriation of their property or a reduction of their control over the product. If compelled expression offends the Charter because it is experienced as an invasion of one's personal sphere, or an interference with one's 'freedom of mind,' a multinational cigarette company cannot have the same claim as an individual to be free from compulsion to communicate.[14]

Even if we thought this law compelled cigarette companies to express views they do not wish to express, there may be good reasons for requiring them to publicly acknowledge or disclose the risks of smoking. The majority judgment assumed that the state's purpose in requiring the manufacturer to place warnings on its packages is simply to ensure that other voices are heard in the smoking debate, voices that inform consumers about the risks of smoking. Or, at least, their assumption was that this is the only purpose that could legitimately support the warnings requirement.[15] However, the requirement might better be understood and defended as an attempt to force cigarette manufacturers to publicly acknowledge the risks of smoking.

Imposing such an obligation on cigarette manufacturers seems more than justified, given their past efforts to suppress information about the fatal consequences of smoking. Canadian law requires disclosures of many different kinds. The law requires house sellers to reveal latent defects, drug manufacturers to disclose risks and side effects, and doctors to inform their patients of the risks of different procedures.[16] It would seem strange if a manufacturer, vendor, or doctor objected to these disclosure requirements on the ground that the information about product or procedure risks was not attributed to the government. Consumers do not have independent access to specialized information nor do they have the expertise to assess the information that may be provided and so they depend on (and place trust in) producers or professionals to disclose accurate information about risks. This is why, when a manufacturer provides inaccurate and harmful product information, liability is imposed without any issue of freedom of expression being raised (Post 1995, 1254).

The claim that health warnings on cigarette packages are objectionable because they are not attributed to the government assumes that these warnings are contestable statements of opinion; an assumption that, until recently at least, cigarette manufacturers sought to reinforce. Attribution matters only if we think that these health warnings are just the views or opinions of the government and that it is unfair when they are passed off as the views of the manufacturer. Indeed, if the majority was correct that manufacturers must have the freedom to disassociate themselves from the warnings, then surely the manufacturers should also be free to include on the packaging a contradiction of the warning.

LaForest J., in his dissent, rejected the companies' claim that they must have the right to 'engage in counter-speech.' He recognized that warnings 'do nothing more than bring the dangerous nature of these products to the attention of consumers' (*RJR Macdonald* 1995, 322). He saw the purpose of the warnings as 'simply to increase the likelihood that every literate consumer of tobacco products will be made aware of the risks entailed by the use of that product' (*RJR Macdonald* 1995, 322). In his view, these warnings have 'no political, social or religious content' and so are very different from the statements of opinion that were the focus in most compelled expression cases (*RJR Macdonald* 1995, 322).[17]

We depend on regulation to ensure that the information we receive from manufacturers is reliable. The health damage caused by tobacco use is well established and should not be contested by manufacturers in the public presentation of their product. This 'issue' should be removed from the scope of protected product advertising or presentation because manufacturers have an incentive to distort the truth, because other participants in the marketplace have neither the resources nor the incentive to contest factual misstatements, and because the general public has neither the time nor expertise to determine the accuracy of the claims made to them.[18]

4. Extending the Doctrine to Protect Exclusive Control of Property

The *RJR Macdonald* 1995 decision raised the question of whether the 'right not to speak' prohibits the state from making use of an individual's (or corporation's) property for its own communication. The communicative use of property is vital to the individual's (and the corporation's) ability to communicate effectively with others and so is generally protected from state restriction. As the Supreme Court of Canada said in *Libman* 1997, 594, freedom of expression also protects the means of expression. It does not follow, however, that a law granting communicative access to an individual's property compels expression contrary to the Charter. Such a law is better understood as a limitation on the individual's exclusive control over her or his property, which does not automatically raise concerns about dignity and personal invasion.

However, some properties are so closely tied to the individual and to her ability to express her views that a law granting other members of the community the right to use one of these properties for communication may be experienced by its owner as an invasion of her 'sphere of intellect.'[19] Perhaps, then, we should see state use of, or state-granted access to, certain 'personal' properties as amounting to compelled expression. This should apply, however, only to a very narrow category of properties. If legislated access to any property, including the holdings of large corporations, was seen as compelled expression violating section 2(b) of the Charter, state efforts to distribute communicative opportunities more widely in the community would be significantly impeded.

A law compelling an individual to carry a message on his or her person – for example, a political button worn on the person's clothing – would be experienced as an invasion no less significant than a requirement to salute the flag and would be seen as compelled expression violating section 2(b). Wearing a political button is a very common and very personal way of expressing one's political views. An individual who is required to wear a political button will suffer the indignity of carrying on his person a message that is not his and that others might attribute to him (although once again knowledge of such a requirement would avoid this second concern).

A larger personal sphere was recognized in the U.S. Supreme Court judgment of *Wooley* 1977. A couple, who were members of the Jehovah's Witness faith, covered up the 'Live free or die' slogan on their New Hampshire licence plate. They were charged under state law with altering their licence plate. The United States Supreme Court held that the application of the law in this case violated the couple's free speech, because it compelled them to communicate against their will. A majority of the court thought that it is a violation of the right to free speech 'for the state to require an individual to participate in the dissemination of an ideological message by displaying it on his private property in a manner and for the express purpose that it be observed and read by the public' (*Wooley* 1977, 713). The court acknowledged that this sort of compulsion is less serious an infringement of the freedom than compelling the 'affirmative act of a flag salute.' Nevertheless, it considered that: 'Here as in *Barnette*, we are faced with a state measure which forces an individual, as part of his daily life – indeed constantly while his automobile is in public view – to be an instrument for fostering public adherence to an ideological point of view he finds unacceptable. In doing so, the State invades the sphere of intellect and spirit which it is the purpose of the First Amendment to our Constitution to reserve from all official control' (*Wooley* 1977, 715).

But why is a law that requires an individual to carry a message on her car seen as compelling her to speak? Very little is required of the individual. She must attach the licence plate to the bumper and when she travels about in the car, the message will go with her. Most people are aware that the state uses licence plates to carry certain messages and so it is unlikely that anyone who reads the message on the car will assume that it originates with the owner of the car. (Of course, the message is usually so innocuous that no one thinks much about it.) Only if car owners were given a right, which was sometimes exercised, to alter the message on their licence plates, might we see the message on a particular plate as reflecting the owner's personal views. Failure to cover up the message, then, might be seen as an acceptance or affirmation of it.

In a case such as *Wooley* 1977, the car owner is not compelled to communicate against her will, inasmuch as she is not required to speak or write any words. She has simply lost exclusive control over the use of her property, which is not such an extraordinary thing. Property rights are defined and redefined by state laws in a variety of ways. The state law at issue here might be seen as nothing more than a limit on the scope of a particular property right or an expropriation of a property right that should be addressed on the basis of principles of fairness appropriate to this sort of issue. Yet the majority of the court saw the display of a state message on an individual's private property as an invasion of his or her personal sphere, as compelled expression.

The state use of a car bumper may be experienced as an invasion of the individual's personal sphere because a car bumper is an important extension of the individual into the public world. The communicative use of one's car by the state is experienced as an invasion, as compelled expression, because the car is often used by the owner to communicate with others. The car bumper, in particular, is an important and personal platform for expression by the individual owner.

An individual must have exclusive control over a certain realm of property rights if he is to communicate effectively with others. Without some exclusive rights, the individual would be without a secure place from which to communicate (or the means with which to communicate) and he would be in constant competition with others for communicative opportunities. The bumper of one's car, and perhaps also the front lawn of one's house, are, by convention, significant means of communication, identifying the car owner and home occupier with the view expressed there. If an individual does not have exclusive control over the messages that appear on his lawn or car, it may be difficult sometimes for others to know what messages originate with him or represent his views.

The link to compelled expression rests on a recognition that a car bumper, like a front lawn, is an established platform from which individuals sometimes express themselves to others. State use of a car bumper to communicate its own message, or state-enforced access for the benefit of someone other than the owner is experienced by the owner as a personal invasion or interference because this property is an important extension of the person into the public realm. In this way, the use by the state, or by others, of a car bumper, or other basic and personal platforms, resembles or amounts to compelled expression. These means of communication are so important to the individual's opportunity for expression that their use by the state is an affront to her, an invasion of her 'sphere of intellect and spirit' (Moon 1988, 253).

In *Pruneyard* 1980, the U.S. Supreme Court upheld the requirement of the California constitution (as interpreted by the Supreme Court of California) that shopping centres, including those that are privately owned, permit speech and petitioning that is 'reasonably exercised.' The Pruneyard Center claimed that the California access requirement violated its First Amendment right not to speak. The center argued that it would be 'associated' with the views expressed on its property.

Rehnquist J., for the court, rejected this argument. He distinguished this case from *Wooley* 1977 in a number of ways. He observed that in *Wooley* 1977 the government prescribed a message to be displayed on the *personal* property of the individual. In contrast, the shopping centre, by choice of its owner, is not limited to his/her/its personal use. As well, because the public comes and goes as they please, '[t]he views expressed by members of the public ... will not likely be identified with those of the owner' (*Pruneyard* 1980, 87). In any event, the shopping centre 'can easily disavow any connection with the message by simply posting signs in the area where the speakers and handbillers stand' (*Pruneyard* 1980, 87). Finally, in *Pruneyard* 1980 the state had not dictated a particular message to be displayed on the property; rather, it had created a forum for the expression of views by members of the community.

Nevertheless, the communicative access in *Pruneyard* 1980 interferes with the mall owner's use (and in a very loose sense, its communicative use) of its property. Shopping malls are designed and operated in a way that encourages the notion that shopping/consumption is an important means of self-realization (Schiller 1989, 101; Schnably 1993, 367).[20] It is hardly surprising that the mall owners wanted to prevent the expression of controversial views on their property. They wanted their property to be a place that sets the right mood for buying. Speech concerning important and controversial issues may not directly counter an explicit message of the mall owners. But this sort of speech is inconsistent with the owners' implicit message that all problems can be resolved through consumption and their general interest in creating an environment conducive to buying.

In the subsequent U.S. Supreme Court judgment of *Pacific Gas* 1986, the court took a different view of legislated access to corporate property. In *Pacific Gas* 1986, the court considered whether a California public utility could be required by the state to enclose literature from consumer advocacy groups in the 'extra space' of its billing envelopes.[21] Consumer advocacy groups had asked the California Public Utilities Commission to order the utility to stop enclosing political editorials along with its monthly bills to consumers. The commission rejected this request. Instead, the Commission decided that the 'extra space' in the envelopes should be apportioned between the utility and designated consumer groups, and it ordered the utility to enclose material from these groups at least four times a year. In effect, the commission gave public interest groups limited access to a property otherwise under the exclusive control of a large corporation that held a monopoly position. The U.S. Supreme Court ruled that this requirement violates the First Amendment because it compels the utility 'to use *its* property as a vehicle for spreading a message with which it disagrees' and because it might discourage the utility from expressing any potentially controversial views for fear that a consumer advocacy group might choose to respond (*Pacific Gas* 1986, 912).[22]

The consumer groups would almost certainly have used their access right to counteract the specific claims and arguments of the utility. Nevertheless, it is unclear why this access should be seen as compelling the utility to express itself. Since there was no real possibility that the occasional enclosure of consumer group messages in the billing envelopes would curtail the utility's ability to communicate with its consumers, and since these messages would be attributed to the particular consumer group, the wrong in *Pacific Gas* 1986 is simply that a large corporation was being required to open its property to communication by others, and in particular the communication of information that might be contrary to the corporation's interests.[23]

A large corporate property holder, whether a mall corporation or a private utility, is not in the same position as an individual car owner to complain that the communicative use of its property by another is an affront to its dignity and an invasion of its personal sphere.[24] While communicative access may interfere with the corporate owner's business interests, this is not the same as an invasion of personal space or an affront to human dignity. The argument against communicative access to corporate property rests on the peculiar assumption that human dignity is compromised whenever property rights are restricted or redefined.

5. Freedom of the Press and Compelled Access

The courts in both the United States and Canada have held that freedom of expression precludes the state from requiring a newspaper to publish a story or statement. The courts have struck down legislation granting limited public access to the print media, in the form of a right of reply to political criticism, and a right against discrimination in the purchase of advertising space.

In *Miami Herald* 1974, the U.S. Supreme Court struck down a Florida law that gave a political candidate the right to reply to editorial criticism of his or her candidacy.[25] The court held that access legislation of this kind violates freedom of the press. Chief Justice Burger, who wrote for the majority, recognized that entry into publishing has become so expensive, and concentration of media ownership has grown to such an extent, that 'the power to inform the American people and shape public opinion' is now 'in a few hands' (*Miami Herald* 1974, 250). He acknowledged, but was not convinced by, the argument that right-of-reply laws might add to the diversity of views put before the public. He considered that even if this argument was valid, the implementation of such laws by government would involve 'a confrontation with the express provisions of the First Amendment' (*Miami Herald* 1974, 254). Editors or publishers should not be compelled to publish that which '"reason" tells them should not be published':

> Even if a newspaper would face no additional costs to comply with a compulsory access law and would not be forced to forgo publication of news or opinion by the inclusion of a reply, the Florida statute fails to clear the barriers of the First Amendment because of its intrusion into the function of editors. A newspaper is more than a passive receptacle or conduit for news, comment, and advertising. The choice of material to go into a newspaper, and the decisions made as to the limitations on size and content of the paper, and treatment of public issues and officials – whether fair or unfair – constitute the exercise of editorial control and judgment. (*Miami Herald* 1974, 258)

The court viewed state-ordered access as an interference with the owner's/editor's judgment about what should go into the paper and therefore as a violation of his/her/its freedom of speech.

In the course of his judgment, Chief Justice Burger pointed to the costs that such a law imposes on the newspaper,[26] as well as its potential chilling effect. Access, in the form of a right of reply, is triggered by a critical or controversial position taken by the newspaper. Because editors will sometimes decide that the safe course is to avoid controversy, a '[g]overnment-enforced right of access inescapably "dampens the vigor and limits the variety of public debate"' (*Miami Herald* 1974, 257).

The Supreme Court of Canada adopted a similar view in the pre-Charter case of *Gay Alliance* 1979. The *Vancouver Sun*, in carrying out its 'duty to protect the morals of the community' had refused to accept for publication a short advertisement for a gay newspaper.[27] ('Subs to GAY TIDE, a gay lib paper. $1.00 for 6 issues. 2146 Yew St., Vancouver.') A complaint against the *Sun* was filed under the B.C. Human Rights Code. A board of inquiry found that the *Sun* had contravened section 3 of the B.C. Human Rights Code 1973,[28] which prohibits discrimination 'against any person or class of persons with respect to any accommodation, service or facility customarily available to the public.' The board considered the advertising pages of the newspaper to be such a service or facility.

The Supreme Court of Canada, however, decided that section 3 of the Code should not be interpreted as requiring a newspaper to sell advertising space to a particular individual or group. Martland J., who wrote for the majority, thought that 'the service which is customarily available to the public in the case of a newspaper which accepts advertising is a service subject to the right of the newspaper to control the content of such advertising' (*Gay Alliance* 1979, 455). The nature and scope of the service which is offered, including the advertising service, 'is determined by the newspaper itself' (*Gay Alliance* 1979, 456). According to Martland J., all that section 3 does is ensure that when a service, as defined by the newspaper, is offered to the public, the newspaper does not deny access to any particular member of the public without reasonable cause. Martland J. found that the *Sun* had adopted a policy of not accepting ads that 'advocate' homosexuality and so the service that the newspaper offered to the public, and which is subject to the requirement of non-discriminatory access, does not include advertising with gay or lesbian content.

Martland J. was led to this rather peculiar (and circular) interpretation of section 3 because he believed that a wider reading might violate freedom of the press. He took from *Miami Herald* 1974 the principle that there should be no state interference with the newspaper's editorial control, and he argued that if the Code were interpreted as limiting the newspaper's control over the content of the advertising pages, it would violate freedom of the press and might well be ultra vires the province:

> The law has recognized the freedom of the press to propagate its views and ideas on any issue and to select the material which it publishes. As a corollary to that a newspaper also has the right to refuse to publish material which runs contrary to the views which it expresses ... A newspaper supporting certain political views does not have to publish an advertisement advancing contrary views. In fact, the judgments of Duff C.J., Davis J. and Cannon J. in the *Alberta Press* case ... suggest that provincial legislation to compel such publication may be unconstitutional. (*Gay Alliance* 1979, 455)

In his dissenting judgment, Mr Justice Dickson acknowledged the importance of freedom of the press but considered that the advertising section of a newspaper might not deserve the same protection from legislated access as the news and editorial sections.[29] He saw an 'important distinction' between legislation designed to control the editorial content of a newspaper and legislation designed to control discriminatory practices in the sale of advertising space. The newspaper sells advertising in order to raise revenue. The advertising part of the paper 'is not concerned with freedom of speech on matters of public concern as a condition of democratic polity, but rather with the provision of a "service or facility customarily available to the public" with a view to profit' (*Gay Alliance* 1979, 469). In contrast, the news and editorial sections of the paper are not open to the public and so are not subject to the non-discriminatory access required by section 3 of the Code.

The distinction drawn by Dickson J. between the advertising and the editorial/news sections of the paper has some appeal but is not without problems. It is true that newspapers are happy to publish almost any paid ad that is submitted and that the readership will not usually attribute the views expressed in the ad (ordinarily a commercial message) to the newspaper's editors/owners. However, the growing use of political ads has led to a blurring of the distinction between advertising and editorial sections. Jerome Barron argues that if the point of an ad is to make a political statement or if the ad reflects a controversial perspective 'that is in conflict with the views of the private newspaper to which access is sought, the right to refuse to publish such advertising material is, arguably, still central to a protected status for editorial freedom' (Barron 1986, 193). I will leave for discussion later in this chapter the other way in which the distinction between the sections is problematic: that the choice of editorial content in large daily newspapers is driven significantly by a desire to maximize advertising revenue.

The court in *Gay Alliance* 1979 relied on the Supreme Court of Canada judgment in *Re Alberta Statutes* 1938. In that case, the Supreme Court ruled that a variety of legislative bills put forward by the Alberta government, including the Alberta Accurate News and Information Act [the Press Bill], were unconstitutional. A majority of the court held that the Press Bill could not stand because its administrative structure was borrowed from the Social Credit Act, an Act which the court had decided was ultra vires the province because it was related to federal banking and monetary powers. However, three members of the court also held that the Press Bill was ultra vires the province because it interfered in a significant way with freedom of the press and hence with the operation of the Parliament of Canada. Chief Justice Duff, for example, argued that while the province has the power to engage in 'some degree of regulation of newspapers,' the limit is reached 'when legislation effects such a curtailment of the exercise of public discussion as substantially to interfere with the working of the parliamentary institutions of Canada as contemplated by the provisions of the *British North America Act*' (*Re Alberta Statutes* 1938, 134).

The Press Bill gave the chairman of the Social Credit Board the power to require a newspaper to publish statements 'correcting or amplifying' material published by the paper that related to the activities or policies of the government. The chairman could also require a newspaper to identify every source from which it obtained information and to provide the names, addresses, and occupations of all persons who provided such information to the newspaper and of the writers of any editorial, article, or news item.

Mr Justice Cannon believed that the purpose of the Press Bill was to discourage or neutralize criticism of the government. In his view, the government's object was to make Social Credit doctrine 'a sort of religious dogma of which a free and uncontrolled discussion is not permissible' (*Re Alberta Statutes* 1938, 144). He noted that 'the bill does not regulate the relations of the newspapers' owners with private individual members of the public, but deals exclusively with expressions of opinion by the newspapers concerning government policies and activities' (*Re Alberta Statutes* 1938, 144). In this way, the case is very different from *Gay Alliance* 1979.[30] In *Gay Alliance* 1979 the issue was whether the Human Rights Code should be interpreted to require fairer access to the media for different members of the community. The Code was not intended to neutralize or suppress criticism of the government.

The *Miami Herald* 1974 and *Gay Alliance* 1979 cases decided that a newspaper should not be compelled to print a story or an advertisement.[31] Because a newspaper is a vehicle for communication, the courts regard any interference with the owners/editors' judgment as to what it should contain as a violation of freedom of the press, analogous to the violations considered in *Barnette* 1946 and *Wooley* 1977. There was no suggestion in either *Miami Herald* 1974 or *Gay Alliance* 1979 that the access granted would, in any noticeable way, displace material that the newspapers would otherwise have printed.[32] In *Miami Herald* 1974, Chief Justice Burger stated very clearly that in his mind the legislation would have been unconstitutional '[e]ven if a newspaper would face no additional costs to comply with a compulsory access law and would not be forced to forgo publication of news or opinion by the inclusion of a reply' (*Miami Herald* 1974, 258). He also suggested that, even if access resulted in greater diversity in the views expressed (which he did not accept), there would still be no justification for interference with freedom of the press, understood as the editor's/owner's right to control the content of the newspaper.

Yet does access legislation of the sort considered in either *Miami Herald* 1974 or *Gay Alliance* 1977 compel someone to communicate against his or her will? Does it 'put words in someone's mouth'? The owners and managers do not have to speak or write any words. Nor is it likely that the message the paper is compelled to publish, particularly if it is an advertisement, will be identified with the owners or managers of the paper. Most large-scale newspapers present themselves, and are viewed, as carriers of a broad range of information and ideas concerning matters of public interest. Readers do not assume that every statement that appears in the paper reflects the views of the owners or managers.

While daily newspapers are vehicles for communication, the connection between the individual (corporate) owner and his (its) newspaper is not analogous to the personal connection between the car owner and his car bumper or the home owner and his front lawn. Not only do very few people have control over, or access to, a newspaper, so that a newspaper cannot be considered a basic and personal vehicle for individual communication, but as well, daily newspapers are large-scale operations that involve many employees in the different stages of production and distribution. For its owner(s), the newspaper is more a profit-making enterprise than a vehicle for personal expression. Occasionally, a newspaper or chain of newspapers is controlled by an individual who is closely linked to the operation and identity of the paper(s). But, even in these cases, the link is selectively downplayed because the success and profitability of a large daily newspaper, particularly if it holds a monopoly position, depends on its being presented and perceived as a general vehicle for the communication of all relevant news and opinion.

For these reasons, it takes some imagination to see the access requirement as an affront to the dignity of the newspaper owner, generally a large corporation, or as something that would be experienced by *it* as an invasion of its 'sphere of intellect and spirit.' While the owners or managers may feel very powerfully that their control of the paper should not be interfered with, this concern rests on the sanctity of property and not on the dignity of the individual, which is invaded when expression is compelled (Moon 1988b, 256). Indeed, it seems likely that a greater loss of dignity would result from the effective exclusion of certain views and voices from public discourse than from minor limits on the newspaper owner's exclusive control over a central communicative resource.

The distribution of communicative power in the community is a relevant consideration when deciding whether access compromises the individual's dignity interests and amounts to compelled expression. The more important a property is to an individual's ability or opportunity to communicate with others, the greater his or her sense of invasion when the state seeks to use the property for its own message or to make the property available for the communicative use of others. Front lawns and car bumpers matter to the individual, and their communicative expropriation is invasive, because they are the only platforms most individuals have to communicate their views to the general public.

Those operating a smaller scale publication might reasonably experience access legislation as invasive. In the case of a small weekly or monthly newspaper that is directed to a particular audience, that adopts a particular perspective, and that is directly (hands-on) managed by its owner or a small group of managers, the similarity to the front lawn or car bumper becomes stronger.[33] There is also a greater risk that displacement might be a problem in the case of a smaller paper with limited resources and space. It is relevant, as well, that these smaller publications do not have a monopoly position so that there are alternative places for competing views to be expressed. These papers often present themselves as partisan and not as neutral or common carriers of public information and debate. We might reasonably suspect that the real purpose behind a requirement of access to a smaller scale publication is to neutralize or hinder its advocacy of a particular viewpoint.

By equating legislated access with compelled expression, the courts avoid having to respond to the claim that access actually advances important freedom of expression interests by enlarging the range of publicly expressed views. The assertion that access amounts to compelled expression operates to pre-empt claims about the consequences of press autonomy. If access legislation interferes with an individual right, then 'policy arguments' are irrelevant. They are trumped by the claim of right.

Yet the compelled expression argument seems strained when applied to large daily newspapers, and it is often supplemented by general and unsupported claims that 'autonomy' of the press is necessary to free and open debate of public issues. For example, Chief Justice Burger in *Miami Herald* 1974 claimed that access legislation, or more specifically right-of-reply legislation, discouraged debate and discussion of issues or candidates because a newspaper would be reluctant to criticize a public official, or to discuss a controversial matter, if doing so would give rise to a right of reply.

The claim that 'press autonomy' is necessary to free and open debate is made more directly in another version of the argument against access legislation. In the United States, it is sometimes argued that the print media have a special constitutional status that precludes any state interference with their institutional 'autonomy.' At the very least, they must be free from interference with their editorial judgment. The print media have a special constitutional role because they perform the important task of supervising the governing process and because they are able to communicate a wide range of ideas and information to a large audience (Bollinger 1991, 20).

In the United States, the argument for press autonomy is strengthened by the specific inclusion in the First Amendment of the right to a free press. In Canada, however, the Charter of Rights does not appear to establish a special, independent press freedom. The language of section 2(b) indicates that freedom of the press is simply an aspect or implication of freedom of expression. The section protects 'freedom of thought, belief, opinion and expression, including freedom of the press and other media of communication.' The term 'media' seems to refer to a method of communication rather than to certain institutions. An individual has the right to express him/herself by speaking to others face to face or by using the press, radio, or television. However, even in the absence of a special press provision, protection of press 'autonomy' may follow from the central role of the press in facilitating public debate and the exchange of information.[34]

On the surface, the argument that press autonomy must be protected because of the important role the press plays in facilitating public discussion contrasts sharply with the central claim in *Miami Herald* 1974 and *Gay Alliance* 1979 that access legislation is unconstitutional because it compels expression (and is similar to a requirement to salute a flag or carry a message on a car bumper). The compelled expression argument rests on a concern for the integrity of the individual and his or her control over essential platforms for communication – over certain personal spaces. In contrast, the special status argument rests on the public function of the press and the contribution of press autonomy to free and open public discourse.

Of course, if press autonomy does not advance the public interest (i.e., if it does not contribute to a free and open public discourse) then this justification for its protection disappears. Those who put forward a public function argument for press autonomy (joining public interest and private right) see no tension between the private (and for profit) character of the press and the public function it performs and no need to address the question of the press's responsibility to support an open public discourse. They assume that the market is the most effective mechanism for distributing goods and opportunities, including communicative opportunities. They take it for granted that any interference with ownership rights or market operation will inhibit free and open expression. Access legislation upsets the balance of an otherwise free and voluntary system for determining who speaks and what gets said. The market is viewed as 'an invisible and unbiased medium for the free circulation of public opinions' (Keane 1991, 45).

The courts' suspicious attitude towards legislated access is supported by a nineteenth-century view of the relationship between state and press, in which the small-scale newspaper fights a heroic struggle against state efforts to suppress free and open debate; in which the freedom and independence of the press is contrasted with state control (Barron 1973, 5; Keane 1991, 37). Today, however, daily newspapers are neither many nor small in scale. The move towards larger scale publications has been pushed along by technological developments and the advantage of lower per unit production costs. The desire to obtain higher advertising revenues has also encouraged both the growth of scale (a larger audience) and the movement towards monopoly in a particular geographic area (Kent Commission 1981, 72). Entry costs are now so high that control over, and communicative access to, daily newspapers belongs to a remarkably small group of people/corporations.

A century ago it was not uncommon for a newspaper to adopt a partisan political position. However, at the time, there were a variety of newspapers produced and so a range of views were published and available for public consideration.[35] In contrast, the small number of daily newspapers that now dominate the public sphere increasingly present themselves as common carriers of information, providing not only neutral and objective news reporting on a wide range matters but also a forum for the expression of different views, in the letters to the editor section and the advertising section. This shift in image from partisan proponent to objective reporter and common carrier has broadened the appeal of particular newspapers and supported their growth in scale. At the same time, this shift in image has been an important defence against attempts to regulate newspapers that operate as a monopoly in particular geographic areas (de Sola Pool 1983, 238).

However genuine the aspiration to objectivity, the result of ownership concentration is that the values of a small group of corporations play a significant role in shaping public debate. There is no need to see evil intent behind this. A newspaper must decide what to include and what to exclude, what to treat with emphasis or in depth and what to treat superficially on the back pages (Bagdikian 1992, 16). This selection is bound to reflect the values, concerns, and interests of those who make the decisions and those who employ the decision makers.[36]

Because daily newspapers are generally owned by large conglomerates (companies with non-media holdings), there is always potential for conflict of interest.[37] There are numerous cases where newspapers have declined to examine critically the behaviour of their owners. However, the conscious suppression of a story that is damaging to the owner's interests is far less significant than the tendency of newspapers to advance the market values that seem obvious and right to newspaper owners.

Newspapers are a business and so they are concerned primarily with the production of profit. Daily newspapers obtain far more revenue from advertising than from circulation. As a consequence, the selection of newspaper content is significantly influenced by a desire to attract and retain advertising revenue. As Roy Megary, former publisher of the *Globe and Mail*, has said: 'publishers of mass circulation daily newspapers ... are primarily in the business of carrying advertising messages' (quoted in Bagdikian 1992, 195).

Newspapers must appeal to readers but also to advertisers.[38] While it is true that advertisers want a large audience, so that appealing to readers is crucial, that is not all that they want. Sometimes advertisers want newspapers to suppress stories contrary to their interests; for example, the cigarette manufacturers who worked very hard to ensure that newspaper content was censored to obscure the link between tobacco and death (Bagdikian 1992, 173).[39] More often, advertisers simply want the news content of the paper to complement their message. If a newspaper is to be an effective vehicle for commercial messages, it must not be too harsh and opinionated. It must set the mood for buying

(Jhally 1990, 91; Baker 1994, 62). It must appeal to the more affluent, those in a position to purchase advertised goods and services. And it must not question the central message of advertisers, that self-realization is achieved through consumption.

The public function argument for press autonomy rests on a recognition that the daily newspaper is not simply a private commodity; it is also a key part of the public sphere where discussion about the affairs of the community takes place (Garnham 1986, 37). The newspaper is not simply a participant in public discourse, it is a forum where public discourse occurs, a medium for public discourse. Not only is the discussion of public affairs constrained by corporate faith in market ordering and consumerism, but it takes place with no direct input from the vast majority of the population. Most members of the community simply receive information from the press and have no opportunity to participate as speakers in public discussion (except occasionally through the controlled letters to the editor and advertising sections of the paper) and define their interests in their own terms (Ruggles 1994, 147).[40] In this light, access legislation in the form of a limited right of reply or a requirement of non-discrimination in the sale of advertising seems like the most minor incursion into the control exercised by large corporate interests over the shape of public discourse.

A law that gives the state the right to use a car bumper or a front lawn for its own communication or that opens these places up to others for communication will not contribute to a fairer (or wider) distribution of communicative opportunities. If anything, state intervention into the communicative use of these properties, which are basic to the individual's opportunity to express him/herself, will only reduce the already limited communicative power of the average person. In contrast, the purpose behind the state's effort to cut into a wealthy minority's exclusive control over the principal channels of public communication is to distribute, more widely, opportunities for participation in public discourse. Access legislation attempts to limit the potential for private censorship (such as discrimination in the sale of advertising space or the failure to set out more than one side of an issue) which comes with the concentration of media ownership. It seeks to open up important forums to a wider range of voices and views. While the constitutional right to freedom of expression may not require that members of the community be given access to privately owned property (*CBS* 1973, 94), this right should not be understood as prohibiting the state from legislating a wider distribution of opportunities for communication.

In *Miami Herald* 1974 and *Gay Alliance* 1979, legislated access is characterized as an invasion of individual right. The compelled expression argument is used to avoid difficult questions about the distribution of communicative power. However, access to the press does not involve a clear and direct violation of freedom of expression. No words are put in the mouth of another. There is no invasion of the individual's sphere of spirit and intellect. The only issue then is whether legislated access contributes to or detracts from the goal of a free and open public debate.

Access legislation can take many forms, including a requirement of non-discrimination in advertising, a right of reply to editorial criticism, and a requirement of balanced reporting. Different schemes will raise different concerns. Any time an administrative agency is involved there may be concerns about unfair pressure or favouritism. In the case of a right of reply triggered by a story or editorial, there may be concern that the newspaper will simply avoid controversy in order to avoid a situation in which the right might be invoked. Nevertheless, if the issue is whether legislated access assists or hinders public discussion of issues, the courts should in general defer to the legislature's judgment. Any attempt to determine whether a particular form of access inhibits public debate (its openness and diversity) will be speculative and will rest on a variety of assumptions and judgments about institutional and individual behaviour. Judicial intervention should be limited to cases of clear bad faith, where it appears that the real purpose (and not simply the possible effect) of the access law is to stifle debate, and, in particular, to limit effective criticism of government policy. Space for legislative judgment and experiment is crucial given the enormous control that a small number of corporate owners exercise over public debate.

6. Access to the Broadcast Media

The courts in both Canada and the United States have taken a different view of legislation requiring access to the broadcast media. American and Canadian courts have recognized that the broadcast spectrum is a scarce resource and accepted that the state is justified in imposing public responsibilities on those who have been given the right to use a part of that resource.

From the 1930s on, it has generally been accepted that 'Canada's airwaves are owned by the public, and should be administered by the national government in trust' (Canada 1986, 8).[41] The federal Broad-

casting Act gives authority to the Canadian Radio-television and Telecommunications Commission (CRTC) to 'regulate and supervise all
aspects of the Canadian broadcasting system' including the grant of
renewable licences to broadcasters (Broadcasting Act 1991, section 5).
Radio and television licences are granted by the CRTC subject to various conditions, including a requirement that the broadcaster produce
a certain amount of Canadian programming.[42] As well, the CRTC has
the power to make general regulations 'respecting the proportion of
time that shall be devoted to the broadcasting of Canadian programs,'
'respecting the character of advertising and the amount of broadcasting time that may be devoted to advertising' and respecting the amount
of time devoted to political programming (Broadcasting Act, section
10(1)).[43]

The CRTC requires broadcasters 'to devote a reasonable amount of
time to the coverage of public issues.' This coverage must be balanced
and it must provide an opportunity for the 'presentation of contrasting
points of view.' However, the Commission has said that 'the determination of what is reasonable, of what constitutes balance, which are matters of public concern, which views merit to be aired, is the broadcaster's
responsibility, subject to possible public evaluation' (CRTC 1977). According to the Commission, the 'balance' requirement in the Broadcasting Act 1991 does not mean that every program must, of necessity,
describe all sides of an issue. Balance is achieved if 'in the context of
total programming, legitimately controversial issues are dealt with fairly
and honestly' (CRTC 1970).

In the few cases where broadcast regulation has been challenged on
freedom of expression grounds, the courts have dismissed the challenge fairly quickly. In the pre-Charter case of *CTV Ltd.* 1981, the Federal Court of Appeal held that a licence condition that the CTV network produce ten hours of original drama did not violate the network's
freedom of expression, which was recognized in the federal broadcasting legislation.[44] Similarly, in *CJMF-FM Ltée* 1984 the Federal Court of
Appeal rejected the argument of the radio station that a refusal to
renew its licence, because it had not fulfilled certain conditions, did
not violate freedom of expression under the Charter.[45] The court noted
that the applicant had obtained its licence because it had promised to
broadcast certain types of musical programs and that it had not kept its
promise. In the court's view the CRTC 'could base its refusal to renew
the licence on the [applicant's] conduct without infringing [its] freedom of expression' (*CJMF-FM Ltée* 1984).

The American courts have taken the constitutional challenge to broadcast regulation more seriously but have reached the same conclusion as the Canadian courts. In *Red Lion* 1969, the U.S. Supreme Court held that a Federal Communications Commission (FCC) regulation (the subsequently repealed 'fairness doctrine') that required broadcasters to spend a reasonable amount of time covering controversial issues of public importance, to give a fair and balanced presentation to each side of a public issue, and to allow members of the public an opportunity to respond to personal attacks or political editorials was consistent with the First Amendment.

The court in *Red Lion* 1969 focused on the interests of the audience and the value of diversity in public discourse and held that the public's right 'to receive suitable access to social, political, esthetic, moral, and other ideas and experiences ... is crucial' (*Red Lion* 1969, 390). This was in stark contrast with *Miami Herald* 1974, where the court insisted that the access requirement was an unjustified interference with the owner's free speech rights, even though it might open the newspaper up to a wider range of views and speakers. As well, the court in *Red Lion* 1969 was unmoved by the chilling effect argument that was invoked in *Miami Herald* 1974: 'And if experience with the administration of these doctrines indicates that they have the effect of reducing rather than enhancing the volume and quality of coverage, there will be time enough to reconsider the constitutional implications. The fairness doctrine in the past has had no such overall effect' (*Red Lion* 1969, 393).

This difference in focus (in *Miami Herald* 1974, the speaker threatened by the state, and in *Red Lion* 1969, the audience exposed to only some views by the broadcaster) rests on the characterization of a newspaper as a private property and a television station as a public trust. These contrasting characterizations are based on the courts' perception of the technological differences between print and broadcast media. In *Red Lion* 1969, the court said that because the spectrum of broadcast frequencies is limited, it is necessary for the state to distribute broadcasting opportunities by renewable licence and to impose public responsibilities upon licence holders. The broadcast spectrum is distributed under licence by the state and held as a 'public trust' because 'there are substantially more individuals who want to broadcast than there are frequencies to allocate' (*Red Lion* 1969, 388).

Yet, with any market commodity, there is always some level of scarcity. Not everyone can afford to purchase a daily newspaper or even a printing press. The legislature could have created property rights in the broadcast spectrum which, like daily newspapers or printing presses, could have been distributed in the market to the highest bidder. In any event, technology has changed. The arrival of cable and other technologies has created the possibility of a far greater number of television and radio stations. If the courts are to continue supporting legislated access to the broadcast media, they must base their support on something other than technological limitation.

The assumption that property, privately owned and exclusively controlled, is the natural or proper way to order social affairs (and organize public discourse) underlies the belief that access legislation, of the sort considered in *Miami Herald* 1974 or *Gay Alliance* 1979, interferes with the expression rights of newspaper owners. Yet private property claims have not blocked public interest regulation of television and radio facilities. Aside from the scarcity argument, there are many reasons why the courts may have been willing to attach public responsibility to broadcasting.

Attitudes towards the press are shaped by the traditional view of the press as small scale and accessible. More than a century ago it seemed possible that public opinion, in all its diversity, could find expression in a remarkably wide range of publications. Even today there is at least the theoretical possibility that any individual can produce a small newspaper or a pamphlet. This possibility has obscured the reality that daily newspapers are a key part of the public sphere, the place where public debate takes place, and not simply a participant in public debate. In contrast, broadcasting has always been seen as a large-scale enterprise that has significant power to influence public opinion, although local cable production may be changing this by providing a lower cost and smaller scale television alternative.

In Canada, the public responsibility of broadcasters also rests on a recognition that regulation, and in particular the Canadian content requirement, is necessary to ensure the preservation and development of Canadian culture and identity. According to the Broadcasting Task Force of 1986: 'The assignment of radio frequencies for broadcasting in Canada is an essential component of national sovereignty' (Canada 1986, 147).[46] Canadian identity and sovereignty would be at risk if American or other foreign programs displaced discussion of Canadian issues and expression of Canadian culture. Implicit in the assumption that broadcasting is central to Canadian cultural identity is a recognition that broadcasting frequencies are an important part of the public sphere, the place where public discussion takes place and where public culture is forged. Once we recognize this, it seems to follow that the use of broadcast frequencies should carry public responsibility.

Other factors may also account for the courts' willingness to recognize that broadcast frequency use carries public responsibility. Broadcast ownership did not precede regulation. The emergence of broadcast technology came hand-in-hand with regulation so that the property rights allocated to broadcasters were shaped by public interest concerns (Bollinger 1991, 98). In contrast, the property rights of newspaper or printing press owners are so well established that we tend to see them as natural and fixed rather than as the product of political choice. Finally, the differential treatment may be based on our attitudes towards print and visual imagery as means of communication. While the printed word is seen as appealing to reason, visual imagery is seen as capable of manipulating its viewers.

In the absence of some form of public regulation, television and radio may simply become advertising vehicles. Commercial television and radio operations are funded almost entirely by advertising revenue. It is not surprising then that advertising has had a significant effect on programming. This impact is most obvious in the evolution of children's programming and news programming. Children's television is now significantly made up of program-length commercials conceived and designed to sell toys and other products (Engelhardt 1986, 75). But even programs not specifically designed to sell products must not 'disturb' audiences and interfere with their ability 'to receive, recall and respond to the commercial messages' (Miller 1986, 191). In part, this is why public interest programming has become increasingly indistinguishable from the ads and prime time programs that surround it, with their 'cheery and speedy' images. As Mark Crispin Miller observes: 'the news has been turned into a mere extension of prime time, relying on the same techniques and rhetoric that define the ads' (Miller 1986, 194).

Recognition that broadcasters have a public responsibility does not mean that state access and balance requirements are immune from freedom of expression review. It should mean, however, that the legislature is given ample room to manoeuvre when its object is to ensure that a wider range of voices and views are given access to the public sphere.[47]

7. A Note on the Internet

It is sometimes suggested that the emergence of new and decentralized media, such as the Internet, means that newspaper and broadcast con-

212 The Constitutional Protection of Freedom of Expression

centration will become less and less a concern. The Internet, it is said, has the potential to be a 'truly' democratic forum. As the costs of computer technology continue to fall, the Internet will become broadly accessible. While advertising and commercial sites will continue to proliferate on the Internet, the decentralized character of the medium makes censorship nearly impossible and commercial capture very difficult.[48] Non-commercial 'speakers' cannot easily be frozen out. Web sites can be established at fairly low cost and can offer a wide range of views and information that may not be available in the mainstream media. Individuals with particular interests and perspectives can exchange information and ideas at specialized sites, although it is sometimes difficult to find relevant information and to know whether the information found is reliable.

Yet the decentralized character of the Internet, which makes censorship and commercial capture difficult, may also limit the value of this medium as a forum for democratic debate. Democratic discourse must involve something more than a series of separate face-to-face conversations ('private' conversations) between individuals or groups of individuals. It requires a general meeting place or forum where different views can be exchanged and considered in a public way. The sheer size of our political community means that democratic discourse must be 'mediated' in some way. Newspapers and broadcast stations now provide, or purport to provide, such a 'meeting place' where large sections of the population are exposed to a common body of ideas and information. One of the concerns described earlier is that at these 'meeting places' (newspapers and broadcast stations) there is no dialogue, only monologue, with most individuals participating only as readers or viewers.[49] The other, and more important, concern is that newspapers and broadcasters do not provide a full range of perspectives on community issues.

While the Internet facilitates conversations between individuals who may be geographically remote and is sometimes a useful source of information and ideas, it may be just too fragmented to serve as a public meeting place.[50] It is of course possible that over time particular sites on the Internet may become important forums, not unlike daily newspapers or television stations. However, it seems likely that popular sites will come under the control of corporate/commercial interests. The costs of operating a site that provides comprehensive and reliable information or popular entertainment and that draws a large and general audience would be significant and would probably require advertising support.

The dilemma then, is that Internet discourse is either too fragmented to serve democratic interests or sufficiently focused (in particular sites) but controlled by commercial interests. The scale of modern cultural/economic/political communities means that 'mediated' expression is a fact of life. (Of course, the scale of community is in part the consequence of communication technology.) The goal should be to democratize the communicative process not by demolishing key public forums or abolishing any form of control or selection but rather by ensuring that our public forums carry a wide range of views concerning public issues from all segments of the community.

8. Compelled Monetary Support for Expression: Union Dues

It has been argued that an individual's freedom of expression is violated when he or she is required to pay dues to a union and the union spends some of this money on political speech. This argument has been accepted in the United States but rejected in Canada.

In *Abood* 1977, the U.S. Supreme Court reviewed the constitutionality of a collective agreement between a teachers' union and a school board.[51] The agreement required the payment of dues by all employees represented by the union, whether or not they were union members. Mr Justice Stewart held that this 'agency-shop clause' was valid insofar as the compelled dues went to support 'collective-bargaining' activities. While the compulsion to pay union dues raises First Amendment concerns, 'such interference as exists is constitutionally justified by the legislative assessment of the important contribution of the union shop to the system of labor relations' (*Abood* 1977, 222). However, the court said that a violation of the First Amendment occurs when money paid to the union under compulsion is used for political speech.

According to Mr Justice Stewart: '[A]t the heart of the First Amendment is the notion that an individual should be free to believe as he will, and that in a free society one's beliefs should be shaped by his mind and his conscience rather than coerced by the state' (*Abood* 1977, 234–5). In the view of Stewart J., this principle prohibited the school board from requiring its teachers to contribute 'to the support of an ideological cause as a condition of retaining their teaching job' (*Abood* 1977, 235). It did not matter that the teachers were not required 'to join the Union, espouse the cause of unionism or participate in any other way in Union affairs' (*Abood* 1977, 212). Nor did it matter that an employee who disagrees with the views expressed by the union representing him or her 'is not barred from expressing his[/her] viewpoint' (*Abood* 1977, 230).

Stewart J. drew from *Buckley* 1976, and other judgments of the court, the principle that 'contributing [money] to an organization for the purpose of spreading a political message is protected by the First Amendment' (*Abood* 1977, 234). He then considered this principle in light of *Barnette* 1943, which held that freedom of speech protects an individual from state compulsion to speak against his will. He reasoned that if the state violates the individual's free speech rights when it prevents him from contributing money to support political speech, it also violates the individual's right when it compels him to contribute money to support political speech.

This argument, I think, rests on a very basic mistake. While money, or property generally, may be necessary for effective communication so that limits on spending money for communication (e.g., election spending ceilings) interfere with freedom of expression, it does not follow that the payment or contribution of money is itself speech/expression (Moon 1988b, 261). To be considered expression an act must be intended to convey a message to others. While a contribution of money may indicate support for an organization, such as the Liberal Party or Oxfam, or a cause such as famine relief or tax cuts, ordinarily it is not intended to communicate a message to an audience, except in the weakest sense that any voluntary act communicates or expresses something.

Money may be contributed to support the speech of a particular organization. For this reason a limitation on contributions may sometimes be considered a restriction (albeit indirect) on expression. Contributions are protected because expression is a valued activity, the exercise of which requires resources. However, there is not the same reason to extend freedom of expression protection to the refusal to contribute money. The individual dues payer, in a case such as *Abood* 1977, does not have to attend meetings or participate in the union's speech. Since the dues are compulsory, others will not assume that the statements made by the union represent the individual contributor's thinking, particularly if he or she is not a member of the union. It may seem unfair to take away an individual's money to support a cause he or she does not agree with, but this unfairness has nothing to do with compelled expression.

The only possible freedom of expression concern here is that the compelled payment may reduce the individual's resources to such a degree that he or she is unable to communicate with others. The argument would be that compulsory dues are objectionable not because they involve compelled speech but rather because they limit the individual's ability to communicate effectively with others. However, if the objection to compulsory dues is that they reduce the resources available to the individual for communication, why should anything turn on the way in which the dues are expended by the union? Indeed, this concern could also apply to taxes and to housing costs, both of which reduce an individual's resources.

In *Lavigne* 1991, the Supreme Court of Canada addressed the issue of compulsory dues. Mr Lavigne was an employee at a community college. As a member of the bargaining unit, though not of the union, he was subject to mandatory dues check-off (the 'Rand Formula'). He challenged certain expenditures made by the union, including contributions to the NDP, to the striking National Union of Mineworkers in the United Kingdom, and to pro-choice groups. He argued that his freedom of expression was violated when his compulsory contribution to the union was spent on political speech not directly related to collective bargaining.

All the members of the court agreed that compelled union dues do not violate freedom of expression under section 2(b).[52] According to Laforest J., Mr Lavigne's contribution to the union was not intended to convey meaning nor would anyone be likely to see it as such. As well, no one would consider that Mr Lavigne (particularly as a non-member) was in any way responsible for the way the money was spent or for the union's speech (*Lavigne* 1991, 340).

Similarly, Madame Justice Wilson found that section 2(b) was not violated because no one would attribute the views of the union to an involuntary contributor such as Mr Lavigne. She considered it a 'built-in feature' of the Rand Formula that the union's activities are only the expression of the union as the representative of the majority of employees. As well, Wilson J. noted that the payment of dues pursuant to the agency shop clause did not have the effect of depriving Mr Lavigne of his right to express himself. He retained the power to disassociate himself from the views and actions of the union.

Wilson J. did acknowledge that the compulsion to pay dues might mean that Mr Lavigne could not communicate his views through a boycott of the union (*Lavigne* 1991, 271). However, she found that this sort of restriction on expression is so minor or so peripheral that it should not be considered a violation of section 2(b). In any event, this is not an argument that compulsory payment of dues is objectionable because it amounts to compelled expression. It rests instead on the idea that silence or inaction can sometimes be expression and that requiring an individual to act or speak may prevent her from being able to express herself in this way.

In deciding that Lavigne's section 2(b) rights had not been violated, that the mandatory dues check-off did not amount to compelled expression, the court stressed that others were unlikely to attribute to Mr Lavigne the views expressed by the union and that he had plenty of opportunity to disassociate himself from those views. However, as suggested earlier, compelled expression is objectionable, even when others are unlikely to attribute the message to the speaker. The central objection to compelled expression is the indignity to the individual of having to utter words that are not his or her own.

The real issue, then, is not whether the union's views will be attributed to the dues payer, but rather whether the contribution of money is a central and conventional way in which individuals communicate their views to others, the way that saluting a flag or carrying a message on one's lapel or one's car bumper are conventional ways of communicating. If monetary contribution is an important method of communication (as both Wilson and Laforest JJ. seemed to suggest),[53] then being required to contribute money might well be seen as compelled expression contrary to section 2(b). It will involve the indignity of having to express views that are not your own, regardless of how the contributed money is spent.

However, the contribution of money is not a standard way in which people communicate their views. Through the contribution of money individuals give support to an organization, but they do not usually think of their contribution, not primarily at least, as communication to others of particular views or attitudes. Certainly money is given and taken in all kinds of situations where no one imagines there is expressive intent, in the section 2(b) sense. As well, because the act of paying money is often performed with very little personal involvement or commitment, it is difficult to imagine compulsion to pay money being experienced as an invasion of the individual's personal sphere. The compulsion to contribute money, particularly when all that happens is a payroll deduction, should not ordinarily be seen as compelled expression.[54]

9. Conclusion

The right not to speak rests on the value of speech. Compelled expression is experienced by the individual as an invasion of his 'personal sphere' because expression is so important to the realization of an individual's ideas and feelings and, more generally, to his identity. Compelled expression is objectionable even if others are aware that the views expressed by the individual are not her or his own.

If compelled expression is objectionable because it amounts to an invasion of the individual's personal sphere, there may be less concern when a large corporate entity is 'compelled' to speak or when the state gives communicative access to corporate property. Even if we were to view access to corporate property as a taking of property, which interferes with the corporation's interests, there is no dignitary harm and thus no violation of freedom of expression.

Some properties, such as a car bumper or a front lawn, are so personal and so important to an individual's opportunity to communicate with others and to define him/herself in the public world that legislation requiring the individual owner to grant access to others for communication diminishes the value of the property to the owner as a means of communication and amounts to an invasion of the individual's 'personal sphere.' However, the courts have gone well beyond this extension of the compelled expression principle and have struck down laws requiring access to the print media (and, in the United States, compelling payment of union dues that are spent on political speech) without considering whether the legislation is actually experienced by the owner as a personal invasion or whether it reduces the owner's opportunity to communicate effectively with others. This extension of the principle undermines state efforts to create space for a wider range of views and speakers in a public discourse dominated by a small group of media corporations.

Finally, if the right *not* to express oneself is protected because expression is an activity of central importance to the individual, it may not have the same breadth as the right of expression. While freedom of expression may give some protection to basic opportunities for expression, or conditions necessary for effective expression (for example, the ability of individuals to pool their resources in order to communicate more effectively), it does not follow that the freedom should protect the individual from being compelled to support, or to provide resources for, expression by other members of the community.

Chapter Eight

Conclusion: Freedom of Expression and Judicial Review

Most contemporary defences of judicial review regard constitutional rights, such as freedom of expression, as aspects of the individual's personal sphere (or autonomy) or basic conditions of democratic government, which should be insulated from the give and take of ordinary preference-based politics. According to these accounts, what judges do when enforcing a constitutional right is very different from what elected legislators do when enacting legislation. Judges interpret and apply limited and value-based constraints on the pragmatic, preference-based, decision making of legislators. The judicial role under the Charter of Rights is said to be compatible with democratic principles because it is limited in its scope and distinct from the role performed by elected officials.

Yet, as the discussion in the preceding chapters shows, freedom of expression is not a discrete concern that can be isolated from larger questions of social/economic power. The definition of the scope of freedom of expression and the assessment of its limits involve complex questions that go to the heart of the social/economic order. These are not simple issues that can be neatly separated from ordinary politics and easily dealt with by the courts. For both structural and political reasons, the courts are not well-positioned to engage in a review of the distribution of communicative resources or to assess the relative harm or value of expression, which turns in part on social/economic conditions.

The tension between freedom of expression and the structure of constitutional review is the source of two significant concerns. The first concern is that, in seeking to deal with complex freedom of expression issues within the adjudicative framework, not only will the courts fail to give full effect to the freedom's demands but they may also obstruct genuine legislative efforts to respond to the harms of expression or to the gross maldistribution of communicative power. This can be seen in a variety of cases. For example, in the pre-Charter case of *Gay Alliance* 1979, the court found that freedom of expression precluded legislated access to the media. This conclusion seemed plausible only because the court regarded the existing distribution of communicative resources as the fixed background against which state interference with freedom of expression should be judged. And in *RJR Macdonald* 1995, because the Supreme Court was unable to draw a workable distinction between rational and manipulative expression, it decided that some or all cigarette advertising should be considered valuable expression – expression that communicates ideas and information. Of course, the same difficulty in distinguishing rational and non-rational or non-cognitive expression may have the opposite result. This was the case in *Butler* 1992, where the court upheld a vague restriction on sexually explicit imagery, a restriction that has subsequently been applied by some lower courts in a very broad way, catching material that arguably involves a legitimate exploration of sexual issues and identities.

The second and more significant concern is that the practical constraints of constitutional adjudication may begin to limit our understanding of the demands and possibilities of freedom of expression. We need only look to the United States to see a collapsing of the distinction between freedom of expression as political ideal and constitutional right. Concern that our conception of freedom of expression may become compressed within the parameters of constitutional adjudication rests not on the persuasive force of judicial decisions but rather on our increasing reliance on the courts to resolve familiar freedom of expression issues. As more and more of our discussion of freedom of expression is framed as constitutional argument, it may become natural to think of the freedom as an individual right against state interference.

Notes

1: Truth, Democracy, and Autonomy

1 See for example Redish 1982, 593–4: 'The position taken in this article is that the constitutional guarantee of free speech ultimately serves only one true value, which I have labelled "self-realization" ... My contention is that these other values [political process and marketplace of ideas], though perfectly legitimate, are in reality subvalues of self-realization. To the extent that they are legitimate, each can be explained by – and only by – reference to the primary value: individual self-realization. It is thus inaccurate to say that "the commitment to freedom of expression embodies a complex of values".'

2 McLachlin. J. in *Keegstra* 1990, 806: 'First it may be noted that the broad wording of s.2(b) of the Charter is arguably inconsistent with a justification based on a single facet of expression. This suggests that there is no need to adopt any one definitive justification for freedom of expression. Different justifications for freedom of expression may assume varying degrees of importance in different fact situations.' See also Sharpe 1987, 232, and Greenawalt 1989, 4: 'no single justification is likely to be adequate.'

    Sunstein 1993, xx: 'We should, of course, recognize the plurality and diversity of values served by a system of free expression. The First Amendment is not concerned only with politics; it has to do with autonomy and self-development as well. Any simple or unitary theory of free speech value would be obtuse.'

3 Before considering the established accounts of freedom of expression, it is important to recognize that some are accounts of a constitutionally entrenched right and existing constitutional practice. As such they are shaped by concerns about the legitimacy of judicial review in the enforce-

ment of constitutional rights and are constrained by the structure of constitutional adjudication. Indeed, the constitutional focus of many accounts of the value of freedom of expression may be partly responsible for the downplaying of the freedom's social character. See Chapter 2 for a discussion.

4 Milton 1927 [1644], 36, also defends free debate and discussion as essential to the realization of truth. If men and women were permitted to engage in a free and open exchange of ideas and information, truth would prevail: 'And though all the winds of doctrine were let loose to play upon the earth, so Truth be in the field, we do injuriously by licensing and prohibiting to misdoubt her strength. Let her and Falsehood grapple; who ever knew Truth put to the worse in a free and open encounter?'

5 Mill 1982, 79: 'There is the greatest difference between presuming an opinion to be true because, with every opportunity for contesting it, it has not been refuted, and assuming its truth for the purpose of not permitting its refutation. Complete liberty of contradicting and disproving our opinion is the very condition that justifies us in assuming its truth for purposes of action; and on no other terms can a being with human faculties have any rational assurance of being right.'

6 Schauer 1982, 26: 'It is hardly surprising that the search for truth was so central in the writings of Milton, Locke, Voltaire and Jefferson. They placed their faith in the ability of reason to solve problems and distinguish truth from falsehood. They had confidence in the reasoning power of *all* people, if only the power was allowed to flourish. The argument from truth is very much a child of the Enlightenment, and of the optimistic view of the rationality and the perfectibility of humanity it embodied.'

7 Schauer 1982, 16, describing the common theme of truth-based arguments says: 'They all share a belief that freedom of speech is not an end but a means, a means of identifying and accepting truth.'

8 Mill 1982, 106, recognized that general agreement may at some point be reached about the truth of certain claims: 'As mankind improve, the number of doctrines which are no longer disputed or doubted will be constantly on the increase; and the well-being of mankind may almost be measured by the number and gravity of the truths which have reached the point of being uncontested.'

9 For a brief description of the bizarre racist views of James Keegstra see Chapter 4 below.

10 See Chapter 5 for an extended discussion of this point.

11 Mill recognized that if the individual does not understand the grounds for her opinions, her commitment to these opinions will be either unstable or

dogmatic (Mill 1982, 116). He believed that 'even if the received opinion be not only true, but the whole truth; unless it is suffered to be, and actually is, vigorously and earnestly contested, it will, by most of those who receive it, be held in the manner of a prejudice' (Mill 1982, 106). See also Mill 1982, 97: 'This is not knowing the truth.' 'Truth, thus held, is but one superstition the more, accidentally clinging to the words which enunciate the truth.'

12 Similarly, Milton 1927, 13, argued that the true nature of humans resides in their capacity for reason. God has trusted man 'with the gift of reason to be his own chooser.' For Milton, the life of reason was in discussion and debate. The free exchange of ideas and information is necessary to the realization of human reason and to the development of society. Certainly truth is not to be valued unless it is the outcome of the reasoned judgment of men and women. Milton could not see the value of truth if it is simply, 'a fugitive and cloistered virtue unexercised and unbreathed, that never sallies out and seeks her adversary, but slinks out of the race, where that immortal garland is to be run for, not without dust and heat. Assuredly we bring not innocence into the world, we bring impurity much rather, that which purifies us is trial, and trial is by what is contrary' (Milton 1927, 13).

13 Dworkin 1996, 201, observes that 'John Stuart Mill endorsed both [instrumental and 'constitutive' arguments] in *On Liberty.*' These arguments Dworkin believes 'are not mutually exclusive.' But the point is not that the arguments are compatible; rather, they are inseparable – they are different sides of a single argument. See below at p. 25.

14 McLachlin J. in *Keegstra* 1990, 804, used this language: 'freedom of expression can be justified at least in part on the basis that it promotes the "marketplace of ideas".'

15 A similar view is expressed by Fiss 1996, 3, and by Sunstein 1993, xvii: 'Indeed, we might understand the extraordinary protection now given to political speech to be an elaboration of the American understanding of sovereignty.'

16 Meiklejohn 1965, 14, also says: 'At the bottom of every plan of self-government is a basic agreement, in which all the citizens have joined, that all matters of public policy shall be decided by corporate action, that such decisions shall be binding on all citizens, whether they agree with them or not, and that, if need be, they shall, by due legal procedure, be enforced upon anyone who refuses to conform to them.'

17 Meiklejohn 1965, 21, also says that the First Amendment 'does not forbid the abridging of speech. But, at the same time, it does forbid the abridging of freedom of speech.'

18 Madame Justice McLachlin in *Keegstra* 1990, 805: 'They [governments] have an interest in stilling criticism of themselves, or even in enhancing their own popularity by silencing unpopular expression. These motives may render them unable to carefully weigh the advantages and disadvantages of suppression in many instances.' And see Sunstein 1993, 134: 'An insistence that government's burden is greatest for regulating political speech is based on a sensible view of government's incentives. It is in this setting that government is most likely to be biased or to be acting on the basis of illegitimate, venal or partial considerations. Government is rightly distrusted when it is regulating speech that might harm its own interests; and when the speech at issue is political its own interests are almost always at stake. It follows that the premise of distrust of government is strongest when politics is at issue. And when the premise of distrust is strongest, the burden of justification is highest.'

19 Sunstein 1993, 130, says that speech is political 'when it is both intended and received as a contribution to public deliberation about some issue.' This definition, says Sunstein 1993, 152, 'would encompass not simply political tracts, but all art and literature that have the characteristics of social commentary.'

20 Meiklejohn 1965, 14: 'We must recognize that there are many forms of communication, which, since they are not being used as activities of governing are wholly outside the scope of the First Amendment.' Meiklejohn thought that these would include yelling fire in a crowded theatre, perjury, libel, false advertising, and obscenity. See also Meiklejohn 1965, 16: '[I]f the interests of a self-governing society are to be served, vituperation which fixes attention on the defects of an opponent's character or intelligence and thereby distracts attention from the question of policy under discussion may be forbidden as a deadly enemy of peaceable assembly.'

21 Consider the criticism of Post 1995, 274: 'His [Meiklejohn's] paradigm of the town meeting specifically presupposes that the function of American democracy is to achieve an orderly, efficient, and rational dispatch of common business, and it consequently implies that aspects of public discourse incompatible with that function are constitutionally expendable. To the extent public discourse is thus truncated, a particular concept of national identity is placed beyond the reach of the communicative processes of self-determination.'

22 But see Meiklejohn 1965, 84: 'The principle of the unqualified freedom of public speech is, then, valid only in and for a society which is self-governing. It has no political justification where men are governed without their

consent. For example, in such social institutions as an army or a prison or an insane asylum, the principle of freedom of speech is neither relevant nor valid.'

23 The recent Supreme Court of Canada judgment in *K-Mart* 1999 takes this view: 'For workers, a form of expression which deals with their working conditions and treatment by their employer is a statement about their working environment. Thus it relates to their well-being and dignity in the workplace' (para. 29).

24 Fiss 1996, 3, argues that the First Amendment protects 'popular sovereignty.' Citizens exercising the power of self-government must be exposed to a wide range of different perspectives on public issues. Fiss contrasts his democratic account with what he describes as a 'libertarian' account. The libertarian account, according to Fiss, protects the individual interest in self-expression or self-actualization. Fiss, however, seems to ignore the fact that self-government is about individuals speaking and listening, and, ideally, making wise judgments. He offers only the most abstract explanation of how speech advances democratic values and in this way avoids coming to grips with the relationship between the individual and the self-governing collective.

Post does not seem to fall into this trap and argues powerfully that 'the function of public discussion is to reconcile, to the extent possible, the will of individuals with the general will' (Post 1995, 299). Freedom of expression 'enables a culturally heterogenous society to forge a common democratic will' (Post 1995, 116).

Post, however, takes little account of the fact that public discourse is mediated and that the significant media are controlled by a relatively small group of individuals who hold a narrow range of perspectives. (See Chapter 7). This must matter if Post is right that '[i]ndividual citizens can identify with the creation of a collective will only if they believe that collective-decision-making is in some way connected to their own individual self-determination' (Post 1997, 1524) and that 'although there may be no determinate fusion of individual and collective will, citizens can nevertheless embrace the government as rightfully "their own" because of their engagement in these communicative processes' (Post 1995, 273).

Post recognizes that individual thought is changed in the process of public discussion – otherwise there could be no reconciliation of individual and collective wills. Yet, at the same time, he seems to regard individual agency (autonomy) as preformed – as prior to and independent of public discourse. According to Post, the 'self' necessary to self-determination is created through a process of socialization into community life or inculcation of community values in school and family environments (Post 1995, 330). Post, however, may be underestimating both the constitutive character of public discourse (and the risks we assume when the forums of public discourse are controlled by a small number of people) and the role of reason and deliberation in the shaping of individual values in school and family environments.

25 Dickson C.J. in *Keegstra* 1990, 764: 'Freedom of expression is a crucial aspect of the democratic commitment, not merely because it permits the best policies to be chosen from among a wide array of preferred options, but additionally because it helps to ensure that participation in the political process is open to all persons.'

26 Sunstein 1993, 18–9: 'In such a system, politics is not supposed merely to protect preexisting private rights or to reflect the outcomes of interest group pressures. It is not intended to aggregate existing private preferences, or to produce compromises among various affected groups with self-interested stakes in the outcome. Instead it is designed to have an important deliberative feature, in which new information and perspectives influence social judgments about possible courses of action. Through exposure to such information and perspectives, both collective and individual decisions can be shaped and improved.'

27 Scanlon 1977, 162: 'To regard himself as autonomous ... a person must see himself as sovereign in deciding what to believe and in weighing competing reasons for action.'

28 Dworkin 1985, 386: 'Anyone who holds this theory must, of course, show why censorship is a more serious injury than other forms of regulation. He must show why someone who is forbidden to speak his mind on politics suffers harm that is graver than when he is forbidden, for example, to drive at high speed or trespass on others' property or combine to restrain trade. Different theories might be proposed: that censorship is degrading because it suggests that the speaker or writer is not worthy of equal concern as a citizen, or that his ideas are not worthy of equal respect; that censorship is insulting because it denies the speaker an equal voice in politics and therefore denies his standing as a free and equal citizen; or that censorship is grave because it inhibits an individual's development of his own personality.'

29 Weinrib 1990, 341–2: '[A] constitutional guarantee of free speech reflects the understanding that language and other forms of meaningful expression actualize the capacity for human self-realization. The focus is, thus, on the meaningful expression of the thinking faculty, rather than on the system of communication itself or the correlative activity of receiving and responding to what has been communicated.' See also Baker 1989, 53:

'[A]ny time a person engages in chosen meaningful conduct, whether public or private, the conduct usually expresses and further defines the actor's identity and contributes to his or her self-realization.'

30 Haiman 1993, 85: 'It is because words, pictures, and other symbolic behaviours are, by their very nature, far less likely than physically conse-quential conduct to reach that level of harmfulness, that we must presume, in our minds and the minds of those who make and administer our laws, the distinction between speech and action.' See also Baker 1989, 56: 'Arguably, a reason for focussing on speech as a specially protected liberty relates to the implicit recognition that speech behaviour is normally non-coercive. Speech typically depends for its power on increasing the speaker's own awareness or the voluntary acceptance of listeners.'

31 Mill 1982, 68: 'the only purpose for which power can be rightfully exer-cised over any member of a civilized community, against his will, is to prevent harm to others. His own good, either physical or moral, is not a sufficient warrant.'

32 By focusing on the censor's motives – his or her lack of respect for the speaker or listener – rather than on the value of expressive activity, proponents of autonomy-based accounts avoid having to address the problem of communicative opportunity.

33 Greenawalt 1989, 33–4 also states: 'The concerns about dignity and equality may seem not to be specially related to speech but to be argu-ments, perhaps rather weak ones, in favour of liberty generally. There may, however, be a tighter connection between restrictions on communications and affronts to dignity and equality. Expressions of beliefs and feelings lie closer to the core of our persons than do most actions we perform; restrictions of expression may offend dignity to a greater degree than most other restrictions; and selective restrictions based on the content of our ideas may imply a specially significant inequality. So put, the notion of affront to dignity and equality bears a plausible relationship to free speech, though it also reaches other forms of liberty, such as liberty of sexual involvement and liberty of personal appearances, which lie close to how we conceive ourselves.

34 Taylor 1985, 229: an individual's 'ideas do not properly exist before their expression in language or some other range of media men deploy. That is what is meant by saying that language, or expression in general, is constitu-tive of thought.' See also Hutchinson 1995a, 191: 'Language is not a transparency through which the world is observed or a catalogue of labels to be attached velcro-like to the appropriate contents of the world. There is no form of pure communication that merely represents instead of creating.

The world is within language and the language is within the world. Language is a social medium. It shapes society and its individuals as they work to reshape it. No one is free to describe the world as they wish; they are always and already constrained by the prevailing ways of speaking. As such, discourse is as much constitutive of society, both personal and collective, as it is constituted by that society.'

35 Taylor 1985, 232: '[Language is a] pattern of activity, by which we realize a certain way of being in the world, that of reflective awareness, but a pattern which can only be deployed against a background which we can never fully dominate; and yet a background that we are not fully dominated by, because we are constantly reshaping it. Reshaping it without dominating it, or being able to oversee it, means that we never fully know what we are doing to it; we develop language without knowing fully what we are making it into.' See also Taylor 1985, 231: The words we use 'only have sense through their place in the whole web [of language]' and so 'we can never have a clear oversight of the implications of what we say at any moment.'

36 See also Ricoeur 1976, 19: 'To mean is what the speaker does. But it is also what the sentence does. The utterance meaning – in the sense of the propositional content – is the "objective" side of this meaning. The utterer's meaning in the three-fold sense of the self-reference of the sentence, the illocutionary dimension of the speech act, and the intention of recognition by the hearer – is the "subjective" side of the meaning.' We recognize that a speaker may use the "wrong" words to express her ideas and a listener may misunderstand the speaker's words or her intended meaning or he may interpret those words in a very personal, even idiosyncratic, way. See also Butler 1997, 140: 'One speaks a language that is never fully one's own, but that language only persists through repeated occasions of that invoca-tion. That language gains tempered life only in and through the utterances that reinvoke and restructure the conditions of its own possibility.'

37 Gadamer 1986, 404: Language has its true being only in conversation, 'in the exercise of understanding between people.'

38 Ricoeur 1976, 30: 'If the intentional fallacy overlooks the semantic au-tonomy of the text, the opposite fallacy forgets that a text remains a discourse told by somebody, said by someone to someone else about something. It is impossible to cancel out this main characteristic of discourse without reducing texts to natural objects, i.e. to things which are not man made, but which, like pebbles, are found in the sand.' And see Butler 1997, 133: 'every text or expression is in part structured through a process of selection that is determined in part by decision of an author or

speaker and in part by a language that operates according to selective and differential rules that no individual speaker ever made ...'

39 Taylor 1985, 233: 'The development of new modes of expression enables us to have new feelings, more powerful and more refined, and certainly more self-aware. In being able to express our feelings, we give them a reflective dimension that transforms them. The language user can feel not only anger but indignation, not only love but admiration.'

40 Bruner 1990, 33: '[Human agency (intentional state)] is realized only through participation in the symbolic systems of the culture. Indeed, the very shape of our lives – the rough and perpetually changing draft of our autobiography that we carry in our minds – is understandable to ourselves and to others only by virtue of those cultural systems of interpretation.' And see Voloshinov 1995, 125: Only in 'the stream of verbal communication' does consciousness 'begin to operate.'

41 Steiner 1975, 172: 'Even the most public of languages will always have personal meanings and associations ... Active inside the "public" vocabulary and conventions of grammar are pressures of vital association, of latent or realized content. Much of this content is irreducibly individual and, in the common sense of the term, private. When we speak to others we speak "at the surface" of ourselves. We normally use a shorthand beneath which there lies a wealth of subconscious, deliberately concealed or declared associations so extensive and intricate that they probably equal the sum and uniqueness of our status as an individual person.'

42 Voloshinov 1995, 130: 'In point of fact, word is a two-sided act. It is determined equally by whose word it is and for whom it is meant. As word, it is precisely the product of the reciprocal relationship between speaker and listener, addresser and addressee. Each and every word expresses the one in relation to the "other".'

43 Thompson 1995, 42: 'To appropriate a message is to take hold of its meaningful content and make it one's own. It is to assimilate the message and incorporate it into one's life – a process that sometimes takes place effortlessly, and sometimes involves deliberate application. In incorporating a message we adapt it to our own lives and life contexts.'

44 Thompson 1995, 43: 'In receiving and appropriating media messages, individuals are also involved in a process of self-formation and self-understanding ... By taking hold of messages and routinely incorporating them into our lives, we are implicitly involved in constructing a sense of self, a sense of who we are and where we are situated in space and time. We are constantly shaping and reshaping our skills and stocks of knowledge,

testing our feelings and tastes and expanding the horizons of our
experience.'

45 McLachlin J. in *Keegstra* 1990, 806, noted the importance of both intrinsic
and instrumental accounts: 'The interpretation which has been placed on
s.2(b) of the Charter confirms the relevance of both instrumental and
intrinsic justifications for freedom of expression.' And in *Keegstra* 1990, 802:
'Various philosophical justifications exist for freedom of expression. Some
of these posit free expression as a means to other ends. Others see freedom
of expression as an end in itself.'

46 Self-realization theories are sometimes described in instrumental terms.
For example, Greenawalt 1989, 26: 'By affording people an opportunity to
hear and digest competing positions and to explore options in conversation with others, freedom of discussion is thought to promote independent
judgment and considerate decision, what might be characterized as
autonomy. This is a consequentialist argument that connects free speech to
autonomy.'

47 Instrumental accounts of freedom of expression do not fit well with
contemporary defences of judicial review, which argue that judicial review
is acceptable insofar as it involves the insulation of fundamental liberties
from the give and take of ordinary preference-based politics.

48 Trakman 1995a, 938, describes speech as 'an instrument of social solidarity.' He focuses on the 'relationship between the right to speak and the
responsibility for it.'

49 In their writing about freedom of expression Milton 1927 and Mill 1982
were concerned principally with the freedom to produce and distribute
books, pamphlets, newspapers, and other printed materials without
interference from the state. Milton 1927, 4–5, regarded the printed word as
the expression of reason: '[B]ooks are not absolutely dead things, but do
contain a potency of life in them to be as active as that soul whose progeny
they are; nay they do preserve as in a vial the purest efficacy and extraction
of that living intellect that bred them ... [U]nless wariness be used, as good
almost kill a man as kill a good book: who kills a man, kills a reasonable
creature, God's image; but he who destroys a good book, kills reason itself,
kills the image of God, as it were in the eye.'

50 In the view of Ong 1982, 46, because '[w]riting separates the knower from
the known' it permits 'the conditions for objectivity, ... personal disengagement or distancing.' See also Havelock 1988, 38.
  Communication by print is more individualized and more distanced
from immediate circumstances and so allows space for more thoughtful
reflection by the reader and correction by other writers. Oral communica-

tion, on the other hand, is more likely to involve circumstances that exclude or limit the opportunity for rational reflection and permit an irrational or emotional response. The audience's 'natural reason' is more likely to be distorted by the passion and immediacy of the spoken word.

51 Schauer 1982, 104, refers to statements of 'pure emotive content' and suggests that such statements might not fall within the scope of freedom of expression. But even so-called emotive statements such as 'that's crap' involve more than emotion.

52 As Taylor 1989b, 168 points out: 'Intimacy is an essentially dialogic phenomenon: it is a matter of what we share, of what's for us. One could never describe what it is to be on an intimate footing with someone in terms of monological states.'

53 In *Weisfeld* 1995, Linden J. of the Federal Court of Appeal argued that the freedom of expression 'claimant' 'need not establish that his or her message was received and subjectively understood and appreciated by others. It is the conveying or the attempted conveying of the meaning, not its receipt, that triggers the guarantee under paragraph 2(b).' See also Schauer 1982, 98: 'Communication is a joint enterprise, and only that joint enterprise triggers the principle of free speech. Without communicative intent, a communicated message, and a recipient of the communication there is no complete communicative act, and no occasion to talk about freedom of speech.' And see Sunstein 1993, 131: 'Both intent and receipt must be shown. It seems implausible to say that words warrant the highest form of protection if the speaker does not even intend to communicate a message. The First Amendment should not be taken to put gibberish at the core even if it is taken, by some in the audience, to mean something. By requiring intent, however, I do not mean to require individual trials on subjective motivation. Generally this issue should be resolved by making reasonable inferences from the speech at issue.'

54 This account is derived from Searle 1983 and Grice 1989. It is offered as an account of expression rather than of meaning. See also Green 1994, 138: 'Generally, an act counts as expression only if it attempts to get others to understand or share some proposition or attitude, and only if it does this communicatively, that is by trying to get them to recognize that it is done with that intention.'

55 See above at p. 22. Eagleton 1983, 114, argues that: 'To ask in such a situation "What do you mean?" is really to ask what effects my language is trying to bring about: it is a way of understanding the situation itself, not an attempt to tune into ghostly impulses within my skull. Understanding my intention is grasping my speech and behaviour in relation to a signifi-

cant context. When we understand the "intentions" of a piece of language, we interpret it as being in some sense oriented, structured to achieve certain effects; and none of this can be grasped apart from the practical conditions in which the language operates.'

56 In *Spence* 1974, 409, the U.S. Supreme Court said that an act such as flag burning receives prima facie protection under the First Amendment if 'an intent to convey a particularized message was present, and in the surrounding circumstances the likelihood was great that the message would be understood by those who viewed it.'

57 In *Irwin Toy* 1989, 607, Chief Justice Dickson for the majority of the Supreme Court of Canada argued that 'while most human activity combines expressive and physical elements, some human activity is purely physical and does not convey or attempt to convey meaning.'

Restrictions on dress and personal style illustrate the difficulty in defining a clear category of protected expression on the basis of the actor's intention/awareness.(According to Schauer 1982, 52, mode of dress is not an act of communication protected under the First Amendment.) Sometimes an individual may quite consciously see her choice of clothing as a form of expression (communication); she may even intend to make a definite statement with her clothing, for example, when she wears the national costume of an oppressed group. More often the individual's clothing choices simply reflect a partly conscious 'decision' to follow certain social conventions or practices or to associate him/herself with different social groups or traits. This identification or association with social practice can only weakly be described as the communication of a message to others. Of course, if the state were to impose a restriction on dress we might suspect that it was motivated by a desire to suppress the expression of a particular message. And if such a ban were imposed, an individual might come to regard his mode of dress more clearly as a statement to others. If a ban on a particular style of clothing were meant to prevent a particular image or message or group association, then almost certainly we would regard it as a restriction on expression. As well, when a ban on a style of dress is intended to prevent or inhibit certain kinds of group identification, freedom of expression arguments may be reinforced by concerns about religious or ethnic discrimination.

Haiman 1981, 37, does not believe that 'there must have been a conscious intent to communicate on the part of the actor at the time of the event. The Indian children in Pawnee, Oklahoma may not have been aware that they were advertising their culture by going to school with their hair in braids. It should suffice if their parents testify on their behalf that this hairstyle was a meaningful mode of expressing their tribal values.'

In *Ford* 1988 the Supreme Court of Canada held that language choice is protected under freedom of expression. However, in most cases a person's choice of language is not meant itself to communicate something to others. While use of a particular language is central to group association/identification, individuals do not generally choose between different languages. They use the language they know and which is known by the individuals to whom they wish to communicate. Yet, as the court in *Ford* 1988 noted, language is a vehicle for communication – and it is a vehicle that shapes the message communicated. As well, restrictions on language choice interfere with the communicative relationship and group association among language speakers.

58 Schauer 1982, 110, questions whether art should be regarded as communication. He sets up a contrast between self-expression and communication and suggests that art, at least sometimes, may be self-expression rather than communication.

59 Wollheim 1980, 87: 'the artist is active, but so also is the spectator, and the spectator's activity consists in interpretation.'

60 The medium is integral to the work of art. Henri Matisse, quoted in Geertz 1983, 96, described the connection between form and meaning in this way: 'The purpose of a painter must not be conceived as separate from his pictorial means and these pictorial means must be more complete (I do not mean more complicated) the deeper his thought. I am unable to distinguish the feeling I have for life and my way of expressing it.'

61 Wollheim 1980, 124: 'In creating his forms, the artist is operating inside a continuing activity or enterprise, and this enterprise has its own repertoire, imposes stringencies, offers its own opportunities, and thereby provides occasions, inconceivable outside it, for invention and audacity.'

62 However, it has been argued that the current child pornography law does exactly this. See *Sharpe* 1999.

63 Grice 1989, 26: 'Our talk exchanges do not normally consist of a succession of disconnected remarks, and would not be rational if they did. They are characteristically, to some degree at least, cooperative efforts; and each participant recognizes in them, to some extent, a common purpose or set of purposes, or at least a mutually accepted direction.'

64 Post 1995, 313: '[P]rotecting uncivil speech does not automatically destroy the possibility of rational deliberation. The visceral shock of uncivil speech can sometimes actually serve constructive purposes, as when it causes

individuals to question the community standards into which they have been socialized ... There is in fact a long tradition of oppressed and marginalized groups using uncivil speech to force recognition of the intensity and urgency of their needs.'

65 For example, Meiklejohn 1975, 14, excluded expression that is deceptive or manipulative from the scope of the freedom. He called it non-political and asserted that it did not contribute to political deliberation.

2: The Constitutional Adjudication of Freedom of Expression

1 Dickson C.J. in *Keegstra* 1990, 760: 'Content is irrelevant to this interpretation, the result of a high value being placed on freedom of expression in the abstract.'

2 Dickson C.J. in *Irwin Toy* 1989, 969: 'It might be difficult to characterize certain day-to-day tasks, like parking a car, as having expressive content. To bring such an activity within the protected sphere, the plaintiff would have to show that it was performed to convey meaning. For example, an unmarried person might, as part of a public protest, park in a zone reserved for spouses of government employees in order to express dissatisfaction or outrage at the chosen method of allocating a limited resource. If that person could demonstrate that his activity did in fact have expressive content, he would, at this stage, be within the protected sphere and the s.2(b) challenge would proceed.'

In some cases the 'statement' may not be simply parking but illegal or unauthorized parking. In other words a critical part of the message is the breach of law or rule itself. Even if we consider illegal parking to be an act of expression under section 2(b), it may be that the law restricting the particular form of parking should not be considered as simply a restriction on expression that must be justified under the terms of section 1. After all, the act of expression (its meaning and significance) depends on the law's existence. Perhaps the individual should not be able to argue that the law should not be enforced because it has restricted her expression, since her act of expression depends on the law's existence.'

3 Dickson C.J. in *Irwin Toy* 1989, 974: 'If the government's purpose is to restrict the content of expression by singling out particular meanings that are not to be conveyed, it necessarily limits the guarantee of free expression. If the government's purpose is to restrict a form of expression in order to control access by others to the meaning being conveyed or to control the ability of the one conveying the meaning to do so, it also limits the guarantee. On the other hand, where the government aims to control

only the physical consequences of certain human activity, regardless of the meaning being conveyed its purpose is not to control expression.'

4 The parallel may not be perfect because under the *Irwin Toy* 1989 test a restriction on a particular form of expression, such as street demonstrations or leafleting, might be regarded as a restriction on expression (as having the purpose rather than simply the effect of restricting expression), even though not aimed at the content of the expression.

However, it is not clear that a workable distinction can be drawn between a restriction aimed at a form of expression (which will automatically violate section 2(b)) and a restriction which, although not aimed at expression per se, nevertheless has the effect of restricting a certain form of expression (which will not automatically violate section 2(b)). If a particular restriction is intended to protect privacy or peace and quiet for example (and we do not doubt that this is the real purpose) should it matter if the restricted activity is almost always or only sometimes used to convey a message? – should it matter whether the law bans megaphone use at night (assuming that megaphones are almost always used to convey a message) or loud noises at night?

5 Dickson C.J., *Irwin Toy* 1989, 979: 'To make this claim, the plaintiff must at least identify the meaning being conveyed and how it relates to the pursuit of truth, participation in the community, or individual self-fulfillment and human flourishing.'

6 For example, LaForest J. in *Ross* 1996, 864: 'freedom of expression should only be restricted in the clearest of circumstances.'

7 Lamer C.J. in *Dagenais* 1994, 878: 'To assess the validity of the order in the case at bar, it is necessary to consider the objective of the order, to examine the availability of reasonable alternative measures that could achieve this objective, and to consider whether the salutary effects of the publication ban outweigh the deleterious impact of the ban on freedom of expression.'

Lamer C.J. in *Dagenais* 1994, 889: 'there must be proportionality between the deleterious effects of the measures which are responsible for limiting the rights or freedoms in question and the objective, and there must be a proportionality between the deleterious and salutary effects of the measures.'

8 However, in a concurring judgment McLachlin J. in *Lucas* 1998, 486, argues, against the majority opinion, that the marginal value of a particular form or instance of expression should be taken into account only at the end of the section 1 analysis and not when the court is considering the minimal impairment and rational connection issues: 'To allow the per-

ceived low value of the expression to lower the bar of justification from the outset of the s.1 analysis is to run the risk that a judge's subjective conclusion that the expression is of little worth may undermine the intellectual rigour of the *Oakes* test.'

9 Cory J. in *Lucas* 1998, 459: 'Quite simply, the level of protection to which expression may be entitled will vary with the nature of the expression. The further that expression is from the core values of this right the greater will be the ability to justify the state's restrictive action.' See also Bastarache J. in *Thompson* 1998, 943: 'Another contextual factor to be considered is the nature of the activity which is infringed. The degree of constitutional protection may vary depending on the nature of the expression at issue ... This is not because a lower standard is applied, but because the low value of the expression may be more easily outweighed by the government objective.'

10 Dickson C.J. in *Irwin Toy* 1989, 990: 'Where the legislature mediates between the competing claims of different groups in the community, it will inevitably be called upon to draw a line where one set of claims legitimately begins and the other fades away without access to complete knowledge as to its precise location. If the legislature has made a reasonable assessment as to where the line is most properly drawn, especially if that assessment involves weighing conflicting scientific evidence and allocating scarce resources on this basis, it is not for the court to second guess. That would only be to substitute one estimate for another.'

Deference is appropriate, said Dickson C.J. at 994, because '[w]hen striking a balance between the claims of competing groups, the choice of means, like the choice of ends, frequently will require an assessment of conflicting scientific evidence and differing justified demands on scarce resources. Democratic institutions are meant to let us all share in the responsibility for these difficult choices. Thus, as courts review the results of the legislature's deliberations, particularly with respect to the protection of vulnerable groups, they must be mindful of the legislature's representation function.'

But note also the concern of McLachlin J. in *RJR Macdonald* 1995, 332 that deference not go so far as to preclude meaningful judicial review: 'care must be taken not to extend the notion of deference too far. Deference must not be carried to the point of relieving the government of the burden which the *Charter* places upon it of demonstrating that the limits it has imposed on guaranteed rights are reasonable and justifiable.'

11 I note that Lepofsky 1993 does not argue that violent acts should be protected under section 2(b) but only that the logic of the court's approach to section 2(b) would seem to require their inclusion.

12 For example, Cameron 1997, 65, says that 'section 2(b) cannot be compromised by a concept of harm that is diffuse, pervasive, indeterminate or speculative.' The harm must be other than 'general offence to social values.'

13 The Supreme Court assumes that the limitations issue under section 1 turns principally or entirely on factual findings. This is most obvious when the court says that the burden of proving that a limit is justified falls on the state (or the party seeking to uphold the limit) and that the standard of proof is 'on a balance of probabilities' (*Oakes* 1986, 137). However, it may be that limitations issues are viewed as fact-based only because the court has adopted a 'causal' approach, in which it asks 'does this expression cause this harm?'

14 See for example *Ford* 1988, 767: 'Over and above its intrinsic value as expression, commercial expression which, as has been pointed out, protects listeners as well as speakers plays a significant role in enabling individuals to make informed economic choices, an important aspect of individual self-fulfillment and personal autonomy.'

15 Taylor 1989b, 167: 'A conversation is not the co-ordination of actions of different individuals, but a common action in this strong irreducible sense; it is *our* action.' McLachlin J. in *Zundel* 1992, 756, came close to recognizing this: 'Moreover, meaning is not a datum so much as an interactive process, depending on the listener as well as the speaker. Different people may draw from the same statement different meanings at different times. The guarantee of freedom of expression seeks to protect not only the meaning intended to be communicated by the publisher but also the meaning or meanings understood by the reader.'

16 *Ford* 1988, 766: 'These [scope and justification] are two distinct questions and call for two distinct analytical processes ... First consideration will be given to the interests and purposes that are meant to be protected by the particular right or freedom in order to determine whether the right or freedom has been infringed in the context presented to the court. If the particular right or freedom is found to have been infringed, the second step is to determine whether the infringement can be justified by the state within the constraints of s.1. It is within the perimeters of s.1 that courts will in most instances weigh competing values in order to determine which should prevail.'

17 Even when the alleged injury is to a third party, that is, an individual who is not a party to the communication (for example, injury to an individual's reputation in the case of defamatory expression or violence and discrimination against women in the case of pornography), the character of the communicative relationship may be a factor in the court's decision that the

'expression' is harmful and properly subject to restriction under section 1. Pornography and defamation are restricted because they 'cause' harm to third parties. Yet freedom of expression is said to protect the audience's right to hear and assess the views of others. If the audience agrees with the views expressed and acts on those views, the audience and not the speaker is responsible for any resulting harm. Part of the justification for restricting pornography and defamation may be that these forms of expression appeal to the irrational or occur in circumstances in which the exercise of independent judgment is more difficult. In these circumstances the speaker may be seen as bearing some responsibility for the actions of the audience.

18 In *Irwin Toy* 1989, 970, because the violent expression exception was not applicable on the facts, and was only introduced for future guidance, Dickson C.J. considered that '[i]t is not necessary to delineate precisely when and on what basis a form of expression chosen to convey a meaning falls outside the sphere of the guarantee. But it is clear, for example, that a murderer or rapist cannot invoke freedom of expression in justification of the form of expression he has chosen.'

19 Dickson C.J. in *Keegstra* 1990, 733: 'While the line between form and content is not always easily drawn, in my opinion threats of violence can only be so classified by reference to the content of their meaning. As such, they do not fall within the exception spoken of in *Irwin Toy*, and their suppression must be justified under s.1. As I do not find threats of violence to be excluded from the definition of expression envisioned by s.2(b), it is unnecessary to determine whether the threatening aspects of hate propaganda can be seen as threats of violence, or analogous to such threats, so as to deny it protection under s.2(b).'

20 While this may or may not have been true of James Keegstra's expression, it is certainly not true of a large amount of hateful communication, which can be understood as threatening. Much of what is called hate propaganda is meant to intimidate the members of a particular group. The Nazi march in the suburb with a large Jewish population or the swastikas painted on walls are not meant to engage the viewer in dialogue or to stimulate his or her reflection.

21 Cameron 1989, 269: 'Because "violent forms" do not exist in the abstract, the threat which they pose to society can only be assessed contextually.'

22 Dickson C.J. in *Keegstra* 1990, 734, acknowledged 'the danger of balancing competing values without the benefit of context.'

23 Strauss 1991, 354, makes the point in the strongest terms: 'Lying creates a kind of mental slavery that is an offense against the victim's humanity for many of the reasons that physical slavery is.'

24 Ironically, freedom of expression is generally regarded as an anti-paternalistic measure. Censorship is wrong because it prevents the individual from making his or her own judgments about particular ideas or issues. However, for McLachlin J., it seems that freedom of expression may sometimes rest on the value of paternalism.

Reference to *The Satanic Verses* (Rushdie 1988) seems out of place here. It is a work of fiction. As well, even if Rushdie could be said to have made factual claims, these claims were not made to deceive the audience and so were very different from those of the doctor or animal rights defender.

Perhaps what McLachlin J. really wanted to argue here was not that these lies are valuable and so deserve protection but rather that lies may have to be protected because it is so often difficult to prove when someone is lying and when he or she is simply mistaken.

The dissenting judges in *Zundel* 1992, 839, Cory and Iacobucci JJ., seemed to agree with McLachlin J. that lies may sometimes be beneficial: 'McLachlin J. referred to the doctor who exaggerates the number of persons infected with a virus in order to persuade people to be inoculated against a burgeoning epidemic and to the person who knowingly cites false statistics in order to prevent cruelty to animals. Both examples of expression not only fail to raise the possibility of injury to a public interest but, indeed, they would have an overall beneficial or neutral effect on society.'

25 Dickson C.J. in *Irwin Toy* 1989, 976:

In determining whether the government's purpose aims simply at harmful physical consequences, the question becomes: does the mischief consist in the meaning of the activity or the purported influence that meaning has on the behaviour of others, or does it consist, rather, only in the direct physical result of the activity.

Even if the government's purpose was not to control or restrict attempts to convey a meaning, the court must still decide whether the effect of the government action was to restrict the plaintiff's freedom of expression. Here, the burden is on the plaintiff to demonstrate that such an effect occurred. In order to so demonstrate, a plaintiff must state her claim with reference to the principles and values underlying the freedom.

Madame Justice McLachlin in *Commonwealth of Canada* 1991, 239, described the test in this way: 'If ... the restriction is content-neutral, it may well not infringe freedom of expression at all. In this case, the jurisprudence laid down in *Irwin Toy* requires that the claimant establish that the expression in question (including its time, place and manner) promote one of the purposes underlying the guarantee of free expression.'

26 Most individuals do not have an adequate opportunity to express themselves. However, the issue is whether there are alternatives to the particular

time or location of expression and not whether the individual, in the absence of a particular restriction, has plenty of opportunities to communicate his or her views.

27 This discussion applies to the issue of communicative access to public property, which is the subject of Chapter 6.

28 As noted above, *RJR Macdonald* 1995 may represent a move away from a strongly deferential approach. McLachlin J. in *RJR Macdonald* 1995, 331, stated: 'Context is essential in determining legislative objective and proportionality, but it cannot be carried to the extreme of treating the challenged law as a unique socio-economic phenomenon, of which Parliament is deemed the best judge. This would be to undercut the obligation on Parliament to justify limitations which it places on *Charter* rights and would be to substitute ad hoc judicial discretion for the reasoned demonstration contemplated by the *Charter*.'

29 The dispute came under federal jurisdiction. However, federal labour legislation did not deal specifically with picketing and so the common law rules concerning picketing were applicable. *Dolphin Delivery* 1986, 578–9.

30 Beetz J. in *Dupond* 1978, 348, held that: '[d]emonstrations are not a form of speech but of collective action. They are of the nature of a display of force rather than an appeal to reason; their inarticulateness prevents them from becoming part of the language and from reaching the level of discourse.'

31 One might wonder whether the court's view has really changed since *Dupond* 1978. The issue for Mr Justice Beetz in *Dupond* 1978 was not the meaning of freedom of expression under the Charter, where the issues of scope and limits are separated (section 2(b) and section 1). In *Dupond* 1978 the issue was whether a Montreal by-law was a restriction on freedom of expression that was ultra vires the province (municipality). In both cases the bottom line is the same. Speech of this sort is not deserving of protection because it is harmful or because it does not appeal to reason.

32 Arthurs 1963, 581, points out that '[the business's] commercial success does not necessarily coincide with the interests of the community at large; so long as [the particular product or service] can easily be purchased elsewhere the community may be quite indifferent ...'

33 McIntyre J. in *Dolphin Delivery* 1986, 582, agreed with the lower court that 'the purpose of the picketing was tortious and ... the dominant purpose was to injure the plaintiff rather than the dissemination of information and the protection of the defendant's interest.' In McIntyre's view there is speech meant to convey information or promote 'dialogue and discourse' and

speech meant to cause harm (e.g. damaging the business of the employer). The first is deserving of protection, while the second is not. But it may not be an either/or issue. With one and the same expressive act an individual may communicate information, promote dialogue, and cause injury. An injurious effect can be brought about by convincing others (without deception and without force) of the correctness of certain ideas.

34 McIntyre J. in *Dolphin Delivery* 1986, 588, stated: 'On the basis of the findings of fact I have referred to above, it is evident that the purpose of the picketing in this case was to induce a breach of contract between the respondent and SuperCourier and thus to exert some economic pressure to force it to cease doing business with SuperCourier. It is equally evident that, *if successful*, the picketing would have done serious injury to the respondent' [emphasis added].

35 In the recent case of *K-Mart* 1999 the Supreme Court of Canada saw leafleting during a labour dispute as quite different from labour picketing. In *K-Mart* the court held: 'Consumer leafleting is very different from a picket line. It seeks to persuade members of the public to take a certain course of action. It does so through informed and rational discourse which is the very essence of freedom of expression. Leafleting does not trigger the "signal" effect inherent in the picket line and it certainly does not have the same coercive component (para 43).'

In *K-Mart* 1999, the court drew a distinction between expression that appealed to reason (leafleting) and expression that caused the audience to act in a particular way (picketing). There are a variety of reasons why the court may have chosen to treat leafleting differently from picketing (as appealing to reason or as not causing harm) some of which are suggested in the judgment. Leaflets make written arguments; as such, the court was bound to view them as rational in their appeal, particularly given the important role leafleting played in the early development of freedom of expression jurisprudence in Canada and the United States. While picketing is a collective act, the passing and reading of a leaflet is a more 'individualized' act. In contrast to *Dolphin* 1986 (but not to *BCGEU* 1988), the expression in *K-Mart* 1999 was directed at the general public and not exclusively at other unionized workers. And in this particular case, the court may well have been sympathetic to the appeals of the underpaid K-Mart workers, who had been locked out for six months while trying to negotiate a first collective agreement. Although the union action took place not at the workplace of the locked-out employees, and was therefore like a secondary picket, the other site was owned and operated by K-Mart.

One might well wonder how workable the leafleting/picketing distinction is?

36 The injunction restrained all persons from 'gathering, congregating or picketing at the entrances to the Law Court of the Provincial, County, Supreme, or Appeal Courts of British Columbia or within the precincts of the said Courts; or from engaging in any activities whatsoever which are calculated to interfere with the operations of any Court of Justice in the province or to restrict or limit access of the Courts and their precincts' (*BCGEU* 1988, 222).

37 The contrast here between, on the one hand, the individual and private right of expression and, on the other hand, the public interest in court access is striking. Dickson C.J. in *BCGEU* 1988, 229, continued: 'How can the courts independently maintain the rule of law and effectively discharge the duties imposed by the *Charter* if court access is hindered, impeded or denied? The *Charter* protections would become merely illusory, the entire *Charter* undermined.'

38 Dickson C.J. in *BCGEU* 1988, 232: 'Picketing a court-house to urge the public not to enter, except by permission of the picketers, could only lead to a massive interference with the legal and constitutional rights of the citizens of British Columbia.'

As noted, the union was willing to give picket passes to those who, for various reasons, needed to enter the court building. Dickson C.J. took great exception to the union practice of issuing passes. He declared that the union did not have the right to decide who should enter the court-house. This, however, missed the point of the pass system. Anyone who wanted to enter the courthouse could do so without the union's permission (Chief Justice McEachern, who issued the original injunction, for example). Only those who wanted to honour the picket line and show their support for the union would request a pass. It is not a matter of the union controlling access to the building; it is a matter of giving an individual, who must for certain reasons enter the court buildings, an opportunity to show his or her support for the union.

39 Dickson C.J. said elsewhere in his judgment: 'The very purpose and intent of the picket line in a labour dispute is to discourage and dissuade individuals from entering the premises which are being picketed (*BCGEU* 1988, 231). And 'A picket line is designed to publicize the labour dispute in which the striking workers are embroiled and to mount a show of solidarity of the workers to their goal' (*BCGEU* 1988, 230).

40 The Supreme Court omitted the rest of Weiler's statement on the issue. He continued: 'That [automatic] response is triggered by a number of factors:

the sense of solidarity among members of the general trade union movement; an appreciation that it is in the self-interest of each to honour the
other fellow's picket line because in their own dispute they will want the
same reaction from other workers; a concern for the social pressures and
ostracism of other workers if they do not conform to the trade union ethic;
the likelihood that they will face serious discipline from their own trade
union. It might even cost them their jobs, if they defy that ethic and cross a
picket line approved by the trade union movement' (Weiler 1980, 79). It
seems misleading to call the decision to respect the picket line 'automatic'
or Pavlovian' if it is based on these kinds of considerations.

41 See also St Antoine 1982, 902: 'the notion of an automatic response to a
signal does not square with the realities of picketing addressed to the
atomized and heterogeneous membership of a pluralistic society ...'

42 In a single paragraph the Chief Justice Dickson in *BCGEU* 1988, 231,
seemed at one point to praise the value, and recognize the nobility, of
worker solidarity and at another point to discount it as automatic or self-
interested: 'One of the great strengths of the trade union movement is the
spirit of solidarity. By standing together as a collective whole, trade
unionists are able to aspire to improved wages and working conditions,
unattainable if each individual member were left to his or her own devices.
Solidarity is made manifest when one group of workers is on strike. Fellow
unionists and other sympathetic members of the public are made aware of
the strike by the presence of the pickets. Picketing sends a strong and
automatic signal; do not cross the line lest you undermine our struggle;
this time we ask you to help by not doing business with our employer; next
time when you are on strike, we will respect your picket line and refuse to
conduct business with your employer.'

43 *Devine* 1988 addressed more directly the constitutionality of the requirement of French. The plaintiffs in *Ford* 1988 limited their challenge to the
prohibition of other languages.

44 While the Quebec government had invoked the 'notwithstanding' clause
(section 33 of the Charter) to partially insulate its language law from review
under the Canadian Charter of Rights and Freedoms, the court found that
the Quebec Charter of Human Rights and Freedoms, R.S.Q., c. C-12 was
applicable and that it had provisions equivalent to section 2(b) and section
1 of the Charter.

45 It may be a little misleading to talk about language 'choice.' Most individuals do not simply choose to speak one language or another. They speak the
language first learned and best known, except when they want to communicate with someone outside their language group. Whether or not we

think of the individual's use of a particular language as an expressive choice that is interfered with by a law restricting language use, it is undeniable that such a restriction interferes with the individual's capacity to express her/himself and to identify, or associate, with other members of his or her language community.

46 The court in *Ford* 1988, 748, continued: 'Language is so intimately related to the form and content of expression that there cannot be true freedom of expression by means of language if one is prohibited from using the language of one's choice.'

47 The issue of compelled expression is discussed in Chapter 7.

48 The court in *Ford* 1988, 779: 'In the opinion of this Court it has not been demonstrated that the prohibition of the use of any language other than French ... is necessary to the defence and enhancement of the status of the French language in Quebec or that it is proportionate to that legislative purpose.'

According to the court, if the concern was that the language of the majority community is not adequately reflected in the '*visage linguistique*' of the province, 'the governmental response could well have been tailored to meet that specific problem and to impair the freedom minimally.' Businesses could have been required to use French in addition to any other language or to give more visibility to French than to other languages. Such measures would have ensured that the '*visage linguistique*' reflected the demography of Quebec.

49 The court in *Ford* 1988, 779: '[The section 1 evidence indicates] a rational connection between protecting the French language and assuring the reality of Quebec society is communicated through the "visage linguistique". The section 1 and s. 9(1) materials do not, however, demonstrate that the requirement of the use of French only is either necessary for the achievement of the legislative objective or proportionate to it. That specific question is simply not addressed by the materials. Indeed, in his factum and oral argument, the Attorney General of Quebec did not attempt to justify the requirement of the exclusive use of French.'

50 The court in *Ford* 1988, 778: 'The causal factors for the threatened position of the French language that have been generally identified are: (a) the declining birthrate of Quebec Francophone ... (b) the decline of the Francophone population outside Quebec as a result of assimilation; (c) the greater rate of assimilation of immigrants to Quebec by the Anglophone community of Quebec and (d) the continuing dominance of English at the higher levels of the economic sector. These factors have favoured the use

of the English language despite the predominance in Quebec of a
Francophone population.'

51 Dickson C.J. in *Irwin Toy* 1989, 988–9:

The Attorney General filed a number of studies reaching somewhat
different conclusions about the age at which children generally develop
the cognitive ability to recognize the persuasive nature of advertising and
to evaluate its comparative worth. The studies suggest that at some point
between age seven and adolescence, children become as capable as adults
of understanding and responding to advertisements.

[T]he evidence was strongest with respect to the younger age category
[children six or younger]. Opinion is more divided when children in the
older age category are involved. But the legislature was not obliged to
confine itself solely to protecting the most clearly vulnerable group. It was
only required to exercise a reasonable judgment in specifying the vulnerable group.

52 Dickson C.J. in *Irwin Toy* 1989, 987: 'The concern is for the protection of a
group which is particularly vulnerable to the techniques of seduction and
manipulation abundant in advertising.' This may fit with J.S. Mill's view
that there is a threshold of reason necessary to the exercise of liberty. Mill
stated: 'Liberty, as a principle, has no application to any state of things
anterior to the time when mankind have become capable of being improved by free and equal discussion' (Mill 1982, 69). This kind of categorical exclusion of pre-rational or irrational persons or communities may be
necessary to maintain the doctrine's uncomplicated understanding of
rationality.

53 See also Ramsay 1996, 107: 'This approach may overemphasize the
distinction between the ability of adults and children to "argue against"
advertising, positing a sharp contrast between adult rationality and
childlike credulousness.'

54 Similarly, in *RJR Macdonald* 1995, the Supreme Court's decision to strike
down a general ban on cigarette advertising was based on the absence of
evidence establishing a link between certain forms of advertising and the
decision to take up or continue smoking. The court indicated that it would
have upheld a ban directed exclusively at lifestyle advertising, because
common sense suggested a link between this form of advertising and the
decision to smoke. However, the court found that the general ban was over
inclusive because it also covered brand-name and informational advertising. According to the court, the social science evidence did not clearly
establish a link between these forms of advertising and the consumer's

decision to take up or continue smoking. The court said that it was not willing to defer to Parliament's judgment on these matters. *RJR Macdonald* 1995 is discussed in greater detail in Chapter 3.

55 Language is not an instrument that lies within our perfect control. As Charles Taylor observes: 'our activity in speaking is never entirely under our conscious control. Conscious speech is like the tip of the iceberg. Much of what is going on in shaping our activity is not in our purview. Our deployment of language reposes on much that is preconscious or unconscious' (Taylor 1985, 232).

3: The Regulation of Commercial and Political Advertising

1 Commercial expression encourages others to buy a product or service. Sharpe 1987, 230, defines commercial expression in the following way: 'A commercial message is one which promotes or attempts to entice a specific decision on the part of the recipient of the message to agree to an economic exchange of money in return for goods and services.'

2 Baker 1989, 196: '[I]n our present historical setting, commercial speech reflects the market forces that require enterprises to be profit-oriented. This forced profit orientation is not a manifestation of individual freedom of choice. Unlike the broad categories of protected speech, commercial speech does not represent an attempt to create or affect the world in a way that has any logical or intrinsic connection to anyone's substantive values or personal wishes. Rather, it is logically and intrinsically connected to the structurally enforced requirements of the market.'

3 The court in *Ford* 1988, 767, said that: 'Over and above its intrinsic value as expression, commercial expression which, as has been pointed out, protects listeners as well as speakers, plays a significant role in enabling individuals to make informed economic choices, an important aspect of individual self-fulfilment and personal autonomy. The Court accordingly rejects the view that commercial expression serves no individual or societal value in a free and democratic society and for this reason is undeserving of any constitutional protection.'

4 The quotation is from the judgment of Blackmun J. of the U.S. Supreme Court in *Virginia Pharmacy* 1976, 763.

5 But see Shiner 1994, 102, who argues: 'However much sympathy one may have for [Valerie Ford] personally, and no matter how much personal satisfaction she derived from running her wool shop, the wool shop is still a commercial business and part of the economic market-place and not the "market-place of ideas".'

6 McLachlin J. in *Rocket* 1990, 241: 'Although it has been clearly held that commercial expression does not fall outside the ambit of s.2(b), the fact that expression is commercial is not necessarily without constitutional significance ... It is at [the section 1] stage that the competing values – the value of the limitation and the value of free expression – are weighed in the context of the case. Part of the context, in the case of regulation of advertising, is the fact that the expression is wholly within the commercial sphere.'

7 McLachlin J. in *Rocket* 1990, 247–8, continued: 'In *Irwin Toy*, for example, the majority did not emphasize the consumer choice aspect, because the expression in question was advertising aimed at children and the majority clearly felt that protection of consumer choice in children was much less important than it would be in adults. That left the relatively weak value of protecting the appellant's interest in advertising to increase profits to be pitted against the strong countervailing value of protecting children from economic exploitation.'

8 Sharpe 1987, 237, makes the point: 'Advertising provides consumers with information they need to make important choices. It shapes attitudes, tastes and preferences. While some might despair of the effects of advertising, that merely reinforces the point that it is a powerful influence in our culture. Individuals define important parts of their lives in terms of the availability and acquisition of material goods, and advertising is the way they acquire the information or are persuaded to live in a chosen way. However banal or trivial the message of advertising seems, it is in our society an institution which has a powerful influence on the way citizens define their lives.'

But see Schneiderman 1996, 178, who argues that: 'By privileging the consumer interest to receive information about commercial products, the Court arguably endorses (however unwittingly) the postmodernist conception of consumer culture, in which consumers are social agents who express their individuality by their patterns of consumption under "conditions of freedom".'

9 In the United States begging has been regarded as 'commercial' or 'profit-motivated' in character. Restrictions on begging have been supported under the test for restricting commercial expression. However, none of the reasons for giving lesser protection to commercial expression would seem to apply to begging.

10 These concerns may also account for the intuitive appeal of the arguments discussed earlier for excluding commercial expression from the scope of the freedom. Commercial expression may not seem 'expressive,' if we see it

as an instrument intended to have an 'impact' upon potential consumers. It may not seem part of democratic discourse, if it is nothing more than a monologue generated by corporate interests and does not seek any real engagement with its 'audience.' The plausibility of the democratic and self-expression arguments against protection of commercial expression may rest on a recognition that advertisers want to generate sales/profits and will use the most effective means to achieve this end – persuasion or otherwise.

11 Sharpe 1987, 259, also states: '[R]egulation of commercial speech designed to ensure fair and truthful advertising is consistent with the very purpose of protecting commercial speech ... Hence, while there is a place for judicial review of restraints on commercial expression, a level of constitutional protection significantly lower than that appropriate for other forms of expression is called for.'

12 Mill 1982, 119: '[E]ven opinions lose their immunity when the circumstances in which they are expressed are such as to constitute their expression a positive instigation to some mischievous act. An opinion that corn dealers are starvers of the poor, or that private property is robbery, ought to be unmolested when simply circulated through the press, but may justly incur punishment when delivered orally to an excited mob assembled before the house of a corn dealer, or when handed about the same mob in the form of a placard.'

13 The shift in language from the mob (of Mill's corn merchant speech) to the masses suggests a problem that is deeper and more fixed. It suggests a general condition of manipulation or irrational prejudice rather than an isolated failure of rational agency in a very specific context.

14 The Quebec Consumer Protection Act, S.Q. 1978, c.9, s. 248.

15 Dickson C.J. in *Irwin Toy* 1989, 621: 'the concerns which motivated both legislature and voluntary regulation in this area are the particular susceptibility of young children to media manipulation, their inability to differentiate between reality and fiction and to grasp the persuasive intention behind the message, and the secondary effects of exterior influences on the family and parental authority.'

Dickson C.J. in *Irwin Toy* 1989, 623: 'the legislature reasonably concluded that advertisers should be precluded from taking advantage of children both by inciting them to make purchases and by inciting them to have their parents make purchases. Either way the advertiser would not be able to capitalize upon children's credulity.'

16 Mr Justice McIntyre dissenting in *Irwin Toy* 1989, 636, described the law as a restriction on childrens' freedom of expression rights rather than simply a restriction on the rights of advertisers: 'It is ironic that most attempts to

limit freedom of expression and hence freedom of knowledge and information are justified on the basis that the limitation is for the benefit of those whose rights will be limited. '

...

'There was evidence that children are incapable of distinguishing fact from fiction in advertising. This is hardly surprising; many adults have the same problem. Children, however, do not remain children. They grow up and, while advertising directed at children may be a source of irritation to parents, no case has been shown here that children suffer harm.'

17 Tobacco Products Control Act, S.C. 1988, (35–36–37 Elizabeth II), c. 20.

18 The health warnings requirement is considered in Chapter 7. I note that restrictions on alcohol advertising have also had some difficulties in the courts. In *Assn. of Canadian Distillers* 1995 Dubé J. of the Federal Court – Trial Division struck down section 6(2) of the Television Broadcasting Regulations 1987, which prohibited the broadcast on television of advertisements for spirits containing more than 7% alcohol. Other alcohol products could be advertised, even though they might contain a higher amount of alcohol. The court held that the restriction was arbitrary and irrational. All forms of beverage alcohol are equally susceptible of abuse.

19 Strictly speaking this was the judgment of a plurality of the court. Sopinka and Major JJ. concurred with McLachlin J. on the freedom of expression issues. Iacobucci J. wrote a concurring judgment. Lamer C.J. concurred with Iacobucci J. on the freedom of expression issues. However, Iacobucci J. said that he agreed with many of Justice McLachlin's general conclusions.

20 Cory, L'Heureux-Dubé, and Gonthier JJ. concurred with LaForest J. on the freedom of expression issues.

21 McLachlin J. in *RJR Macdonald* 1995, 343, also said: 'It extends to advertising which arguably produces benefits to the consumer, while having little or no conceivable impact on consumption. Purely informational advertising, simple reminders of package appearance, advertising for new brands and advertising showing relative tar content of different brands – all these are included in the ban. Smoking is a legal activity yet consumers are deprived of an important means of learning about product availability to suit their preferences and to compare brand content with an aim to reducing the risk to their health.'

22 The government had refused to disclose background studies, which assessed alternatives to a total ban on advertising. For McLachlin J. this weighed against the government's argument that the ban was not over inclusive.

McLachlin J. acknowledged that it was difficult to draw firm factual conclusions from social science evidence predictive of human behaviour and she accepted that deference should be shown to Parliament's assessment of this evidence. However, she insisted that judicial deference should not go so far as to exclude any form of scrutiny: 'the courts must nevertheless insist that before the state can override constitutional rights, there be a reasoned demonstration of the good which the law may achieve in relation to the seriousness of the infringement' (*RJR Macdonald* 1995, 329). In her view, to have required less would have been an abdication of the responsibility placed upon the courts to ensure that laws are consistent with the basic rights and freedoms set out in the Charter.

23 LaForest J. in *RJR Macdonald* 1995, 306: 'This type of expression, which is directed solely toward the pursuit of profit, is neither political not artistic in nature, and therefore falls very far from the core of freedom of expression values.'

Laforest J. in *RJR Macdonald* 1995, 282–3: 'the harm engendered by tobacco and the profit motive underlying its promotion, place this form of expression as far from the 'core' of freedom of expression values as prostitution, hate mongering or pornography, and thus entitle it to a very low degree of protection under s.1.'

24 Laforest J. in *RJR Macdonald* 1995, 279: '[T]he Act is the very type of legislation to which this Court has generally accorded a high degree of deference. In drafting this legislation, which is directed towards a laudable social goal and is designed to protect vulnerable groups, Parliament was required to compile and assess complex social science evidence and to mediate between competing social interests.' At 290–1 Laforest J. said: 'Although the appellants observe, quite correctly, that there has not to date been a definitive study conducted with respect to the connection between tobacco advertising and tobacco consumption, I believe there was sufficient evidence adduced at trial to conclude that the objective of reducing tobacco consumption is logically furthered by the prohibition under the Act ...'

25 Laforest J. in *RJR Macdonald* 1995, 278, noted that 'advertising, by its very nature is intended to influence consumers and create demand ...'

26 Laforest J. in *RJR Macdonald* 1995, 291: 'it is difficult to believe that Canadian tobacco companies would spend over 75 million dollars every year on advertising if they did not know that advertising increases the consumption of their product.'

27 LaForest J. *RJR Macdonald* 1995, 291, rejected the companies' argument that their advertising was directed solely at preserving or expanding brand

loyalty among smokers and not at expanding the tobacco market by inducing non-smokers to start: 'First brand loyalty alone will not, and logically cannot, maintain the profit levels of these companies if the overall numbers of smokers declines.' At 291–2 he suggested that 'even commercials targeted solely at brand loyalty may also serve as inducements for smokers not to quit. The government's concern with the health effects of tobacco can quite reasonably extend not only to potential smokers who are considering starting, but also to current smokers who would prefer to quit but cannot.'

28 LaForest J. *RJR Macdonald* 1995, 317, made the point: 'Although the appellants argue that informational advertising allows smokers to make informed health choices by giving them information about tobacco product content, and thereby permitting them to choose tobacco products with lower tar levels, they submit no evidence that such products are actually healthier, nor logically could they, since the evidence appears to point in the opposite direction; such products are no safer than high tar products and serve mainly to induce smokers who might otherwise quit to keep smoking "lighter" brands.'

29 McLachlin J. in *RJR Macdonald* 1995, 339: 'The causal relationship between the infringement of rights and the benefit sought may sometimes be proved by scientific evidence showing that as a matter of repeated observation, one affects the other. Where, however, legislation is directed at changing human behaviour, as in the case of the *Tobacco Products Control Act*, the causal relationship may not be scientifically measurable. In such cases, this Court has been prepared to find a causal connection between the infringement and benefit sought on the basis of reason or logic, without insisting on direct proof of a relationship between the infringing measure and the legislative objective.'

LaForest J. in *RJR Macdonald* 1995, 273, recognized the psychological complexity of the link between advertising and consumption but still saw this in behavioural terms – as a matter of gaining greater knowledge of the 'causes of human behaviour': 'At this point, there is no definitive scientific explanation for tobacco addiction, nor is there a clearly understood causal connection between advertising and consumption, or between tobacco and addiction, without probing into the mysteries of human psychology. Many of the workings of the human mind, and causes of human behaviour remain hidden to our understanding and will no doubt remain so for quite some time.'

30 Concern about manipulation almost reached the surface in Justice Laforest's dissenting judgment in *RJR Macdonald* 1995, 283: 'The large

sums these [cigarette] companies spend on advertising allow them to employ the most advanced advertising and social psychology techniques to convince potential buyers to buy their products. The sophistication of the advertising campaigns employed by these corporations, in my view, undermines their claim to freedom of expression protection because it creates an enormous power differential between these companies and tobacco consumers in the "marketplace of ideas".'

31 But see the judgment of Bastarache J. in *Thomson* 1998, 957, in which he described the finding in *RJR Macdonald* 1995 and two other cases 'where advertisers encouraged choices which served their particular interests': 'Although it was legal for each of them to pursue those interests, and therefore legitimate to do so, there was a danger of undue manipulation in the first two cases [*Irwin Toy* 1989 and *Libman* 1997], and of serious health consequences for individual Canadians in the third [*RJR Macdonald* 1995].'

32 In *Irwin Toy* 1989, the harm of the advertising at issue was not that children might be persuaded to use a harmful product – toys that are in some way dangerous. As McIntyre J. observed in his dissenting judgment in *Irwin Toy* 1989, 636: 'no case has been made that children are at risk' or 'that children suffer harm.' Instead, the ban was concerned with the process of persuasion; the attempt by advertisers to manipulate the behaviour of children.

33 The harmful or wrongful character of an activity does not justify suppression of expression encouraging that activity. In *Iorfida* 1994, the Ontario Court (General Division) held that section 462.2 of the Criminal Code infringed section 2(b) and was not justified under section 1. The Code provision prohibited the distribution of material intended to promote, encourage, or advocate the production or consumption of illicit drugs. The court in *Iorfida* 1994, 201, found that '[t]he objective of the section is to restrict debate about drug use and, accordingly, it is aimed at the very heart of the Charter right enshrined in s.2(b).'

34 The dissenting judgment of LaForest J. in *RJR Macdonald* 1995, 283, did question the companies' reliance on this more idealized form of expression. Specifically, LaForest J. made reference to the 'sophisticated marketing and social psychology techniques' used by the cigarette companies. In his view, the character of cigarette advertising 'undermines [the] claim to freedom of expression protection because it creates an enormous power differential between these companies and tobacco consumers in the "marketplace of ideas".'

35 Postman 1985, 131: '[T]he commercial disdains exposition, for that takes time and invites argument. It is a very bad commercial indeed that engages

the viewer in wondering about the validity of the point being made.' The advertisement makes no particular claims or assertions and so offers nothing that can be refuted or rejected. Ads rely on visual images and visual images make no assertions, contain no propositions.

See also Postman 1985, 72: 'When applied to a photograph, the question, Is it true? means only, Is this a reproduction of a real slice of space-time? If the answer is "Yes", there are no grounds for argument for it makes no sense to disagree with an unfaked photograph.' A visual image does not carry a message in an obvious or direct way. Yet as the saying 'a picture is worth a thousand words' suggests, a visual image can sometimes communicate in a way that words cannot.

36 It is true, of course, that cigarette manufacturers seem to be caught in the dilemma that if, on the one hand, their advertisements do not convey a message then they cannot fall within the protection of freedom of expression but if, on the other hand, their advertisements do convey a message then that message is almost certainly false or deceiving (cigarettes are like the healthy outdoors, cigarettes make you sexually attractive). Sometimes the companies try to escape this dilemma by claiming that the advertisements are aesthetic; that the advertisements present the product in an appealing way; that they give form to a feeling or an attitude without making any specific claims or assertions.

37 Leiss et al. 1986, 60, continues: 'An advertisement's composition often connects background imagery with products having not the slightest relation to it – the automobile or cigarette package displayed against a stunning picture of unspoiled wilderness, the liquor bottle set in a farmhouse room full of hand-crafted furniture – in a straightforward attempt to effect a transfer of the positive feelings evoked by the imagery to the product.'

38 In the words of Barthes 1973, 129: '[E]verything happens as if the picture naturally conjured up the concept, as if the signifier gave a foundation to the signified.'

39 Fiske 1987, 101, speaking of television images generally says that: 'Because the sequence and flow are organized according to associative rather than logical relations, the connections are not made explicitly in the text, but are devolved to the viewer where their associative nature will allow them to be made subconsciously.' See also Leiss et al. 1986, 153: 'The meaning of an ad does not float on the surface just waiting to be internalized by the viewer, but is built up out of the ways that different signs are organized and related to each other, both within the ad and through external references to wider belief systems. More specifically, for advertising to create meaning,

the reader or the viewer has to do "work".' And Schudson 1984, 227: 'While viewers are not persuaded, they do alter the structure of their perceptions about a product ...'

40 Fiske 1987, 64: '[I]n paying attention to textual strategies or preferences or closure ... we may lose sight of the gaps and spaces that open television up to meanings not preferred by the total structure, but that result from the social experience of the reader.'

41 See also: Leiss et al. 1986, 244: 'Iconic representation can be absorbed in a sort of "parallel process" without full conscious awareness, and thus it can register an impact without being translated into explicit verbal formulations.'

Barry 1997, 254: 'Without directly stating a causal relationship between Newport cigarettes and an active young lifestyle, for example, the advertiser uses the associative perceptual logic of the viewer to make the product seem an essential part of the visual story, and the product a metaphor for the socially rewarding experience depicted. Linear logic cannot achieve this; rather the success of the ad depends on the formation of a gestalt in which all of the parts become inseparable from the whole.'

Ramsay 1996, 49: 'All of this interpretive work is done almost instantly so that it is thought to be natural or common sense to view the advertisement in this manner.'

Bauman 1988, 64: 'Elements of the final image are carefully pre-assembled before they are put on display; they are shown "in a context", alongside easily recognizable signs of the situations which they promise to provide, so that the link gradually sediments in the customer's mind (or subconscious) as "natural", "evident", calling for no further argument or justification. The situation in question seems from now on to blend with the situation itself; on top of their own attractions, they offer confidence that the situation of which they are an organic part will indeed be achieved.'

42 The use of photographic images encourages the transfer of meaning from the signifier to the product in a way that makes the transfer seem natural rather than artificial or conventional. A photographed object is generally experienced as real by someone looking at the photo. As Sontag 1989, 154, notes, photographs are seen as capturing reality and for good reason: 'Such [photographic] images are indeed able to usurp reality because first of all a photograph is not only an image (as a painting is an image) an interpretation of the real: it is also a trace, something directly stencilled off the real, like a footprint or a death mask. While a painting, even one that meets photographic standards of resemblance, is never more than the stating of an interpretation, a photograph is never less than the registering

of an emanation (light waves reflected by objects) – a material vestige of its subject in a way that no painting can be.' Of course, as Barthes 1985, 355, points out: 'the photographed object is illusively natural.' A photograph is not simply a 'mechanical record,' it is composed by the photographer who selects the subject matter, the angle, the lighting. As well the photographs used in advertising are almost always 'touched-up' to 'improve upon the appearance of reality.'

Barthes notes that because photography has the reputation of literally transcribing reality or a slice of reality, we seldom think about its real power, its true implications.

43 Jamieson 1992, 54: 'Television can pair previously disconnected images with a speed and seamlessness that defies the scrutiny of the suspicious. [It invites] us to impute a causal link to things only associatively tied ...'

44 Schudson 1984, 226: '[I]t is precisely the belief people have that they are detached that makes the power of advertising all the more insidious. Advertising may create attitudes and inclinations even when it does not inspire belief; it succeeds in creating attitudes because it does not make the mistake of asking for belief.'

45 Morley 1992, 21: 'The power of viewers to reinterpret meanings is hardly equivalent to the discursive power of centralized media institutions to construct the texts which the viewer then interprets; to imagine otherwise is simply foolish.' See also Kress and van Leeuwen 1996, 176: 'control over meaning lies in the selection of images and in the sometimes hardly noticeable way in which these images are edited together.' And Thompson 1995, 30: 'the recipients of mediated messages have relatively little power to determine the topic and content of communication.'

46 Schiller 1989, 156: 'Audiences do, in fact, interpret messages variously. They also may transform them to correspond with their individual experiences and tasks. But when they are confronted with a message incessantly repeated in all cultural conduits, issuing from the commanders of the second order, their capacities are overwhelmed.'

47 Leiss et al. 1986, 300: 'Commercial messages have permeated the entire fabric of life during the course of this century, subtly blending their materials and techniques with those of the consumer culture as a whole, until they become virtually identical with it. As a result, the meaning and impact of advertisements considered in isolation is difficult to pin down.' See also Ramsay 1996, 134: 'Because much of the reading of the advertisement will be done without thinking, it is not difficult to understand why many individuals might overlook the significant ideological importance of the cumulation of these everyday interpretations intersecting with domi-

nant cultural norms. The issue here is not a simpler one of manipulation of the innocent by the power of advertising.'

48 Canada Elections Act 1985, c. E-2.

49 The Canada Elections Act 1985, c. E-2, s.2(1) defines 'election expenses' as:

> (a) amounts paid,
> (b) liabilities incurred
> (c) the commercial value of goods and services donated or provided, other than voluntary labour,
>
> ...
>
> (e) the cost of acquiring the right to the use of time on the facilities of any broadcasting undertaking, or of acquiring the right to the publication of an advertisement in any periodical publication
>
> ...
>
> (g) the cost of acquiring meeting space, of provision of light refreshment and of acquiring and distributing mailing objects, material or devices of a promotional nature.'

50 The Canada Elections Act 1985, c. E-2 imposes limits on campaign contributions. Although financial contribution is not usually considered an act of speech, money is necessary to effective speech and so contributions deserve some protection under section 2(b). However, since 'contribution' is not itself an act of expression but is protected only as support for expression, the amount of contribution may be limited provided the purpose/effect of such a limit is not to prevent the candidate from expressing him/herself effectively. There are some very good reasons for restricting contribution amounts, most notably the concern that large contributions can buy a disproportionate amount of political influence. Of course this influence occurs only because, in the current system of political discourse, politicians benefit from large advertising budgets.

51 The law that was reviewed in *Somerville* 1986 was enacted after the Alberta Court of Appeal in *National Citizens Coalition* 1984 struck down an earlier total ban on third-party spending in support of a candidate or party.

52 But see Bakvis and Smith 1997: 'It needs to be kept in mind that, contrary to Justice Conrad's belief, the primary aim of third parties is not to provide an independent voice on the qualities of the candidates and their programs during election campaigns. Rather, it is to use the most effective means possible to help elect the candidate or party of their choice, and more often than not this means contributing money directly to the political campaigns. In other words, the non-partisan rhetoric notwithstanding, the primary aim is to affect the outcome of an election.'

53 Referendum Act, R.S.Q., c. C-64.1 (1981).
54 According to the Supreme Court in *Libman* 1997, 592, the appellant's wish 'to express his opinions on the referendum question independently of the national committees by means of expenses that are included in the definition of "regulated expenses" ... is a form of political expression that is clearly protected by s.2(b) of the Charter.'
55 The court in *Libman* 1997, 599, seemed to think that ceilings increase the speech opportunities of less wealthy candidates: 'Spending limits are also necessary to guarantee the right of electors to be adequately informed of all the political positions advanced by candidates and by the various political parties.'

Similarly Fiss 1996, 11, seems to believe that ceilings involve a transfer of communicative power from the wealthy to the less wealthy candidate: 'Some defend such regulation as a device to prevent corruption, but it can be understood in more generous terms – as a way of enhancing the power of the poor, putting them on a nearly equal political footing with the rich, thus giving them a fair chance to advance their interests and enact measures that will improve their economic position.'
56 Most supporters of campaign ceilings recognize this. Yet perhaps because they see this form of persuasion as an ordinary part of public discourse, they do not identify it as part of the problem that needs to be addressed. See for example, Hiebert 1998, 103: 'Money privileges those who can purchase the kind of "image makers" necessary to ensure a candidate's commercial appeal or ensure the "saleability" of a message in thirty second advertisements. Money also allows for purchase of sufficient advertising time to compete with, or drown out, the message of a partisan rival.'
57 The court in *Libman* 1997, 599, agreed with the Lortie Commission 1991, 324: 'Elections are fair and equitable only if all citizens are reasonably informed of all the possible choices and if parties and candidates are given a reasonable opportunity to present their positions so that election discourse is not dominated by those with access to greater resources.'
58 More generally, this domination has changed the way we think about political participation and citizenship. Voting is now seen by many as a consumer choice resting on subjective preference.

Kline 1993, 34, argues: 'The criteria and polls that guide the performance of candidates at election time, the way government departments influence the discussion of health problems, the images broadcast by the army from the war zone – all these strategically target our thoughts and feelings through the same framework and techniques developed for marketing communication management. Indeed, we live in a time when the job of managing politicians at election time can be compared without irony to the task of selling soap flakes off store shelves and when the political campaign manager for George Bush can declare "Feelings win elections. What I strive for is an emotion not a position".'

59 Of course, since most polling is done on a national or provincial basis, it is unclear whether it provides useful 'strategic voting' information for voters who must decide between competing candidates in a particular constituency.

60 Bastarache J. in *Thomson* 1998, 952, also stated: 'The more polls which appear during this period, the less likely that voters will base their decisions on the inaccurate poll.'

61 Bastarache J. in *Thomson* 1998, 949: 'Canadian voters must be presumed to have a certain degree of maturity and intelligence. They have the right to consider the results of polls as part of a strategic exercise of their vote. It cannot be assumed that in so doing they will be so naive as to forget the issues and interests which motivate them to vote for a particular candidate. Nor can Canadians be presumed to assume that polls are absolutely accurate in predicting outcomes of elections and that they thus will overvalue poll results.' At p. 943 Bastarache J. said: 'While opinion polls may not be the same as political ideas, they are nevertheless an important part of the political discourse, as manifested by the attention such polls receive in the media and in the public at large, and by the fact that political parties themselves purchase and use such information.'

4: The Regulation of Pornography

1 Lacombe 1994, 6: 'The feminist case against pornography became hegemonic in the 1980's, in the sense that it caused conservative and civil liberties organizations to reverse their 1960s position to such an extent that they discussed pornography in terms of women's oppression.'

2 Gonthier J. in *Butler* 1992, 511 (L'Heureux-Dubé J. concurring) wrote a concurring judgment but agreed with Justice Sopinka's 'disposition of the case and with his reasons generally.'

3 Section 163 of the *Criminal Code of Canada*, R.S.C. 1985, c. C-46, provides:
  (1) Every one commits an offence who
  (a) makes, prints, publishes, distributes, circulates ... any obscene written matter, picture, model, phonograph record or other thing whatsoever,
  ...

(3) No person shall be convicted of an offence under this section if he establishes that the public good was served by the acts that are alleged to constitute the offence and that the acts alleged did not extend beyond what served the public good.

(4) For the purposes of this section it is a question of law whether an act served the public good, but it is a question of fact whether the acts did or did not extend beyond what served the public good.

(5) For the purposes of this section the motives of an accused are irrelevant.

(6) Where an accused is charged with an offence under subsection (1) the fact that the accused was ignorant of the nature or presence of the matter, picture, model ... is not a defence to the charge.

...

(8) For the purposes of this Act, any publication a dominant characteristic of which is the undue exploitation of sex, or of sex and any one or more of the following subjects, namely crime, horror, cruelty and violence, shall be deemed to be obscene.

4 Dickson C.J. In *Towne Cinema* 1985, 509, considered that: 'Since the standard is tolerance, I think the audience to which the allegedly obscene material is targeted must be relevant. The operative standards are those of the Canadian community as a whole but since what matters is what other people may see, it is quite conceivable that the Canadian community would tolerate varying degrees of explicitness depending on the audience and the circumstances.' However, the majority of the court disagreed with him on this point and thought that the particular audience was irrelevant.

5 Sopinka J. in *Butler* 1992, 476–7: 'With respect to expert evidence, it is not necessary and is not a fact which the Crown is obliged to prove as part of its case.'

6 Sopinka J. in *Butler* 1992, 480: 'In *Towne Cinema*, Dickson C.J. considered the "degradation" or "dehumanization" test to be the principal indicator of "undueness" without specifying what role the community tolerance test plays in respect of this issue. He did observe, however, that the community might tolerate some forms of exploitation that caused harm that were nevertheless undue.'

7 Sopinka J. in *Butler* 1992, 481, borrowing from the judgment of Wilson J. in *Towne Cinema* 1985, 524: '... at some point the exploitation of sex becomes harmful to the public or at least the public believe it to be so. It is therefore necessary for the protection of the public to put limits on the degree of exploitation and through the application of the community standards

test, the public is made the arbiter of what is harmful to it and what is not. The problem is that we know so little of the consequences we are seeking to avoid. Do obscene movies spawn immoral conduct? Do they degrade women? Do they promote violence? The most that can be said, I think, is that the public has concluded that exposure to material which degrades the human dimensions of life to a subhuman or merely physical dimension and thereby contributes to a process of moral desensitization must be harmful in some way.'

8 Gonthier J. in *Butler* 1992, 520–1, described Mr Justice Sopinka's approach in this way: 'Sopinka J. uses the community standard of tolerance to gauge the risk of harm. In this context, tolerance must be related to the harm. It must mean not only tolerance of the materials, but also tolerance of the harm which they may bring about. It is a more complicated and more reflective form of tolerance than what was considered by Dickson C.J. in *Towne Cinema, supra*. Such a development is fully in accordance with the emphasis put by this court on harm as the central element in the interpretation of s.163(8).'

9 It is unclear what Sopinka J. means here when he says that degrading and dehumanizing material *may* not be tolerated if the risk of harm is substantial. Upon what basis will the community judge whether this material creates a risk of harm other than its degrading or dehumanizing character? Can material be degrading and dehumanizing and not create a risk of harm?

10 Sopinka J. continued in *Butler* 1992, 479: 'While the accuracy of this perception is not susceptible of exact proof, there is a substantial body of opinion that holds that the portrayal of persons being subjected to degrading or dehumanizing sexual treatment results in harm, particularly to women and therefore to society as a whole.'

11 Gonthier J. in *Butler* 1992, 519, took issue with the complete insulation of this third category: 'I would hold that materials falling within Sopinka J.'s third category (explicit sex with neither violence nor degradation or dehumanization), while generally less likely to cause harm than those of the first two categories, may nevertheless come within the definition of obscene at s.163(8) of the *Code*, if their content (child pornography) or their representational element (manner of representation) is found conducive of harm.'

12 In *Big M.* 1985 the issue was whether there was a constitutionally legitimate reason for banning Sunday shopping. The scope of the prohibition was not in dispute. However, in *Butler* the identification of a different purpose for section 163 (to avoid the charge of vagueness or unconstitutional purpose) was bound to affect the scope of the prohibition.'

13 Specifically Sopinka J. in *Butler* 1992, 494–5, said: 'I do not agree that to identify the objective of the impugned legislation as the prevention of harm to society, one must resort to the shifting purpose doctrine. First, the notions of moral corruption and harm to society are not distinct, as the appellant suggests, but are inextricably linked. It is moral corruption of a particular kind which leads to the detrimental affect on society.

Secondly, and more importantly, I am of the view that with the enactment of s.163 Parliament explicitly sought to address the harms which are linked to certain types of obscene materials. The prohibition of such materials was based on a belief that they had a detrimental impact on individuals exposed to them and consequently on society as a whole. Our understanding of the harms caused by these materials has developed considerably since that time, however, this does not detract from the fact that the purpose of this legislation remains, as it was in 1959, the protection of society from harms caused by exposure to obscene materials.

14 For the opposite view see McLaren 1991, 130–1: 'Contrary to subsequent commentary on this provision, which has tended to see its purpose as a move away from the conservative morality enshrined in the *Hicklin* test, it is clear, as Professor Charles has established in his analysis of the parliamentary debates on the new provision, that Mr. Fulton was seeking to toughen up the law ... Mr. Fulton's statements in debate make it clear that the revised subsection was not designed to replace the *Hicklin* test, which he fully expected would be the gauge against which serious literature and art would continue to be judged.'

15 As Cossman 1997, 120, observes: 'The Court spins around a tautological circle: the harms that are intended to be addressed by obscenity legislation are the harms that are caused by obscenity. If this circular reasoning is valid, we now have a generic objective so broad it can be applied to virtually any piece of legislation ... According to this generic, or "no-name" objective of preventing harm, there will be little difficulty avoiding the net of the shifting purpose doctrine whenever it is convenient to do so.'

16 Sopinka J. in *Butler* 1992, 484: 'Because this [what is harmful] is not a matter that is susceptible of proof in the traditional way and because we do not wish to leave it to the individual tastes of judges, we must have a norm that will serve as an arbiter in determining what amounts to an undue exploitation of sex. That arbiter is the community as a whole.'

17 Cockburn C.J. in *Hicklin* 1868, 371: 'I think that the test of obscenity is this, whether the tendency of the matter charged as obscenity is to deprave and corrupt those whose minds are open to such immoral influences, and into whose hands a publication of this sort may fall.'

18 Freedman J.A. (dissenting) in *Dominion News* 1963, 116: 'Community standards must be contemporary. Times change and ideas change with them. Compared to the Victorian era this is a liberal age in which we live. One manifestation of it is the relative freedom with which the whole question of sex is discussed. In books, magazines, movies, television, and sometimes even in parlour conversation, various aspects of sex are made the subject of comment, with a candour that in an earlier day would have been regarded as indecent and intolerable. We cannot and should not ignore these present day attitudes when we face the question whether [the materials] are obscene.'

19 The court's belief that moral judgment is subjective is revealed in a number of statements, including the following: 'Moral disapprobation is recognized as an appropriate response when it has its basis in Charter values' (*Butler* 1992, 493, quoting Dyzenhaus 1991, 376) and 'much of the criminal law is based on moral conceptions of right and wrong and the mere fact that a law is grounded in morality does not automatically render it illegitimate' (*Butler* 1992, 493).

20 Dickson C.J. in *Towne Cinema* 1985, 516: '[T]his inquiry, though involving judgments about values, must be distinguished from the application of the trier of fact's subjective opinions about the tastelessness or impropriety of certain publications. The decision must focus on an objective determination of the community's level of tolerance and whether the publication exceeds such level of tolerance, not the trier of fact's personal views regarding the impugned publication.'

In the same case Wilson J. stated: 'The test by which the trier of fact must assess the community standard is an objective one. The community standard itself, however, necessarily contains an element of subjectivity since what must be objectified are the subjective views of the entire community as to what degree of exploitation of sex is acceptable' (*Towne Cinema* 1985, 520).

21 Sopinka J. in *Butler* 1992, 484: 'Some segments of society would consider that all these categories of pornography cause harm to society because they undermine its moral fibre. Others would contend that none of the categories cause harm. Furthermore, there is a range of opinion as to what is degrading ad dehumanizing.' The court seems to say that because the community cannot agree on the content of the ban, it must rely on community standards to fix the content.

22 Sopinka J. in *Butler* 1992, 494: 'First, the notions of moral corruption and harm to society are not distinct, as the appellant suggests, but are inextrica-

bly linked. It is moral corruption of a certain kind which leads to the detrimental effect on society.'

23 Sopinka J. proceeded through the various steps of the *Oakes* 1986 test, holding that the restriction advances a substantial and compelling purpose, is rationally connected to this purpose, achieves this purpose with minimal impairment to freedom of expression, and advances a value that is proportionate to the detrimental impact on the freedom.

24 Sopinka J. in *Butler* 1992, 479–80, also said: 'It would be reasonable to conclude that there is an appreciable risk of harm to society in the portrayal of such material.'

25 Sopinka J. in *Butler* 1992, 505: 'It [section 163] is designed to catch material that creates a risk of harm to society. It might be suggested that proof of actual harm should be required. It is apparent from what I have said above that it is sufficient in this regard for Parliament to have a reasonable basis for concluding that harm will result and this requirement does not demand actual proof of harm.' Obviously, when the restriction was enacted in 1959, Parliament could not have made a judgment about non-existent empirical studies.

26 Dworkin 1996, 219, states: 'It would plainly be unconstitutional to ban speech directly advocating that women occupy inferior roles, or none at all, in commerce and the professions, even if that speech fell on willing male ears and achieved its goals. So it cannot be a reason for banning pornography that it contributes to an unequal economic and social structure even if we think it does.' See also Cameron 1992, 1149, who argues that the restriction of obscenity is based on the content of the message and is therefore illegitimate: 'Because the Court's objective was advanced at the broadest level of generalization, what s.163(8) fundamentally prohibits is an unacceptable conception of equality and of female sexuality. However, if it is not permissible for Parliament to suppress dirt for dirt's sake, because that would constitute the coercive imposition of a standard of morality, it is difficult to see how it is permissible for Parliament to impose a particular conception of equality.'

27 Sopinka J. in *Butler* 1992, 487, said that the activity in issue 'conveys ideas, opinions, or feelings.' He also said 'The message of obscenity which degrades and dehumanizes is analogous to that of hate propaganda' (501). Yet later he observed: 'In contrast to the hate-monger who may succeed, by the sudden media attention, in gaining an audience, the prohibition of obscene materials does nothing to promote the pornographer's cause' (504). Sopinka J. does not explain the difference between hate promotion

and pornography. The explanation, however, is that pornography, in contrast to hate promotion, makes no explicit claims.

28 Kappeler 1986, 2: 'The aim of realism is to obliterate our awareness of the medium and its conventions and to make us take what is represented for a reflection of natural reality.' See also Coward 1982, 12: 'Visual images are constantly exempted from scrutiny, either they are "real" or they are just "aesthetically pleasing".'

29 See also Diamond 1985, 46: 'There is a prevalent belief in our culture that images represent reality in a literal way, when in fact they are the result of a whole series of manipulations. Camera angles (direct, from above or below); framing (close in to long shot); the composition of the picture (what comprises a scene and what in that scene is included in the final frame) .... These elements work together to provide a specific message, one constructed by the maker of the image, which is then interpreted by the viewers who impose the conventions they have learned to use when "reading" visual symbols.'

30 See also Cossman et al. 1997, 26: 'The meaning of any particular image will depend on the location of the viewer, in a broad range of intersecting discourses that constitute her intersubjectively. Rather than being clear and unequivocal, the meaning of sexual representations is a site of political and discursive struggle.'

31 Kappeler 1986, 2: 'Sex or sexual practices do not just exist out there, waiting to be represented; rather, there is a dialectical relationship between representational practices which construct sexuality, and actual sexual practices, each informing the other.'

32 Lacombe 1994, 36: 'This scientific research is also problematic because it decontextualizes pornography. Rather than being conceived as a practice, as a representation organized in historical, economic, political and social contexts, pornography is studied in the laboratory as though it had an essence that was isolatable from any real situation in which one might produce and consume it.'

33 Hutchinson 1995b, 128: 'Pornography will not be the cause – a *sine qua non* – but one that goes into the mix that cannot be isolated in its effects nor negatived as a possible cause. Pornography does not operate as a one-on-one individualized phenomenon that causes a particular man to rape a particular woman, but it can generate a social environment in which women are devalued as a group and sex is presented as eroticized violence through which men gratify themselves.'

34 Mackinnon 1987, 184: 'Specific pornography does directly cause some assaults. Some rapes *are* performed by men with paperback books in their pockets.'

35 Cole 1989, 38: 'Far from expressing dissent, pornography's message is becoming the cultural norm.'

36 Some writers have drawn an analogy between the risk of violence from pornography and the risk of cancer from cigarette smoking. See for example, Mahoney 1991, 169:

> While hundreds of studies indicate that pornography reinforces sexual attitudes and behaviour antithetical to equality rights and contributes to the perpetuation of violent and dangerous behaviour, the same causal and methodological problems arise in this kind of research as in research which attempts to positively prove that alcohol causes traffic deaths or smoking causes cancer. The links are suggestive, but none of them are dispositive. Uncertainty as to the nature and extent of the link, however, should not be enough to make obscenity laws unconstitutional. Evidence of potentially serious harm has justified government regulation of the tobacco and alcohol industries as well as many others where health and safety are concerned. The effects of pornography on women should be of no less concern when so much evidence suggestive of harm exists.

However, there are important differences between the risk of cancer from smoking and the risk of sexual violence from pornography. Pornography creates this risk because it shapes the thinking and guides the behaviour of a human agent. Pornography has an impact because it contributes to the social construction of sexuality – a systemic process that makes degradation, violence, and subordination appear unexceptional and even natural.

37 In *Little Sisters* 1998, it was argued that certain provisions of the Canadian customs legislation violated section 2(b) of the Charter. These provisions prohibited the importation of material 'deemed to be obscene' under the obscenity provision of the Criminal Code and gave customs officers the power to make this determination (subject to certain appeals).

The British Columbia Court of Appeal found that the legislation had been improperly applied and that non-obscene material destined for Little Sisters Book Store had often been stopped at the border. However, the court held that the overbroad application of the legislation was due not to any flaws in the legislation but simply to improper application by the customs authorities. The court, therefore, refused to strike down the law.

The result is not surprising. At root, the problem is the standard for determining obscenity. But this is the standard the Supreme Court of Canada upheld in *Butler* 1992. Can the courts hold that they can apply this test in a consistent, coherent, and limited way but that other decision makers are not able to do so? The court's focus then must be on improving the process for determining when material is obscene. Yet, if the standard is vague, it will not matter how many procedural safeguards are put in place.

38 Mackinnon 1987, 154, argues: 'The difficulties courts have in framing workable standards to separate "prurient" from other sexual interest, commercial exploitation from art or advertising, sexual speech from sexual conduct, and obscenity from great literature make the feminist point. These lines have proven elusive in law because they do not exist in life. Commercial sex resembles art because both exploit women's sexuality. The liberal's slippery slope is the feminist totality. Whatever obscenity may do, pornography converges with more conventionally acceptable depictions and descriptions just as rape converges with intercourse because both express the same power relation. Just as it is difficult to distinguish literature or art against a background, a standard, of objectification, it is difficult to discern sexual freedom against a background, a standard, of sexual coercion. This does not mean it cannot be done. It means that legal standards will be practically unenforceable, will reproduce this problem rather than solve it, until they address its fundamental issue – gender equality – directly.'

39 In this regard, the concern is sometimes expressed that the image of sex as a dominant/submissive relationship is presented so often and in so many locations that it may affect to some degree how we view any sexual representation.

40 Mackinnon 1987, 151: '[M]ore and more violence has become necessary to keep the progressively desensitized consumer aroused to the illusion that sex is (and he is) daring and dangerous.'

5: The Regulation of Racist Expression

1 Sections 319(2) and (7) of the Criminal Code of Canada, R.S.C. 1985, c. C-46, discussed below, prohibit the wilful promotion of hatred against 'any section of the public distinguished by colour race, religion or ethnic origin.'

2 The language of 'silencing' is used by Laforest J. in *Ross* 1996, 878: 'Such expression silences the views of those in the target group and thereby hinders the free exchange of ideas feeding our search for political truth ... It [hate speech] impedes meaningful participation in social and political decision-making ...'

3 Cory and Iacobucci JJ. in *Zundel* 1992, 826, noted the problems of inequality and dominant messages: 'To protect only the abstract right of minorities

to speak without addressing the majoritarian background noise which makes it impossible for them to be heard is to engage in a partial analysis. The position ignores inequality among speakers and the inclination of listeners to believe messages which are already part of the dominant culture.'

4 Lawrence 1993, 74: 'But Black folks know that no racial incident is "isolated" in the United States. That is what makes the incidents so horrible, so scary. It is the knowledge that they are *not* the unpopular speech of a dissident few that makes them so frightening.'

5 This incident was the subject of the U.S. Supreme Court judgment in *RAV* 1992. The U.S. Supreme Court held that the regulation at issue violated the First Amendment because it was not content neutral.

6 In *Collin* 1978, a neo-Nazi group planned to march through Skokie, a Chicago suburb with a large Jewish population, which included many Holocaust survivors. The Federal Court of Appeals (7th Circuit) held that the parade was protected speech under the First Amendment.

7 Delgado 1993, 105: 'The maker of a racist slur necessarily calls upon the entire history of slavery and racial discrimination in this country to injure the victim.'

8 Section 319(2) of the Criminal Code of Canada 1985 provides that:
Every person who, by communicating statements, other than in private conversation, wilfully promotes hatred against any identifiable group is guilty of
(a) an indictable offence and is liable to imprisonment for a term not exceeding two years; or
(b) an offence punishable on summary conviction.
Section 319(3) of the Code provides a number of defences:
No person shall be convicted of an offence under subsection (2)
(a) if he establishes that the statements communicated were true;
(b) if, in good faith, he expressed or attempted to establish by argument an opinion on a religious subject;
(c) if the statements were relevant to any subject of public interest, the discussion of which was for the public benefit, and if on reasonable grounds he believed them to be true; or
(d) if, in good faith, he intended to point out, for the purpose of removal, matters producing or tending to produce feelings of hatred towards an identifiable group in Canada.
Subsection (7) provides definitions and clarifications of some of the important terms used in the section. In particular 'communicating' is said to include communicating 'by telephone, broadcasting or other audible or

visible means'; 'identifiable group' means any section of the public identified by colour, race, religion, or ethnic origin; 'public place' includes 'any place to which the public have access as of right or by invitation, express or implied'; and finally, the term 'statements' is broadly defined to include 'words spoken or written or recorded electronically or electro-magnetically or otherwise' as well as 'gestures, signs or other visible representations.'

9 For a more detailed description of Keegstra's views see Bercuson and Wertheimer 1985.

10 Dickson C.J. and McLachlin J. adopted different approaches to the rational connection test under section 1. Chief Justice Dickson stated that 'the measures adopted must be carefully designed to achieve the objective in question. They must not be arbitrary, unfair or based on irrational consid-erations' (*Keegstra* 1990, 735, quoting *Oakes* 1986, 139). McLachlin J., in contrast, seemed willing to go further and assess the likely effectiveness of the measure.

11 McLachlin J. in *Keegstra* 1990, 856, disagreed: '"hatred" is a broad term capable of catching a wide variety of emotion.'

12 Dickson C.J. in *Keegstra* 1990, 775, stated that the mental element, wilful promotion of hatred, 'significantly restricts the reach of the provision and thereby reduces the scope of the targeted expression.'

13 Dickson C.J. in *Keegstra* 1990, 776, continued: '[I]t is clearly difficult to prove a causative link between a specific statement and hatred of an identifiable group. In fact to require direct proof of hatred in listeners would severely debilitate the effectiveness of s.319(2) in achieving Parliament's aim.' As Madame Justice McLachlin noted in *Keegstra* 1990, 857: 'The process of "proving" that listeners were moved to hatred has a fictitious air about it.'

14 Dickson C.J. in *Keegstra* 1990, 722, indicated early in the judgment that he used the term 'hate propaganda' 'to denote expression intended or likely to create or circulate extreme feelings of opprobrium and enmity against a racial or religious group.'

15 As Madame Justice McLachlin observed in *Keegstra* 1990, 857: 'A belief that what one says about a group is true and important to political and social debate is quite compatible with, and indeed may inspire an intention to promote, active dislike of that group. Such a belief is equally compatible with foreseeing that promotion of such dislike may stem from one's statements.'

16 The Supreme Court of Canada has said that the restriction of individual defamation is consistent with Charter values (*Hill* 1995). However, it is

often argued that group defamation cannot be restricted without under-mining our basic commitment to freedom of expression. The harm of group defamation (false claims about particular groups) is assumed to be more diffuse than that of individual defamation. As well, group defamation is thought to involve claims that are public in nature and open to debate.

17 Madame Justice McLachlin in *Keegstra* 1990, 853, suggested a more immediate problem with the majority's scepticism about audience reason: 'The argument that criminal prosecution for this kind of expression will reduce racism and foster multiculturalism depends on the assumption that some listeners are gullible enough to believe the expression if exposed to it. But if this assumption is valid, these listeners might be just as likely to believe that there must be some truth in the racist expression because the government is trying to suppress it.'

18 Specifically, McLachlin J. in *Keegstra* 1990, 850, stated: 'The result of a failure to do so [draft the limitation with great precision] may be to deter not only the expression which the prohibition was aimed at, but *legitimate* expression. The law-abiding citizen who does not wish to run afoul of the law will decide not to take the chance in a doubtful case. Creativity and the beneficial exchange of ideas will be adversely affected' [emphasis added]. At p. 859 McLachlin J. said: 'The more vague the language of the prohibi-tion, the greater the danger that right-minded citizens may curtail the range of their expression against the possibility that they may run afoul of the law ... The danger is ... that the legislation may have a chilling effect on legitimate activities important to our society by subjecting innocent persons to constraints born out of a fear of criminal prosecution.'

19 In *The Haj* (Uris 1984), a variety of objectionable statements are made about the Arab 'personality.' For example: 'The short fuse that every Arab carries in his guts had been ignited with consummate ease. Enraged mobs poured into the streets ...' (89). 'The Bedouin was thief, assassin and raider and hard labour was immoral' (29). 'So before I was nine I had learned the basic canon of Arab life. It was me against my brother; me and my brother against my father; my family against my cousins and the clan; the clan against the tribe; and the tribe against the world' (25).

More significant than these descriptions of the Arab personality are the actions of the different characters in the story. In contrast to the Jewish characters, Arab characters lie, cheat, rape, and attack for little or no reason.

20 Jamieson 1992, 42: 'When fear is aroused, attention narrows, simple automatic behaviors are facilitated, complex, effort-filled ones inhibited, and critical thought dampened.'

21 Dickson C.J. in *Keegstra* 1990, 747, observed that 'the alteration of views held by the recipients of hate propaganda may occur subtly, and is not always attendant upon conscious acceptance of the communicated ideas. Even if the message of hate propaganda is outwardly rejected, there is evidence that its premise of racial or religious inferiority may persist in a recipient's mind as an idea that holds some truth ...'

22 McLachlin J. in *Keegstra* 1990, 832, may have been right when she said it was impossible 'to imagine a vigorous political debate ... in which speakers did not seek to undermine the credibility of the ideas, conclusions and judgment of their opponents.' However, the credibility and self-esteem of the target group member is undermined by widely held and subtly expressed racist assumptions and not by anything resembling the specific claims made during a back-and-forth debate between individuals.

23 Dickson C.J. in *Keegstra* 1990, 747 (quoting the Cohen Commission 1965, 8) thought that the restriction of hate promotion rests on the fallibility of human reason in exceptional circumstances: 'The successes of modern advertising, the triumphs of impudent propaganda such as Hitler's have qualified sharply our belief in the rationality of man. We know that under strain and pressure in times of irritation and frustration, the individual is swayed and even swept away by hysterical, emotional appeals. We act irresponsibly if we ignore the way in which emotion can drive reason from the field.'

24 Madame Justice McLachlin in *Zundel* 1992, 753, thought that only minority views would be caught by the ban: 'Thus the guarantee of freedom of expression serves to protect the right of the minority to express its view, however unpopular it may be; adapted to this context, it serves to preclude the majority perception of "truth" or "public interest" from smothering the minority's perception. The view of the majority has no need of constitutional protection; it is tolerated in any event. Viewed thus, a law which forbids expression of a minority or "false" view on pain of criminal prosecution and imprisonment, on its face, offends the purpose of the guarantee of free expression.'

25 For a discussion of some of the problems in regulating hate speech on the Internet see Gosnell 1998.

26 Gates 1994, 52: 'To remove the very formulation of our identities from the messy realm of contestation and debate is an elemental, not incidental, truncation of the ideal of public discourse.'

27 Dickson C.J. in *Keegstra* 1990, 777: 'Hatred ... is a most extreme emotion that belies reason; an emotion that, if exercised against members of an identifiable group, implies that those individuals are to be despised,

scorned, denied respect and made subject to ill-treatment on the basis of group affiliation.'

28 The other noteworthy case involving a teacher is *Ross* 1996. In *Ross* 1996, 873–4 the court noted: 'Young children are especially vulnerable to the messages conveyed by their teachers ... [T]hey are unlikely to distinguish between falsehoods and truth and more likely to accept derogatory views espoused by a teacher.'

29 See for example the Saskatchewan Human Rights Code, S.S. 1979, c. S-24.1, s. 14(1); The Human Rights Code of British Columbia, R.S.B.C. 1996, c. 210, s. 7(1).

30 Section 13(1) of the Canadian Human Rights Act, 1976–77 provides as follows: 'It is a discriminatory practice for a person or group of persons acting in concert to communicate telephonically or to cause to be so communicated, repeatedly, in whole or in part by means of the facilities of a telecommunications undertaking within the legislative authority of Parliament, any matter that is likely to expose a person or persons to hatred or contempt by reason of the fact that that person or those persons are identifiable on the basis of a prohibited ground of discrimination.'

31 E. Taylor, 1995, 182: 'The two-stage approach to hate propaganda results in criminal punishment, not for hate speech, but for breaking a court order.'

6: Access to State-Owned Property

1 L'Heureux-Dubé J. in *Commonwealth of Canada* 1991, 192: 'Unlike the American system whereby delineated tests are required for the various "types" of expression, our s.1 is flexible enough to accommodate all these types, the result depending on what objectives are put forward by the government, and what means are selected to advance these objectives. This enables us to construct a contextual rather than a categorical approach ...'

See also Lamer C.J. in *Commonwealth of Canada* 1991, 152: 'The American experience shows that the "public forum" concept actually results from an attempt to strike a balance between the interests of the individual and the interests of the government. As there is no provision similar to s.1 of our *Charter*, the American "public forum" doctrine is the result of the reconciliation of the individual's interest in expressing himself in a place, which is itself highly propitious to such expression, and of the government's interest in being able to manage effectively the premises it owns.'

Hugessen J. of the Federal Court of Appeal in *Commonwealth of Canada* 1987, 78, stated: 'The concept of a "public forum" is borrowed from American decisions. The *Constitution of the United States* differs appreciably from our own, notably in that it contains no equivalent to our sections 1 and 33. It is neither necessary nor advisable for us in Canada to adopt the categories developed by the U.S. courts to limit the overly absolute formulation of certain rights in their Constitution.'

2 The American doctrine is described in *Perry* 1983 and more recently in *Arkansas Educational Television* 1998. Several American writers have argued that the public/non-public forum distinction should be dropped because it conceals or distorts the proper balancing of competing interests. See, for example, Dienes 1986.

3 As L'Heureux-Dubé J. observed in *Commonwealth of Canada* 1991, 195: 'If property rights alone can be invoked to limit, restrain, or abridge a fundamental freedom on any given place of public property, the Charter's guarantees lose all meaning – only those holding the property-owners permission could express themselves.' McLachlin J. in *Commonwealth of Canada* 1991, 230, expressed the same view. If the government had 'the absolute right to prohibit and regulate expression on all property which it owns ... [l]ittle would remain of the right. Its purpose – to permit members of society to communicate their ideas and values to others – would be subverted.'

4 Section 7 of the Government Airport Concession Operations Regulation, SOR/79-373.
   Under the regulation a person could engage in these activities if 'authorized in writing by the Minister.'

5 The seven members of the court, who heard the appeal, disagreed on the question of whether the regulation restricting advertising and soliciting covered the respondents' activities. Four of the judges, L'Heureux-Dubé, McLachlin, Cory, and Gonthier JJ., thought that the restriction covered political communication of the sort engaged in by the respondents. The other three judges, Lamer C.J., LaForest and Sopinka JJ., thought that the regulation restricted only commercial activities and not political communication.

6 Sopinka and Cory JJ. concurred with the chief justice on the access issue.

7 The decision to give state property use priority over communicative access claims was never clearly explained by Chief Justice Lamer. At one point, he stated that 'the Charter does not protect "expression" itself, but freedom of expression.' However, he did not explain the basis for this distinction and he did not say how it was to be reconciled with the court's earlier judgments, which take a broad view of the scope of protected expression under section 2(b) (excluding only expression that has a violent form) and require that restrictions on expression be justified under the terms of

section 1. The chief justice seemed to assume that the state's use of the property represents the collective interest, which should prevail over the individual's interest in free expression. But why should a restriction on communication that protects the state's use of its property be treated differently from restrictions that protect other public values or concerns? Restrictions on expression that protect racial minorities from harm or children from manipulation are addressed under section 1 and must meet proportionality and minimum impairment standards.

At one point in his discussion of the compatibility test, the chief justice said that '[e]ven before any attempt was made to use [state-owned property] for purposes of expression, such places were intended by the state to perform specific social functions' (*Commonwealth of Canada* 1991, 156). The suggestion here is perhaps that these properties would not be forums for communication if the state had not put them to a use which drew a crowd – the roads, or the legislature – so that those seeking access can hardly complain if their claim is treated as secondary to the state's use of the property. Indeed, the usefulness of the place as a forum for communication might be lost if the state function were undermined by the frequent occurrence of incompatible communication. In some cases, the conflict between the communicative access claimed and the state use of the property is not coincidental. Yelling from the parliamentary gallery may be significant communication only because it disrupts the state's property use.

8 Lamer C.J. in *Commonwealth of Canada* 1991, 158: 'it is only after the complainant proved that his form of expression is compatible with the function of the place that the justifications which may be put forward under s.1 of the *Charter* can be analysed. While the state's main interest is to ensure the effective operation of its property, that is not the only concern; there is, for example, the maintenance of law and order, which is another government objective that might justify certain limitations on s.2(b).' One might wonder why law and order concerns could not be described as property use related.

9 Sometimes it may be difficult to decide whether the restricted expression is incompatible with the state's use of its property or is simply in conflict with a more general interest or value. Put another way, it will sometimes be difficult to distinguish between a restriction that advances or protects the state's property use and a restriction that protects a more general public interest. Is the noise restriction meant to protect the special use of the property or is it simply a way of protecting individuals in a particular context from irritating or undesirable noise? If the restriction protects the state's use of its property, it will *not* violate section 2(b). However, if the

restriction advances a more general value or interest it will violate section 2(b), although it may be justified under section 1.

Similarly, there might be some question as to whether a particular act of communication is incompatible with the state's use of the property, and so outside the protection of section 2(b), or whether it is the combination or cumulation of a number of similar acts that is incompatible, so that the issue falls to be resolved under section 1 – a matter of distributing a limited number of opportunities to communicate. A particular instance of public communication in the airport terminal may be compatible with the movement of travellers but if there were many instances of expression occurring at the same time, the ordinary use of the terminal would be impaired.

10 LaForest J. (with whom Gonthier J. concurred on the access issue) said that 'in dealing with future cases, I would tend to approach them in the manner suggested by McLachlin J.' (*Commonwealth of Canada* 1991, 166).

11 McLachlin J. in *Commonwealth of Canada* 1991, 231, appealed to the intentions of the 'framers' of the Charter and questioned whether they 'intend[ed] s.2(b) to offer protection to the citizen's speech in even the most private state-owned property,' such as 'private government offices, state-owned broadcasting towers and prisons?' And she pointed to the absence of any historical right to communicate in/on these properties: 'Freedom of expression has not traditionally been recognized to apply to such places or means of communication ...' 'To say that the guarantee of free speech extends to such arenas is to surpass anything the framers of the Charter could have intended.'

12 According to McLachlin J. in *Commonwealth of Canada* 1991, 232, the person claiming access must show 'that the expression on the public property in question engages traditional free speech concerns and hence falls within the ambit of s.2(b).'

13 According to McLachlin J. in *Commonwealth of Canada* 1991, 237, the court's task is to define 'what types of government property should *prima facie* be regarded as constitutionally available for forums for public expression.'

14 McLachlin J. in *Commonwealth of Canada* 1991, 228: 'In my view, the guarantee of free expression in s.2(b) of the *Charter* cannot reasonably be read as conferring a constitutional right to use all government property for purposes of public expression.'

15 McLachlin J. in *Commonwealth of Canada* 1991, 242: '[This] represents a value-based approach to determining the content of the guarantee of freedom of expression, focussing on the interests served by permitting a particular type of expression in a particular place.'

16 As argued by Madame Justice McLachlin in *Keegstra* 1990, 832.

17 I note that when criticizing the compatibility test put forward by Lamer C.J., McLachlin J. seemed to assume that restrictions on communication in a library would be subject to evaluation under section 1. (*Commonwealth of Canada* 1991, 235).

18 L'Heureux-Dubé J. in *Commonwealth of Canada* 1991, 198, recognized that '[i]f members of the public had no right whatsoever to distribute leaflets or engage in other expressive activity on government-owned property (except with permission), then there would be little if any opportunity to exercise their rights of freedom of expression. Only those with enough wealth to own land, or mass media facilities (whose ownership is largely concentrated) would be able to engage in free expression.'

19 L'Heureux-Dubé J. in *Commonwealth of Canada* 1991, 222: 'If all restrictions relating to noise, litter, orderliness, and access to property, which may obliquely impinge upon the freedom of expression, had to be predicated upon momentous governmental objectives under the *Oakes* test, government would hardly ever be able to legislate effectively with respect to these matters.'

20 L'Heureux-Dubé in *Commonwealth of Canada* 1991, 220: 'First the measure's purpose must be considered. The more significant the purpose, the greater will be the latitude for regulating time, place and manner of expression. Second, the restriction should be tailored to its objectives, such that it did not overreach its purpose. Third, the courts should consider whether the restrictions are designed in a manner which tends to be free from excessive official discretion or undue arbitrariness. Fourth, courts should assess whether in the circumstances, adequate alternative avenues for expression are left open. Fifth, courts should exclude the extent to which the restriction ensures that the property at issue can be used by the government and the public for the governmental function or activity for which it was intended, apart from its use as a public arena for expression.'

21 L'Heureux-Dubé J. in *Commonwealth of Canada* 1991, 190: 'The public forum discussion alluded to earlier is an important one. It is almost indispensable when evaluating what is a reasonable restriction on "place" in the review of a time, place and manner regulation. Nevertheless, on the bases of our Charter's drafting, structure and subsequent interpretation, such review belongs under section 1 ...'

22 L'Heureux-Dubé J. in *Commonwealth of Canada* 1991, 198, continued: '[W]hile the *Charter* should be given a broad and generous interpretation, "it is important not to overshoot the actual purpose of the right or freedom in question".'

23 Another factor listed by L'Heureux-Dubé in *Commonwealth of Canada* 1991,
   203, was '[t]he symbolic significance of the property for the message being
   communicated.' But this relates to the importance of access for the
   particular speaker and only indirectly to the 'public' character of the
   property.

24 L'Heureux-Dubé J. in *Commonwealth of Canada* 1991, 225: 'While I do not
   entirely endorse the "public forum" doctrine which has found favour in the
   American jurisprudence, the qualified definition of "public arenas" is
   helpful to appraise the reasonableness of any "place" restrictions within
   contested time, place and manner regulations. While clearly not disposi-
   tive, those areas traditionally associated with, or resembling, sites where all
   persons have a right to express their views by any means at their disposal
   should be vigilantly protected from legislative restrictions on speech. This
   is not to say that no encumbrances of any kind can be imposed, but simply
   that any prospective conditions will have to be reasonable having regard to
   all the circumstances.'

25 For example McLachlin J. in *Commonwealth of Canada* 1991, 236–7, said that
   '[t]he analysis under s.2(b) should focus on determining when, as a
   general proposition, the right to government expression on government
   property arises.'

26 See for example *Société de Transport* 1997, 235, where the Quebec Court of
   Appeal decided that while the outer area of the subway station might be a
   public arena, the area beyond a subway turnstile has not traditionally been
   open to the general public for debate and discussion. Rather, it has been
   dedicated to the exclusive benefit of those who have paid a fare to travel
   the subway. The court also held that even if the impugned regulation
   violates freedom of expression, it is a reasonable limit on that right because
   it allows for the distribution of literature in the subway stations up to the
   point at which the fare is paid.

27 Lamer C.J. in *Commonwealth of Canada* 1991, 157–8: 'For example, if a
   person tried to picket in the middle of a busy highway or to set up barri-
   cades on a bridge, it might well be concluded that such a form of expression in such a place is incompatible with the principal function of the
   place, which is to provide for the smooth flow of automobile traffic. In such
   a case, it could not be concluded that freedom of expression had been
   restricted if a government representative obliged the picketer to express
   himself elsewhere.'

28 Lamer C.J. in *Commonwealth of Canada* 1991, 158–9, found that the distribution of pamphlets is 'in no way incompatible with the airport's primary
   function, that of accommodating the needs of the travelling public.' The

form of expression can take place 'without the effectiveness or function of the place being in any way threatened.'

29 McLachlin J. in *Commonwealth of Canada* 1991, 235, was critical of the compatibility test. She wondered, 'Does it mean normal function? Minimal or essential function? Optimum function? At what point does expression become incompatible with function? Presumably, only if the impairment of function were severe would s.2(b) be held inapplicable, with limitations relating to optimal (as opposed to minimal) function falling to be justified under s.1.' She observed that the concept of function is 'a relative one' and involves 'a balancing of interests which arguably serves better as part of the s.1 test than as a threshold for screening out claims which raise no prima facie free expression interest.' She thought that '[i]n some cases, the right of free expression might be considered important enough to interfere to some extent with the function of government property. In others, the impairment of function will be so great in comparison with the interest in free expression as to justify exclusion or limitation of the expression. The concept of function is thus seen to involve a balancing of interests which arguably serves better as part of the s.1 test than as a threshold for screening out claims which raise no prima facie freedom of expression interest' (*Commonwealth of Canada* 1991, 235).

30 Of course, the size of the political community, the definition of political issues, and the character of political involvement are themselves affected by the media's scale.

31 An attitude expressed by Dubin J. in *Kopyto* 1987, 291: 'I do not think that a reasonable person with knowledge of the facts would give any greater heed to what the appellant was stating than would be given to what is stated by those who attend every Sunday in Hyde Park, London, England, and who mount their soapboxes and give vent to their complaints.'

32 As discussed in Chapter 7, laws granting access to private property, most notably the privately owned media, have sometimes been seen as 'compelling expression' and so as violating freedom of expression under the Charter.

33 Most notably *Dolphin Delivery* 1986 and *McKinney* 1990.

34 While a variety of arguments have been put forward to account for this limit on the application of the Charter, the government action doctrine is really nothing more than a pragmatic attempt to limit the scope of judicial review. In the absence of such a limit, the courts would have the power to oversee all activity in the community, second-guessing legislative judgments about the need for, and shape of, private sector regulation.

35 In *McKinney* 1990, 273–4, Laforest J. for the majority of the Supreme Court of Canada found that universities were not government actors subject to

Charter review: 'Though the legislature may determine much of the environment in which universities operate, the reality is that they function as autonomous bodies within the environment.'

36 This may be less clear cut following the Supreme Court of Canada's decision in *Eldridge* 1997. In *Eldridge* 1997, the court said that the Charter applies to hospitals only insofar as they are 'implementing government policy.' However, the court defined government policy in that case very broadly, as the provision of medical services – a very general public function.

37 L'Heureux-Dubé J. in *Commonwealth of Canada* 1991, 195, noted that the U.S. Supreme Court had decided that 'in some extreme circumstances' such as a company town, private ownership may be treated as public ownership for the purposes of expression. This assumes that the absence of communicative opportunity for some members of the community is something that occurs only in extreme (and exceptional) circumstances and is not a systemic problem.

38 In *Trieger* 1988, 279, Campbell J. of the Ontario Court of Justice stated: 'There is a significant constitutional value at stake here in the freedom of the press and other media of communication, particularly the broadcast media. The delicate balancing of their constitutional rights against the constitutional rights asserted by the applicants would involve a very complex factual process of broadcast regulation.'

39 I have not addressed in this chapter the relationship between intellectual property and freedom of expression. For a discussion of this relationship see Fewer 1997.

   In a recent Canadian case, *Michelin* 1997, the Federal Court prevented striking workers from making use of the Michelin man image on their picket signs. In this and other cases, the property in question is not simply a location or platform for expression. It is itself expression. The creation of property rights in 'expression' raises a variety of difficulties, particularly when we recognize that all expression is a response or reaction to the expression of others (Coombe 1991, 1879).

40 Post 1996, 156: 'even though the state may retain the "greater" power to terminate the subsidy (and perhaps also the speech), it does not follow that it also retains the "lesser" power to control the speech in ways that are otherwise inconsistent with First Amendment restraints on government regulations of public discourse.' See also Trakman 1995b, 71: '[The courts] could also adopt a weaker conception [of positive liberty] by requiring the state to perform a positive act towards a party only if the state has already chosen to act.'

41 Trakman 1995b, 74: 'By amplifying the right of expression of one group, but not another, the state not only treats them unequally: it potentially infracts upon the right of the ignored group to express itself ... The guarantee of freedom ... includes the protection from indirect forms of control that the state exerts in favour of some groups. That indirect control is most apparent – and most questionable – when the state assists some groups to express their particular beliefs and practices, but not others.'

42 Kreimer 1984, 1318: 'Revocation of access to the U.S. mails, for example, would more effectively silence a dissident news magazine than either a fine or a prison sentence for the editor. Even a revocation of a subsidized second class mail rate could be as effective.'

43 L'Heureux-Dubé J., in *Haig* 1993, 1039, said this might take the form of legislative intervention 'aimed at preventing certain conditions which muzzle expression, or ensuring public access to certain kinds of information.'

44 Some of this money was earmarked for women's issues and was transferred from the NCC and the AFN to the Native Women's Association of Canada (NWAC). Sometime later in the process, the federal government made direct, but relatively small, payments to the NWAC.

45 According to Sopinka J. in *NWAC* 1994, 663, section 2(b) 'does not guarantee any particular means of expression or place a positive obligation to fund or consult anyone ... The right to a particular platform or means of expression was clearly rejected by this Court in *Haig.*'

46 Sopinka J. in *NWAC* 1994, 664, said: 'Even assuming that in certain extreme circumstances, the provision of a platform of expression to one group may infringe the expression of another and thereby require the Government to provide an equal opportunity for the expression of that group, there was no evidence in this case to suggest that the funding or consultation of the four Aboriginal groups infringed the respondent's equal right to freedom of expression.'

7: Compelled Expression and Freedom of the Press

1 See also *Slaight* 1989, 1080, where Lamer J. stated that 'freedom of expression necessarily entails the right to say nothing or the right not to say certain things.'

2 Referring to freedom of association rather than freedom of expression Laforest J. in *Lavigne* 1991, 625, said that 'freedom from forced association and freedom to associate should not be viewed in opposition, one "negative" and the other "positive".' These are not distinct rights, but two sides of a bilateral freedom which has as its unifying purpose the advancement of

individual aspirations.' The U.S. Supreme Court expressed a similar view in *Wooley* 1977, 714: 'The right to speak and the right to refrain from speaking are complementary components of the broader concept of "individual freedom of mind".'

3 A moment of silence is a public act of personal contemplation or reflection and so can be seen as both speech and non-speech.

Whenever an individual decides not to respond to something that is said or done, his or her silence may be viewed (and it may be intended) as expression. However, it may be that we see silence as expression only when it occurs in circumstances where we would ordinarily expect the individual to speak – for example, when he or she is asked a question. In this way the expressive character of an individual's silence depends on ordinary speech practices.

4 The resolution required a '"stiff-arm" salute, the saluter to keep the right hand raised with palm turned up while the following is repeated: "I pledge allegiance to the Flag of the United States of America and to the Republic for which it stands; one nation, indivisible, with liberty and justice for all" (*Barnette* 1943, 628).

'Failure to conform is "insubordination" dealt with by expulsion. Readmission is denied by statute until compliance. Meanwhile the expelled child is "unlawfully absent" and may be proceeded against as a delinquent. His parents or guardians are liable to prosecution ...' (*Barnette* 1943, 629).

For a similar Canadian case see *Donald* 1945. In that case the relevant legislation provided that no pupil should be required 'to join in any exercises of devotion or religion, objected to by his parent or guardian.' The Ontario Court of Appeal held that for the objecting families singing the national anthem and saluting the flag were religious activities.

5 Oaths required of government employees and new citizens have also been challenged in the American courts. For a discussion see Levinson 1986.

In *Cole* 1972 the U.S. Supreme Court held that the government could not condition employment 'on an oath that one has not engaged or will not engage, in protected speech such as the following: criticizing institutions of government; discussing political doctrine that approves the overthrow of certain forms of government; and supporting candidates for political office' (*Cole* 1972, 680). A minimal oath in which the employee declares that he or she will defend and uphold the constitution and oppose the violent overthrow of the government was found to be acceptable.

In *Roach* 1994, the Canadian Federal Court of Appeal struck out a statement claim in which Mr Roach argued that the oath of allegiance to the Queen, which he was required to make before he could become a

Canadian citizen, violated his Charter rights. The majority found that his claim had no merit. Mr Justice Linden, who dissented, thought that there was a justiciable case and that the statement of claim should not be struck out. In the course of his reasons, Linden J. observed that Mr Roach's freedom of expression argument might have been stronger had he argued that the compulsion to make an oath of allegiance was an 'invasion of his sphere of intellect and spirit.' Instead, Mr Roach had argued that taking the oath was objectionable because it prevented him from communicating his opposition to the monarchy by remaining silent (silence here being expression that Mr Roach was prevented from engaging in). Leave to appeal the judgment to the Supreme Court of Canada was refused.

6 However, Mr Justice Jackson in *Barnette* 1943, 634, stated that the issue did not turn 'on one's possession of particular religious views or the sincerity with which they are held': 'While religion supplies appellees' motive for enduring the discomforts of making the issue in this case, many citizens who do not share these religious views hold such a compulsory rite to infringe constitutional liberty of the individual.'

7 Mr Justice Jackson in *Barnette* 1943, 633: 'It is not clear whether the regulation contemplates that pupils forego any contrary convictions of their own and become unwilling converts to the prescribed ceremony or whether it will be acceptable if they simulate assent by words without belief and by a gesture of barren meaning.'

8 Frankfurter J. in *Barnette* 1943, 664: 'Saluting the flag suppresses no belief nor curbs it. Children and their parents may believe what they please, avow their belief and practice it. It is not even remotely suggested that the requirement for saluting the flag involves the slightest restriction against the fullest opportunity on the part both of the children and of their parents to disavow as publicly as they choose to do so the meaning that others attach to the gesture of salute. All channels of affirmative free expression are open to both children and parents.'

9 See generally Brown 1994, 5/110. In *Pottle* 1954 it was reported that the provincial Minister of Public Welfare had imputed gross immorality to the residents of a particular locality. In *Byron (Lord)* 1816 authorship of an undistinguished poem was attributed to the respected poet.

10 According to the Supreme Court of Canada in *Ford* 1988, 780, if the concern behind this law was that the predominance of the French language was not adequately reflected in the '*visage linguistique*' of Quebec, 'the governmental response could well have been tailored to meet that specific problem and to impair freedom of expression minimally.' French could be required in addition to any other language or it could be re-

quired to have a greater visibility than that accorded to other languages. Such measures would ensure that the '*visage linguistique*' reflected the demography of Quebec.

11 See discussion of *Ford* 1988 in Chapter 3.

12 Section 9 of the Tobacco Products Control Act, 1988, prohibited the sale of tobacco products that did not display on the packaging prescribed messages concerning the health effects of the product as well as a list of the product's toxic constituents. This section also prohibited tobacco manufacturers from displaying on their packages any writing other than the name, trademark, and other information required by legislation.

Section 17(f) of the Act authorized the governor-general in council to adopt regulations prescribing the content of health messages.

The Tobacco Products Control Regulations SOR/93-389, s. 11 provided that every tobacco product must have one warning from a list that included the following:

   (i) Cigarettes are addictive

   (ii) Tobacco smoke can harm your children

   (iii) Cigarettes cause fatal lung disease

   (iv) Cigarettes cause cancer

   ...

   (vii) Smoking can kill you.

13 LaForest J. in *RJR Macdonald* 1995, 321: 'Simply because tobacco manufacturers are required to place unattributed warnings on their products does not mean that they must endorse these messages, or that they are perceived by consumers to endorse them. In a modern state, labelling of products, and especially products for human consumption, are subject to state regulation as a matter of course. It is common knowledge amongst the public at large that such statements emanate from the government, not the tobacco manufacturers. In this respect, there is an important distinction between messages directly attributed to tobacco manufacturers, which would create the impression that the message emanates from the appellants and would violate their right to silence, and the unattributed messages at issue in these cases, which emanate from the government and create no such impression.'

14 LaForest J. in *RJR Macdonald* 1995, 322: 'The Charter was enacted to protect individuals, not corporations. It may, at times it is true, be necessary to protect the rights of corporations so as to protect the rights of the individual. But I do not think this is such a case ...'

15 One of the purposes of the Tobacco Products Control Act, 1988, was 'to enhance public awareness of the hazards of tobacco use by ensuring the

effective communication of pertinent information to consumers of tobacco products.'

16 Laforest J. in *RJR Macdonald* 1995, 321: 'individuals may in certain pre-scribed circumstances be required to place danger signs on facilities used by the public or on construction sites, and so on. This is not really an expression of opinion by the person in control of the facility or the construction site. It is rather a requirement imposed by the government as a condition of participation in a regulated activity.'

17 LaForest J. in *RJR Macdonald* 1995, 322, said that these warnings 'do nothing more than bring the dangerous nature of these products to the attention of consumers. Given that the objective of the unattributed health message requirement is simply to increase the likelihood that every literate consumer of tobacco products will be made aware of the risks entailed by the use of that product, and that these warnings have no political, social or religious content, it is clear that we are a long way in this context from cases where the state seeks to coerce a lone individual to make a political, social or religious statement without a right to respond.'

18 Cohen 1991, 61, notes that absent legal compulsion manufacturers have no great incentive to produce complete information about the product's characteristics and in particular its risks.

19 Radin 1993, 162, argues that cars express one's personal taste and style. They are repositories of personal effects and they form the backdrop for carrying on private thoughts and intimate relations.

20 Schiller 1989, 101: '[The mall] brings masses of people together to buy goods and services and by virtue of its peculiar feudal patterns of owner-ship ... effectively insulates them from seeing, hearing or encountering expression and ideas that might, however slightly, disturb the mood, routines and tranquillity of daily shopping. The mall comes as close as can be managed to a total corporate-commercial environment.'

21 There was 'extra space' in the billing envelope because more material could be enclosed without exceeding the weight limit for the basic postage rate – without additional cost to the utility.

22 Powell J. in *Pacific Gas* 1986, 912, stated: 'The Commission's access order thus clearly requires appellant to use its property as a vehicle for spreading a message with which it disagrees ... [Like the requirement in *Wooley* 1977] the Commission's order requires appellant to use its property – the billing envelopes – to distribute the message of another. This is so whoever is deemed to own the "extra space".'

23 A more recent American case, *Hurley* 1995, was concerned with the decision of the organizing committee of the St Patrick's Day Parade in

Boston not to permit a gay and lesbian group to march in the parade. The trial court held that the Parade Council had violated the state law that prohibited discrimination in public places on grounds of sexual orientation.

The U.S. Supreme Court found that the parade had a common theme, to which the different parts contributed. The court held that to require the parade organizers to include a group, whose message they did not support, would be to compel them to communicate a message that they did not wish to communicate: 'when dissemination of a view contrary to one's own is forced upon a speaker intimately connected with the communication advanced, the speaker's right to autonomy over the message is compromised' (*Hurley* 1995, 2348).

24 As Rehnquist J. pointed out in his dissenting judgment in *Pacific Gas* 1986, 921: 'Extension of the individual freedom of conscience decisions to business corporations strains the rationale of those cases beyond breaking point. To ascribe to such artificial entities an "intellect" or "mind" for freedom of conscience purposes is to confuse metaphor with reality.'

25 The Florida statute under review in *Miami Herald* 1974 provided that if a candidate for nomination or election was assailed regarding his personal character or official record by any newspaper, the candidate had the right to demand that the newspaper print, free of cost to the candidate, any reply the candidate might make to the newspaper's charges. The reply must appear in as conspicuous a place and in the same kind of type as the charges which prompted the reply, provided it did not take up more space than the charges (*Miami Herald* 1974, 244).

26 Chief Justice Burger in *Miami Herald* 1974, 256, identified the costs that are imposed on the newspaper as a consequence of the statutory right: 'The Florida statute exacts a penalty on the basis of content of a newspaper. The first phase of the penalty resulting from the compelled printing of a reply is exacted in terms of the cost in printing and composing time and materials and in taking up space that could be devoted to other material the newspaper might have preferred to print. It is correct ... that a newspaper is not subject to the finite technological limitations of time that confront a broadcaster but it is not correct to say that, as an economic reality, a newspaper can proceed to infinite expansion of its column space to accommodate the replies that a government agency determines or a statute commands the readers should have available.'

27 In rejecting the ad the *Sun* also argued that 'homosexuality is offensive to public decency and that the advertisement would offend some of its subscribers.' It relied on the Code of Advertising standards, which provided

that no ad should be accepted 'which is vulgar, suggestive or in any way offensive to public decency' (*Gay Alliance* 1979, 450).

However, Richstone and Russell 1981, 106, tell us that: 'on the day the Gay Tide advertisement would have appeared had it been accepted for publication, *The Sun* printed several advertisements dealing with pornographic films, along with warnings from the B.C. Film Classification Director indicating that in one case, a film contained "group sex and lesbianism", that another was "completely concerned with sex", and another was described as an "orgy of sex and violence" complete with male nudity & sex.'

28 Human Rights Code of British Columbia, 1973 (B.C. 2nd Sess.), c. 119, ss. 3, 18.

29 In *Pittsburgh Press Co.* 1973 the U.S. Supreme Court held that a Pittsburgh Human Rights Commission ruling that a newspaper had violated the city's human rights ordinance by publishing job ads under headings designating job preference by sex did not violate the First Amendment. The judgment rested on the rule that commercial advertising was not protected under the First Amendment – a rule that has since been discarded.

30 Several authors have distinguished *Re Alberta Statutes* 1938 from *Gay Alliance* 1979 on this basis. See, for example, Richstone and Russell 1981, 103; Black 1979, 664; and Barron 1986, 177. Barron 1986, 177, says: 'Despite the clear language of section 3 giving government the right to publish "corrections" or "amplifications" in a newspaper against a newspaper's wishes, I do not think the *Alberta Press* statute should be seen as a right of reply statute. The statute was viewed by Cannon J. not as an attempt to ensure an expanded debate, but rather as an effort by government to dominate and control public opinion.'

31 An exception to this may be the publication of an apology for (or retraction of) a defamatory statement. See Brown 1994, 25/82: 'A published apology or retraction made by the defendant following his/her defamatory remarks may be offered in mitigation of damages.' See also Brown 1994, 26/10: 'Where the libel has already been published by a newspaper, and a judgment has been entered against the defendant, an appropriate remedy in some jurisdictions is the publication in the same newspaper of the court judgment. Such a remedy is provided for under the *Quebec Press Act* R.S.Q. 1964 c. 48 s.13.'

In the first case the paper is not directly compelled to publish a retraction; however, not doing so may have financial consequences. In the second case, the paper is required to publish the court judgment. It would, of course, be obvious to the reader that the published judgment did not (necessarily) represent the opinion of the newspaper.

32 Lichtenberg 1990, 126: 'In the real world ... not every inability to publish because of having to publish something else would be seriously regarded as censorship. If a network cancels *Wheel of Fortune* to carry a political debate, censorship is not at issue. Moreover, publishing is not a zero sum game; it is sometimes possible just to publish more.'

33 de Sola Pool 1983, 246: 'One would not require the Roman Catholic *Pilot* to carry ads for birth control or a trade union magazine to carry ads against a closed shop. But these cases assume that diverse magazines exist.'

34 A view expressed by Laforest J. for the Supreme Court of Canada in *CBC* 1996, 497: 'Debate in the public domain is predicated on an informed public, which is in turn reliant upon a free and vigorous press. The public's entitlement to be informed imposes on the media the responsibility to inform fairly and accurately. This responsibility is especially grave given that the freedom of the press is, and must be, largely unfettered.'

35 Kent Commission 1981, 22, states that 'in the 19th Century ... even the humblest printer became a gazetteer. But industrial development and the rise of the mass media put an end to the proliferation of papers for every viewpoint. Because of the large amount of capital required to put out a newspaper, the press became concentrated in the hands of big business. Diversity of opinion was placed in jeopardy. Freedom of the press ultimately came to depend on an increasingly restricted ability to publish or be published. As in old authoritarian days, the definition of truth once again risked becoming the prerogative of a few, now the few who had the power of money. It was to ward off this danger that the notion of social responsibility of the media was born.'

36 McQuaig 1995, 12: 'We must always remember that virtually all media outlets are owned by rich, powerful members of the elite. To assume that this fact has no influence on the ideas they present would be equivalent to assuming that, should the entire media be owned by say, labour unions, women's groups or social workers, this would have no impact on editorial content.' See also Glasbeek 1986, 107: 'opinion writers ... feel free to express themselves, but only because their opinions stay within the bounds of tolerance established by their employers. They would not have risen to their positions of eminence and autonomy if their politics had been radically to the left or right of their newspapers ...'

37 Winter 1997, xiii, offers an example: '[H]ow could one rely on the four English-language New Brunswick dailies, all owned by the Irving family, to report fairly on the strikes by workers at the Irving Oil Limited in

Saint John, which began in the spring of 1994 and is still going on two years later.'

38 Curran and Seaton 1985, 41: 'advertisers thus acquired a de facto licensing authority since, without their support, newspapers ceased to be economically viable.'

Herman and Chomsky 1994, 14: 'With the growth of advertising, papers that attracted ads could afford a copy price well below production costs. This put papers lacking in advertising at a serious disadvantage; their prices would tend to be higher, curtailing sales, and they would have less surplus to invest in improving the saleability of the paper ... For this reason, an advertising-based system will tend to drive out of existence or into marginality the media companies and types that depend on revenue from sale alone. With advertising, the free market does not yield a neutral system in which final buyer choice decides. The *advertisers*' choices influence media prosperity and survival. The ad-based media receive an advertising subsidy that gives them a price-marketing-quality edge, which allows them to encroach on and further weaken their adfree (or ad-disadvantaged) rivals.'

39 Another example is offered by Bagdikian 1992, 167: 'In 1978 [Air Canada] notified newspaper advertising managers that its ads would be cancelled as long as any news story of an Air Canada crash or hijacking ran in the paper and if its ads were carried within two pages of a news story of any crash or hijacking on any airline.'

40 Ruggles 1994, 147: 'The interactional structure of the commercial mass media is characterized by privately controlled choice of speakers, topics and formats, and by a rigid separation of roles in which the vast bulk of the public is permitted to participate in public discourse only to the extent of regularly indicating whether they are still attending (ie through audience surveys).'

41 The *Report on Broadcasting Policy* (Canada 1986), 15, also states: 'All broadcasting agencies, both public and private, are recipients of public support in the right to use scarce public assets. They must pay for these valuable rights by giving a responsible performance and the state is fully entitled to ensure that the trust is honoured.'

42 The Broadcasting Act, 1991, s. 9(1)(b) gives the CRTC authority to 'issue licences for such terms not exceeding seven years and subject to such conditions related to the circumstances of the licensee.'

43 See for example the Television Broadcasting Regulations, 1987, s. 4(6), which sets Canadian content requirements.

In addition to the requirements in the Broadcasting Act, 1991, the Canada Elections Act, 1985, ss. 307 and 316, requires broadcasters to make available a specified amount of time for the broadcast of both paid and unpaid political messages during a federal election campaign.

Radio Regulations 1986, Part 1.1, Broadcasting Content/Political Broadcasting provides: 6. During an election period, a licensee shall allocate time for the broadcasting of programs, advertisements or announcements of a partisan political character on an equitable basis to all accredited political parties and rival candidates represented in the election or referendum.

44 *CTV* 1981, 261: 'There is nothing whatever in the condition which interferes with freedom of expression within the meaning of paragraph 3(c) ... [T]he condition concerned as it is with the presentation of Canadian drama and containing no restrictions on freedom of expression in such drama, would not offend it.' Freedom of Expression is now given specific recognition in section 2(3) of the Broadcasting Act, 1991.

45 See also *Re N.B. Broadcasting* 1984, where the Federal Court of Appeal upheld a CRTC policy that denied broadcast licences to the proprietors of newspapers in the same geographic area. In the court's view: 'the argument confuses the freedom guaranteed by the *Charter* with a right to the use of property and is not sustainable. The freedom guaranteed by the Charter is a freedom to express and communicate ideas without restraint, whether orally or in print or by other means of communication ... [I]t gives no right to anyone to use the radio frequencies which, before the enactment of the Charter, had been declared by Parliament to be and had become public property and subject to the licensing and other provisions of the *Broadcasting Act*' (*Re N.B. Broadcasting* 1984, 88).

46 The *Report on Broadcasting Policy* (Canada 1986), 147 also notes: 'The availability of a larger number of channels will do little or nothing to guarantee access or to ensure that airwaves will reflect the Canadian identity or culture.'

...

'There are therefore still very good reasons for maintaining the public character of frequencies used for broadcasting. It is not so much on the ground of scarcity of radio frequencies that this policy is justified, but rather because of the importance of broadcasting in maintaining our national identity and expressing the values upon which our society is based.'

47 An interesting balance issue arose in *Banzhaf* 1969, in which CBS was found to have violated the fairness doctrine by presenting only cigarette company ads, which represented only one side of a controversial issue.

It is difficult to see how this understanding of balance can be reconciled with the operation of private broadcasting and its role as a vehicle for commercial advertising.

48 For a discussion of the potential for commercial domination of the Internet see Bakan 1997, 66–7: 'Nor is it likely that new communications media, such as the internet, will provide truly interactive communications. Most people lack sufficient resources and skills – and computer, computer literacy, money to pay for on-line fees – to log on to the internet. More fundamentally, the Internet cannot escape the pull of market forces towards the highly profitable, and decidedly non-interactive, pay-for-view form of "information super-highway"; it is already taking the shape of a ten-lane highway coming into the home, with only a tiny path leading back out – just wide enough to take a credit card number or to answer multiple choice questions.'

49 Thompson 1995, 244, describes the traditional idea of public life as 'the coming together of individuals in a common space, a shared locale, to engage in debate about matters of general concern ... The very essence of public life, on this account, is the to-and-fro of argument between individuals who confront each other face-to-face.'

50 Audience fragmentation is also occurring with radio and television.

51 In subsequent judgments, the U.S. Supreme Court has tried to determine when expenditures are relevant to collective bargaining and to work out appropriate rebate procedures. See, for example, the judgment in *Lehnert* 1991.

   In *Keller* 1990, the U.S. Supreme Court applied the same principle to a state bar's use of mandatory dues for political speech. The court held that mandatory fees could be used only when 'the officials and members of the Bar are acting essentially as professional advisors to those ultimately charged with the regulation of the legal profession' (*Keller* 1990, 15).

52 In *Lavigne* 1991, Wilson J. considered that *freedom of association*, which is intended to advance 'the collective action of individuals in the pursuit of common goals,' 'should not be expanded to protect a right not to associate' (*Lavigne* 1991, 253). She rejected the argument that 'if s.2(d) protects the right to associate, it should also as a matter of simple logic protect the converse, i.e. the right not to associate' (*Lavigne* 1991, 258–9). She thought that individuals are 'of necessity involved in associations not of [their] own choosing' and that 'it is naive to suggest that the Court can or should enable us to extricate ourselves from all the associations we deem undesirable' (*Lavigne* 1991, 260). In her view, the real objections to compelled association are more properly addressed under section 2(b): '[T]he real

harm produced by compelled association is not the fact of association itself but the enforced support of views, opinions or actions one does not share or approve' *(Lavigne* 1991, 263).

LaForest J. believed that there is a right not to associate. In his view, '[f]orced association will stifle the individual's potential for self-fulfilment and realization as surely as voluntary association will develop it' *(Lavigne* 1991, 318). He considered that the freedom of non-association is violated even when no one is likely to attribute the views expressed by the group to the associated individual *(Lavigne* 1991, 322). He continued: 'Consequently the test should not be whether payments "may reasonably be seen" as association, or must "indicate to any reasonable person" that the individual has associated himself with an ideological cause' *(Lavigne* 1991, 322). However, Laforest J. insisted that the Charter does not create a right to isolation and that it does not protect us 'from any association we may wish to avoid' *(Lavigne* 1991, 320). In particular, 'it does not protect us against the association with others that is a necessary and inevitable part of membership in a democratic community' *(Lavigne* 1991, 320). In his view, there can be no objection under section 2(d) to the payment of compulsory union dues 'insofar as the union addresses itself to the matters, the terms and conditions of employment for members of his bargaining unit, with respect to which he is "naturally" associated with his fellow employees' *(Lavigne* 1991, 329). However, an individual member's freedom of association 'will be violated when he or she is compelled to contribute to causes, ideological or otherwise, that are beyond the immediate concerns of the bargaining unit' *(Lavigne* 1991, 332).

LaForest J. considered that, in this case, the ideological concerns to which union funds were donated were not directly related to collective bargaining. Although section 2(d) is violated in this case, he found that this violation is justified under section 1. In his view, to remove the power of unions to devote resources to different causes – not directly related to collective bargaining – would reduce their ability 'to favourably affect the political, social and economic environment in which collective bargaining and dispute resolution take place' *(Lavigne* 1991, 335).

For McLachlin J., '[f]reedom of association protects the freedom of individuals to interact with, support and be supported by, their fellow humans in the varied activities in which they choose to engage' *(Lavigne* 1991, 343). She thought that the right not to associate rests on 'the individual's interest in being free from enforced association with ideas and values to which he or she does not voluntarily subscribe' *(Lavigne* 1991, 344). In this way, Justice McLachlin's view is similar to that of Wilson J.

53 Laforest J. in *Lavigne* 1991, 340: 'While I have no doubt that the contribution of money to a fund would in many circumstances constitute an activity
capable of expressing meaning, I do not think it does in the circumstances
of the present case.' See also Wilson J. at 270: 'Similarly, for some members
of the bargaining unit represented by OPSEU, the contribution of dues to
the union signifies for them support for the union and perhaps more
generally for the union movement and the interests it supports. Clearly,
therefore, volunteering financial support is expressive for such people.
Particularly in this day and age where money is an extremely powerful way
of expressing support, the channelling of contributions is expressive
indeed.'

54 A similar argument concerning tax credits for election campaigns was
rejected by the Supreme Court of Canada in *McKay* 1989. It was argued
before the court that the Election Finances Act, (S.M. 1982–83–84, c. 45)
of Manitoba violated taxpayers' freedom of expression because it provided
for payment out of the province's tax revenue of a portion of the campaign
expenses of election candidates who received a certain percentage of the
votes in a provincial election. Cory J., for the court, rejected the argument
in a paragraph: 'The Act does not prohibit a taxpayer or anyone else from
holding or expressing any position or their belief in any position. Rather,
the Act seems to foster and encourage the dissemination and expression of
a wide range of views and positions. In this way it enhances public knowledge of diverse views and facilitates public discussion of those views (*McKay*
1989, 366). Whatever concerns may exist about the fairness of such a
scheme, they have nothing to do with the taxpayers' freedom of expression. As Cory J. pointed out, the claim that this arrangement amounts to
compelled expression seems implausible since the taxpayer is not required
to convey a message and the paid-for political messages will not be attributed to him or her.

Cases

Abood v. Detroit Board of Education, 431 U.S. 209 (1977).

Abrams v. United States, 250 U.S. 616 (1919).

Alberta Statutes (Reference Re), [1938] S.C.R. 100; aff'd [1939] A.C. 117.

Arkansas Educational Television Commission v. Forbes, 118 S. Ct. 1633 (1998).

Associated Press v. U.S., 326 U.S. 1 (1945).

Association of Canadian Distillers v. CRTC, [1995] 2 F.C. 778 (F.C.T.D.).

Banzhaf v. F.C.C., 405 F. 2d 1082 (D.C. Cir. Ct.) (1969).

[Barnette] West Virginia State Board of Education v. Barnette, 319 U.S. 624 (1943).

[BCGEU] *British Columbia Government Employees Union v. British Columbia (Attorney-General)*, [1988] 2 S.C.R. 790.

Big M Drug Mart (R. v.), [1985] 1 S.C.R. 295.

Brodie (R. v.), [1962] 1 S.C.R. 681.

Buckley v. Valeo, 424 U.S. 1 (1976).

Butler (R. v.), [1992] 1 S.C.R. 452.

Byron (Lord) v. Johnston (1816), 2 Mer. 28; 35 E.R. 851.

CBC v. N.B. (A.G.), [1996] 3 S.C.R. 480.

CBS v. Democratic National Committee, 412 U.S. 94 (1973).

CJMF-FM Ltée. v. Canada (CRTC), [1984] F.C.J. No. 244.

Cohen v. California, 403 U.S. 15 (1971).

Cole v. Richardson, 405 U.S. 676 (1972).

Collin v. Smith, 578 F.2d 1197 (1978); U.S. 7th Cir. I 11 (1978).

Committee for the Commonwealth of Canada v. Canada, [1985] 2 F.C. 3 (F.C.T.D.); [1987] 2 F.C. 68 (F.C.C.A.); [1991] 1 S.C.R. 139 (S.C.C.).

CTV v. CRTC, [1981] 2 F.C. 248 (Fed. C.A.).

Dagenais v. Canadian Broadcasting Corporation, [1994] 3 S.C.R. 835.

Devine v. AG Quebec, [1988] 2 S.C.R. 790.

Dolphin Delivery (Retail, Wholesale and Department Store Union, Local 580 v.),
  [1986] 2 S.C.R. 573.

Dominion News and Gifts Ltd. (R. v.), [1963] 2 C.C.C. 103.

Donald v. Hamilton Board of Education, [1945] O.R. 518.

Dupond (AG Canada and) v. City of Montreal, [1978] 2 S.C.R. 770.

Edmonton Journal v. Alberta (Attorney-General), [1989] 2 S.C.R. 1326.

Eldridge v. British Columbia (A.-G.), [1997] 3 S.C.R. 624.

Ford v. Quebec (Attorney-General), [1988] 2 S.C.R. 712.

Gay Alliance Toward Equality v. The Vancouver Sun, [1979] S.C.R. 435.

Glad Day Bookshop Inc. v. Deputy Minister of National Revenue, Customs and Excise.
  90 D.L.R. (4th) 527 (1992) (Ont. Gen. Div.).

Haig v. Canada, [1993] 2 S.C.R. 995.

Hicklin (R. v.) (1868), L.R. 3 Q.B. 360.

Hill v. Church of Scientology of Toronto, [1995] 2 S.C.R. 1130.

Hudgens v. NLRB, 424 U.S. 507 (1976).

Hurley v. Irish American Gay, Lesbian and Bisexual Group of Boston, 515 U.S.
  577.

Iorfida v. MacIntyre (1994) 24 C.R.R. (2d) 293.

Irwin Toy Ltd. v. Quebec (Attorney-General), [1989] 1 S.C.R. 927.

K-Mart Canada (United Food and Commercial Workers v.) (1999) (unreported)
  (S.C.C.).

Keegstra (R. v.), [1990] 3 S.C.R. 697.

Keller v. State Bar, 496 U.S. 1 (1990).

Klein and the Law Society of Upper Canada (Re) (1985), 16 D.L.R. (4th) 489
  (Ont. Div. Ct.).

Kopyto (R. v.) (1987), 47 D.L.R. (4th) 213 (Ont. C.A.).

Lavigne v. O.P.S.E.U., [1991] 2 S.C.R. 211.

Lehnert v. Ferris Faculty Association, 500 U.S. 507 (1991).

Libman v. Quebec (Attorney General), [1997] 3 S.C.R. 569.

Little Sisters Book and Art Emporium v. Canada (1998), 160 D.L.R. (4th) 385
  (B.C. C.A.)

[Logan Valley] Food Employees v. Logan Valley Plaza, 391 U.S. 308 (1968).

Lucas (R. v.), [1998] 1 S.C.R. 439.

Marsh v. Alabama, 326 U.S. 501 (1946).

McKay v. Manitoba, [1989] 2 S.C.R. 357.

McKinney v. University of Guelph, [1990] 3 S.C.R. 229.

Miami Herald Publishing v. Tornillo, 418 U.S. 241 (1974).

Michelin and CIE v. A.A.A.T.G.W.U.C. (CAW-Canada), [1997] 2 F.C. 306
  (F.C.T.D.).

National Bank of Canada and Retail Clerks International Union et al. (Re), [1984] 1 S.C.R. 269.

National Citizens Coalition Inc. v. Canada (Attorney-General) (1984), 11 D.L.R. (4th) 481 (Alta. Q.B.).

New Brunswick Broadcasting Co. Ltd. and C.R.T.C. (Re) (1984), 13 D.L.R. 4th 77.

[NWAC] *Native Women's Association of Canada v. Canada*, [1994] 3 S.C.R. 627.

Oakes (R. v.), [1986] 1 S.C.R. 103.

Pacific Gas and Electric v. PUC of California, 475 U.S. 1 (1986).

Perry Education Association v. Perry Local Educators' Association, 460 U.S. 37 (1983).

Pittsburg Press Co. v. Pittsburgh Comm. on Human Rights, 413 U.S. 376 (1973).

Pottle v. Evening Telegram Ltd. (1954), 34 M.P.R. 101 (Nfld. S.C.).

Pruneyard Shopping Center v. Robins, 447 U.S. 74 (1980).

Ramsden v. Peterborough, [1993] 2 S.C.R. 1084.

RAV v. City of St. Paul, 505 U.S. 377 (1992).

Red Hot Video Ltd. (R. v.) (1985), 18 C.C.C. (3d) 1 (B.C.C.A).

Red Lion Broadcasting v. F.C.C., 395 U.S. 367 (1969).

Reform Party of Canada v. Canada (1995), 123 D.L.R. (4th) 366 (Alta. C.A.).

RJR MacDonald Inc. v. Canada (Attorney-General), [1995] 3 S.C.R. 199.

Roach v. Canada (Minister of Multiculturalism and Culture), [1994] 113 D.L.R. (4th) 67 (F.C.A.).

Rocket v. Royal College of Dental Surgeons, [1990] 2 S.C.R. 232.

Ross v. New Brunswick School District No. 15, [1996] 1 S.C.R. 825.

Schenck v. United States, 249 U.S. 47 (1919).

Sharpe (R. v.) (1999) (unreported) (B.C.C.A.).

Shelley v. Kraemer, 344 U.S. 3 (1948).

Slaight Communications v. Davidson, [1989] 1 S.C.R. 1038.

Societé de Transport de la Communauté de Montréal v. Robichaud (1991), 147 D.L.R. (4th) 235 (Que. C.A.).

Somerville v. Canada (Attorney-General) (1996), 136 D.L.R. (4th) 205 (Alta. C.A.).

Spence v. Washington, 418 U.S. 405 (1974).

Taylor (Canada v.), [1990] 3 S.C.R. 892.

Thomson Newspapers Co. v. Canada, [1998] 1 S.C.R. 877.

Towne Cinema Theatres v. The Queen, [1985] 1 S.C.R. 495.

Trieger v. Canadian Broadcasting Corporation (1988), 66 O.R. (2d) 273 (Ont. H.C.).

Virginia State Board of Pharmacy v. Virginia Citizens Consumer Council, 425 U.S. 748 (1976).

Weisfeld v. Canada, [1995] 1 F.C. 68 (Fed. C.A.).

Wooley v. Maynard, 430 U.S. 701 (1977).
Zundel (R. v.), [1992] 2 S.C.R. 731.

Bibliography

Anand, S. 1998. 'Beyond Keegstra: The Constitutionality of the Wilful Promotion of Hatred Revisited.' *National Journal of Constitutional Law* 9:117.

Arthurs, H. 1963. 'Comment on *Hersees of Woodstock* v. *Goldstein*.' *Canadian Bar Review* 41:573.

Bagdikian, B. 1992. *The Media Monopoly*. 4th ed. Boston: Beacon Press.

Bakan, J. 1997. *Constitutional Rights and Social Wrongs*. Toronto: University of Toronto Press.

Baker, C.E. 1989. *Human Liberty and Freedom of Speech*. Oxford: Oxford University Press.

– 1994. *Advertising and a Democratic Press*. Princeton, N.J.: Princeton University Press.

Bakhtin, M.M. 1986. *Speech Genres and Other Late Essays*. Trans. V. McGee. Austin: University of Texas Press.

Bakvis, H., and Smith, J. 1997. 'Third Party Advertising and Electoral Democracy: The Political Theory of the Alberta Court of Appeal in *Somerville* v. *Canada (Attorney-General)*.' *Canadian Public Policy* 23(2):164.

Barron, J. 1973. *Freedom of The Press for Whom?* Bloomington, Ind.: Indiana University Press.

– 1986. 'Public Access to the Media under the Charter: An American Appraisal.' In P. Anisman and A. Linden, eds., *The Media, the Courts and the Charter*. Toronto: Carswell.

Barry, A.M. Seward 1997. *Visual Intelligence*. Albany, N.Y.: State University of New York Press.

Barthes, R. 1973. *Mythologies*. London: Paladin Grafton Books.

– 1985. *The Grain of the Voice*. New York: Hill and Wang.

Bauman, Z. 1988. *Freedom*. Markham: Fitzhenry & Whiteside.

Bercuson, D., and D. Wertheimer. 1985. *A Trust Betrayed: The Keegstra Affair.* Toronto: Doubleday.

Berger, J. 1977. *Ways of Seeing.* London: BBC & Penguin.

Bezanson, R.P. 1998. *Speech Stories.* New York: New York University Press.

Black, W.W. 1979. '*Gay Alliance Toward Equality v. Vancouver Sun.*' *Osgoode Hall Law Journal* 17:649.

Bollinger, L.C. 1991. *Images of a Free Press.* Chicago, Ill.: University of Chicago Press.

Borovoy, A. 1988. *When Freedoms Collide.* Toronto: Lester & Orpen Dennys.

Brown, R. 1994. *The Law of Defamation in Canada.* Vols. 1 and 2. 2nd ed. Toronto: Carswell.

Bruner, J. 1990. *Acts of Meaning.* Cambridge, Mass.: Harvard University Press.

Butler, J. 1997. *Excitable Speech.* London: Routledge.

Cameron, J. 1989. 'The Original Conception of Section 1 and Its Demise: A Comment on *Irwin Toy Ltd.* v. *A-G of Quebec.*' *McGill Law Journal* 35:253.

– 1990. 'The First Amendment and Section 1 of the Charter.' *Media & Communications Law Review* 1:59.

– 1991. 'A Bumpy Landing: The Supreme Court of Canada and Access to Public Airports Under Section 2 (b) of the Charter.' *Media & Communications Law Review* 2:91.

– 1992. 'Abstract Principles v. Contextual Conceptions of Harm: A Comment on *R.* v. *Butler.*' *McGill Law Journal* 37:1135.

– 1997. 'The Past, Present and Future of Expressive Freedom under the Charter.' *Osgoode Hall Law Journal* 35:1.

Canada. 1986. *Report of the Task Force on Broadcasting Policy.* Ottawa: Minister of Supply and Services Canada.

CRTC. 1970. Canadian Radio-television & Telecommunications Commission, *Report of the Special Committee Appointed in Connection with the CBC Program 'Air of Death.'* Ottawa: CRTC.

– 1977. Canadian Radio-television and Telecommunications Commission, *Controversial Programming in the Canadian Broadcasting System – Report on Issues Raised by CFCF's Anti-Bill 22 Campaign.* Ottawa: CRTC.

Cohen Commission. 1965. *Report of the Special Committee on Hate Propaganda.* Ottawa: Queen's Printer.

Cohen, D. 1991. 'Can It Really be Unconstitutional to Regulate Product Safety Information?' *Canadian Business Law Journal* 17:55.

Cole, S. 1989. *Pornography and the Sex Crisis.* Toronto: Amanita.

Coombe, R.J. 1991. 'Objects of Property and Subjects of Politics: Intellectual Property Laws and Democratic Dialogue.' *Texas Law Review* 69:1853.

Cossman, B. 1997. 'Feminist Fashion or Morality in Drag.' In Cossman et al., *Bad Attitudes on Trial.* Toronto: University of Toronto Press, 107.

Cossman, B., S. Bell, L. Gotell, and B. Ross. 1997. *Bad Attitudes on Trial.* Toronto: University of Toronto Press.

Coward, R. 1982. 'Sexual Violence and Sexuality.' *Feminist Review* 11:9.

Curran, J. 1991. 'Mass Media and Democracy: A Reappraisal.' In J. Curran and M. Gurevitch, eds., *Mass Media and Society.* London: Edward Arnold.

Curran, J., and J. Seaton. 1985. *Power without Responsibility: The Press and Broadcasting in Britain.* 2nd ed. London: Metheun.

Delgado, R. 1993. 'Words That Wound: A Tort Action for Racist Insults, Epithets and Name Calling.' In M. Matsuda, C. Lawrence, R. Delgado, and K. Crenshaw, *Words That Wound.* Boulder, Col.: Westview Press.

de Sola Pool, I. 1983. *Technologies of Freedom.* Cambridge, Mass.: Belknap Press.

Devlin, N. 1996. 'Opinion Polls and the Protection of Political Speech – A Comment on *Thomson Newspapers Co.* v. *Canada (Attorney-General).*' *Ottawa Law Review* 28:411.

Diamond, S. 1985. 'Pornography: Image and Reality.' In V. Burstyn, ed. *Women Against Censorship.* Vancouver: Douglas & McIntyre, 40.

Dienes, C.T. 1986. 'The Trashing of the Public Forum: Problematic First Amendment Analysis.' *George Washington Law Review* 55:109.

Dworkin, R. 1985. *A Matter of Principle.* Cambridge, Mass.: Harvard University Press.

– 1996. *Freedom's Law.* Cambridge, Mass.: Harvard University Press.

Dyer, G. 1982. *Advertising as Communication.* London: Methuen.

Dyzenhaus, D. 1991. 'Obscenity and the Charter: Autonomy and Equality.' *Criminal Reports* 1:367.

Eagleton, T. 1983. *Literary Theory.* Oxford: Blackwell.

Eckersley, R. 1987. 'Whither the Feminist Campaign?: An Evaluation of Feminist Critiques of Pornography.' *International Journal of the Sociology of Law* 15:149.

Engelhardt, T. 1986. 'The Shortcake Strategy.' In T. Gitlin, ed., *Watching Television.* New York: Pantheon Books.

Estlund, C. 1997. 'Freedom of Expression in the Workplace and the Problem of Discriminatory Harassment.' *Texas Law Review* 75:687.

Fewer, D. 1997. 'Constitutionalizing Copyright: Freedom of Expression and the Limits of Copyright in Canada.' *University of Toronto Faculty of Law Review* 55:175.

Fiske, J. 1987. *Television Culture.* London: Routledge.

Fiss, O. 1996. *The Irony of Free Speech.* Cambridge, Mass.: Harvard University Press.

Gadamer, H.G. 1986. *Truth and Method.* New York: Crossroad.

Garnham, N. 1986. 'The Media and the Public Sphere.' In P. Golding, G. Murdock, and P. Schlesinger, eds., *Communicating Politics: Mass Communication and the Political Process.* Leicester: Leicester University Press.

Gates, H.L. 1994. 'War of Words: Critical Race Theory and The First Amendment.' In H. Gates, A. Griffin, D. Lively, R. Post, W. Rubenstein, and N. Strossen, *Speaking of Race, Speaking of Sex.* New York: New York University Press.

Geertz, C. 1973. *The Interpretation of Cultures.* New York: Basic Books.

– 1983. *Local Knowledge.* New York: Basic Books.

Glasbeek, H. 1986. 'Comment: Entrenchment of Freedom of the Press – Fettering Freedom of Speech for the People.' In P. Anisman and A. Linden, eds., *The Media, the Courts and the Charter.* Toronto: Carswell.

– 1990. 'Contempt for Workers.' *Osgoode Hall Law Journal* 28:1.

Gombrich, E.H. 1963. *Meditations on a Hobby Horse.* London: Phaidon.

Gosnell, C. 1998. 'Hate Speech on the Internet: A Question of Context.' *Queen's Law Journal* 23:369.

Green, L. 1994. 'Freedom of Expression and Choice of Language.' In W.J. Waluchow, ed., *Free Expression: Essays in Law and Philosophy.* Oxford: Clarendon Press.

Greenawalt, K. 1989. *Speech, Crime, and the Uses of Language.* Oxford University Press.

Grice, P. 1989. *Studies in the Way of Words.* Cambridge, Mass.: Harvard University Press.

Haiman, F.S. 1981. *Speech and Law in a Free Society.* Chicago: University of Chicago Press.

– 1993. *Speech Acts and the First Amendment.* Carbondale: Southern Illinois Press.

Havelock, E. 1988. *The Muse Learns to Write.* New Haven: Yale University Press.

Herman, E., and N. Chomsky. 1994. *Manufacturing Consent: The Political Economy of the Mass Media.* London: Vintage.

Hiebert, J. 1998. 'Money and Elections: Can Citizens Participate on Fair Terms Amidst Unrestricted Spending?' *Canadian Journal of Political Science* 31:91.

Hutchinson, A. 1995a. *Waiting for Coraf: A Critique of Law and Rights.* Toronto: University of Toronto Press.

– 1995b. 'In Other Words: Putting Sex and Pornography in Context.' *Canadian Journal of Law and Jurisprudence* 8:107.

Jamieson, K.H. 1992. *Dirty Politics.* Oxford: Oxford University Press.

Jhally, S. 1990. *The Codes of Advertising.* London: Routledge.

Kanter, M. 1992. 'Balancing Under s.2 (b) of the Charter: Case Comment on *Committee for the Commonwealth of Canada* v. *Canada.*' *Queen's Law Journal* 17:489.

Kappeler, S. 1986. *The Pornography of Representation.* Cambridge: Polity Press.

Keane, J. 1991. *The Media and Democracy.* Cambridge: Polity Press.

Kent Commission. 1981. *Report of the Royal Commission on Newspapers.* Ottawa: Minister of Supply and Services.

Kline, S. 1993. *Out of the Garden.* London: Verso.

Kramer, R. 1992. '*R. v. Butler.* A New Approach to Obscenity Law or Return to the Morality Play?' *Criminal Law Quarterly* 35:77.

Kreimer, S. 1984. 'The Problem of Negative Rights in a Positive State.' *University of Pennsylvania Law Review* 132:1295.

Kress, G., and T. van Leeuwen. 1996. 'Reading Images.' In P. Cobley, ed., *The Communications Theory Reader.* London: Routledge, 172.

Lacombe, D. 1994. *Pornography and the Law.* Toronto: University of Toronto Press.

Lawrence, C. 1993. 'If He Hollers Let Him: Regulating Racist Speech on Campus.' In M. Matsuda, C. Lawrence, R. Delgado, and K. Crenshaw, *Words That Wound.* Boulder, Col.: Westview Press.

Leiss, W., Kline S., and S. Jhally. 1986. *Social Communication in Advertising.* New York: Methuen.

Lepofsky, D. 1993. 'The Supreme Court's Approach to Freedom of Expression – *Irwin Toy* v. *Quebec* – And the Illusion of Section 2 (b) Liberalism.' *National Journal of Constitutional Law* 3:37.

Levinson, S. 1986. 'Constituting Communities through Words That Bind: Reflections on Loyalty Oaths.' *Michigan Law Review* 84:1440.

Lichtenberg, J. 1990. 'Foundations and Limits of Freedom of the Press.' In J. Lichtenberg, ed., *Democracy and the Mass Media.* Cambridge: Cambridge University Press.

Longino, H. 1980. In L. Lederer, ed., *Take Back the Night.* New York: William Morrow.

Lortie Commission. 1991. Royal Commission on Electoral Reform and Party Financing, 1991. *Reforming Electoral Democracy.* Vol. 1. Ottawa: Ministry of Supply and Services.

Mackinnon, C. 1987. *Feminism Unmodified.* Cambridge, Mass.: Harvard University Press.

Macklem, T. 1990. 'Toying with Expression.' *Supreme Court Law Review* 1(2d):547.

Mahoney, K. 1991. 'Canaries in a Coal Mine: Canadian Judges and the Reconstruction of Obscenity Law.' In D. Schneiderman, ed., *Freedom of Expression and the Charter.* Toronto: Thomson.

– 1992. '*R. v. Keegstra*: A Rationale for Regulating Pornography.' *McGill Law Journal* 37:242.

Matsuda, M. 1993. 'Public Response to Racist Speech: Considering the Victim's Story.' In M. Matsuda, C. Lawrence, R. Delgado, and K. Crenshaw, *Words That Wound.* Boulder, Col.: Westview Press.

McLaren, J. 1991. 'Now You See It, Now You Don't: The Historical Record and the Elusive Task of Defining the Obscene.' In D. Schneiderman, ed., *Freedom of Expression and the Charter.* Toronto: Thomson.

McQuaig, L. 1995. *Shooting the Hippo*. Toronto: Viking.

Meiklejohn, A. 1965. *Political Freedom*. New York: Oxford University Press.

– 1975. 'The First Amendment is an Absolute.' In P.B. Kurland, ed., *Free Speech and Association: The Supreme Court and the First Amendment*. Chicago Ill.: University of Chicago Press.

Michelman, F. 1989. 'Conceptions of Democracy in American Constitutional Argument: The Case of Pornography Regulation.' *Tennessee Law Review* 56:291.

Mill, J.S. 1982 [1859]. *On Liberty*. Harmondsworth: Penguin.

Miller, M.C. 1986. 'Deride and Conquer.' In T. Gitlin, ed., *Watching Television*. New York: Pantheon Books. 183.

– 1988. *Boxed In: The Culture of TV*. Evanston, Ill.: Northwestern University Press.

Milton, J. 1927 [1644]. *Aeropagitica and Other Prose Works*. New York: J.M. Dent & Sons, Ltd.

Moon, R. 1985. 'The Scope of Freedom of Expression' (1985) *Osgoode Hall Law Journal* 25:331.

– 1988a. 'Access to Public and Private Property under Freedom of Expression.' *Ottawa Law Review* 20:339.

– 1988b. 'Freedom of Expression and Property Rights.' *Saskatchewan Law Review* 52:243.

– 1991. 'Lifestyle Advertising and Classical Freedom of Expression Doctrine.' *McGill Law Journal* 36:76.

– 1992. 'Drawing Lines in a Culture of Prejudice: *R.* v. *Keegstra* and the Restriction of Hate Propaganda.' *University of British Columbia Law Review* 26:99.

– 1993. '*R.* v. *Butler*: The Limits of the Supreme Court's Feminist Re-Interpretation of Section 163.' *Ottawa Law Review* 25:361.

– 1995. 'The Supreme Court of Canada on the Structure of Freedom of Expression Adjudication.' *University of Toronto Law Journal* 45:419.

– 1998. 'The State of Free Speech.' *University of Toronto Law Journal* 48:125.

Morley, D. 1992. *Television, Audiences and Cultural Studies*. London: Routledge.

Ong, W. 1982. *Orality and Literacy*. New York: Methuen.

Post, R. 1995. *Constitutional Domains*. Cambridge, Mass.: Harvard University Press.

– 1996. 'Subsidized Speech.' *Yale Law Journal* 106:151.

– 1997. 'Equality and Autonomy in First Amendment Jurisprudence.' *Michigan Law Review* 95:1517.

Postman, N. 1985. *Amusing Ourselves to Death*. New York: Penguin.

Radin, M.J. 1993. *Re-Interpreting Property*. Chicago, Ill.: University of Chicago Press.

Ramsay, I. 1996. *Advertising Culture and Law*. London: Sweet and Maxwell.

Raz, J. 1986. *The Morality of Freedom*. Oxford: Clarendon.

Redish, M. 1982. 'The Value of Free Speech.' *University of Pennsylvania Law Review* 130:591.

Richstone, J., and J.S. Russell. 1981. 'Shutting the Gate: Gay Civil Rights in the Supreme Court of Canada.' *McGill Law Journal* (1981):92.

Ricoeur, P. 1976. *Interpretation Theory*. Fort Worth, Tex.: Texas Christian University Press.

Ruggles, M. 1994. *The Audience Reflected in the Medium of Law*. Norwood, N.J.: Ablex Publishing.

Rushdie, S. 1988. *The Satanic Verses*. London: Viking.

St Antoine, T. 1982. 'Free Speech or Economic Weapon?: The Persisting Problem of Picketing.' *Suffolk Law Review* 16:883.

Scanlon, T. 1977. 'A Theory of Freedom of Expression.' In R. Dworkin, ed. *The Philosophy of Law*. Oxford University Press, 161.

Schauer, F. 1982. *Free Speech: A Philosophical Enquiry*. Cambridge: Cambridge University Press.

Schiller, H. 1989. *Culture Inc*. Oxford: Oxford University Press.

Schnably, S. 1993. 'Property and Pragmatism: A Critique of Radin's Theory of Property and Personhood.' *Stanford Law Review* 45:347.

Schneiderman, D. 1996. 'Consumer Interests and Commercial Speech: A Comment on *RJR Macdonald* v. *Canada (A-G)*.' *University of British Columbia Law Review* 30:165.

Schudson, M. 1984. *Advertising, the Uneasy Persuasion*. New York: Basic Books.

Searle, J. 1983. *Intentionality*. Cambridge: Cambridge University Press.

Sharpe, R. 1987. 'Commercial Expansion and the Charter.' *University of Toronto Law Journal* 37:229.

Shiffrin, S. 1990. *The First Amendment, Democracy and Romance*. Princeton, N.J.: Princeton University Press.

Shiner, R. 1994. 'Freedom of Commercial Expression.' In W.J. Waluchow, ed., *Free Expression: Essays in Law and Philosophy*. Oxford: Clarendon Press, 91.

– 1995. 'Advertising and Freedom of Expression.' *University of Toronto Law Journal* 45:179.

Smart, C. 1989. *Feminism and the Power of Law*. London: Routledge.

Smith, S.D. 1987. 'Skepticism, Tolerance and Truth in the Theory of Free Expression.' *Southern California Law Review* 60:649.

Sontag, S. 1989. *On Photography*. New York: Noonday Press.

Steiner, G. 1975. *After Babel.* Oxford: Oxford University Press.

Stevenson, N. 1995. *Understanding Media Cultures.* London: Sage.

Strauss, D. 1991. 'Persuasion, Autonomy and Freedom of Expression.' *Columbia Law Review* 91:334.

Sunstein, C. 1986. 'Pornography and the First Amendment.' *Duke Law Journal* [1986]:589.

– 1993. *Democracy and the Problem of Free Speech.* New York: The Free Press.

Taylor, C. 1985. *Human Agency and Language.* Cambridge: Cambridge University Press.

– 1989a. *Sources of the Self.* Cambridge, Mass.: Harvard University Press.

– 1989b. 'Cross-Purposes: The Liberal-Communitarian Debate.' In N. Rosenblum, ed., *Liberalism and the Moral Life.* Cambridge, Mass.: Harvard University Press.

– 1995. *Philosophical Arguments.* Cambridge, Mass.: Harvard University Press.

Taylor, E. 1995. 'Hanging up on Hate: Contempt of Court as a Tool to Shut Down Hatelines.' *National Journal of Constitutional Law* 5:163.

Ten, C.L. 1980. *Mill on Liberty.* Oxford: Clarendon Press.

Thompson, J.B. 1995. *The Media and Modernity.* Stanford, Cal.: Stanford University Press.

Thornicroft, K. 1992. 'Comment on *Lavigne* v. *OPSEU.*' *Canadian Bar Review* 71:155.

Trakman, L. 1995a. 'Transferring Free Speech: Rights and Responsibilities.' *Ohio State Law Journal* 56:899.

– 1995b. 'The Demise of Positive Liberty? *Native Women's Association of Canada v. Canada.*' *Constitutional Forum* (1995):71.

Uris, L. 1984. *The Haj.* London: Corgi Books.

Valois, M. 1992. 'Hate Propaganda, Section 2(b) and Section 1 of the Charter: A Canadian Constitutional Dilemma.' *Themis* 26:373.

Voloshinov, V.N. 1995. 'Language, Speech and Utterance.' In S. Dentith, ed., *Bakhtinian Thought.* London: Routledge.

Weiler, P. 1980. *Reconcilable Differences.* Toronto: Carswell.

Weinrib, L.E. 1990. 'Does Money Talk? Commercial Expression in the Canadian Constitutional Context.' In D. Schneiderman, ed., *Freedom of Expression and the Charter.* Toronto: Thomson Publishing.

Williamson, J. 1978. *Decoding Advertisements.* London: Marion Boyars.

Winter, J. 1997. *Democracy's Oxygen.* Montreal: Black Rose Books.

Wollheim, R. 1980. *Art and Its Objects.* Cambridge: Cambridge University Press.

Wright, R.G. 1997. *Selling Words: Free Speech in a Commercial Culture.* New York: NYU Press.

Index